There's Always
A Right Job
For Every Woman

There's Always A Right Job For Every Woman

Roberta Roesch

A BERKLEY WINDHOVER BOOK
published by
BERKLEY PUBLISHING CORPORATION

Toni Mendez, Inc.
140 East 56th Street
New York, N.Y. 10022

SBN 425-03193-4

BERKLEY WINDHOVER BOOKS are published by
Berkley Publishing Corporation
200 Madison Avenue
New York, N.Y. 10016

BERKLEY WINDHOVER BOOK ® TM 757,375

Printed in the United States of America

Berkley Windhover Edition, August, 1976

About the Author

Roberta Roesch is a syndicated columnist who specializes in writing about jobs and careers. For her column she has interviewed more than 3,500 working women, and her lengthy tape-recorded conversations with them have supplied her with the best possible research on women and work—the stories and views of women themselves. She has also published two other books on working—*Women In Action* and *Money, Jobs, and Futures*—and written articles for such magazines as *Reader's Digest, Good Housekeeping, Parents,* and *Better Homes and Gardens*. She is a former magazine editor and has appeared on both national and local radio and television. A member of the American Society of Journalists and Authors, she lectures for women's groups and job seminars and teaches at Bergen Community College in New Jersey and Rockland Community College in New York. She lives with her family in Westwood, New Jersey.

Acknowledgments

Many wonderful people participated in this book:

But certainly those at the top of the list are the productive and successful women who so generously shared their stories and views along with their practical advice. Special thanks are also due to *The Record* in Hackensack, New Jersey, which initiated my career-counseling column prior to its syndication. Some of the stories published here originally appeared in that column.

Another vote of thanks belongs to my newspaper readers whose letters and requests for this book motivated me to write it. Equal thanks is extended to the many organizations which assisted me with research and information. Their names are in Chapter 10.

Finally, with gratitude and love, I thank my husband, Phil, and our family—Meredith, Bonnie, and Jeff—for their never-failing help, encouragement, and supportive tasks.

ROBERTA ROESCH

Westwood, New Jersey

Contents

Forethoughts

"Women have aims in a larger world today," actress Helen Hayes said, when I talked with her in her Nyack, New York, home about women and the world of work.

"And in these times when we're all more free to use the gifts we have I don't know of many women who aren't experiencing an interest in working in that larger world."

In my encounters with women I also see, more and more, that the go-and-do life is today's way of life and will be for years to come. As a result of this forecast, women of every age are eager to work—or go back to work—for economic or personal reasons. In the Seventies the women's movement is affecting each of us, and most have been touched to some degree by the questions the movement has raised. Accordingly, those just starting out—as well as those working or going back to work—are looking beyond the stereotyped jobs and, with the assistance of raised consciousness, are struggling to find their personal worth—and their personal liberation—somewhere between the outer extremes of the current women's movement and the obsolete confines of women's roles.

But despite women's rights and the progress we have made, the recession economy of the Seventies has caused some women to give up too soon because of employment setbacks and endless job hunts.

Granted, job crises are bound to exist in recession periods and it's all too easy to listen to the prophets of gloom. But some women swim instead of sink, even when the economy sags, and these are the ones who find their niche and improvise and progress. They're the ones who know that in a tough market it's essential to be resilient and resourceful and equip yourself with a salable skill, based on what you do best. They're positive instead of negative. They cope instead of cop-out.

"Whether you're interested in business, the professions, the arts, or the crafts, I don't go for not starting because of the economy," the successful secretary-treasurer of a large insurance firm told me. "I think you must say, 'This is where it's *at*' and then go ahead and try to push through.

"Actually, when times are less than perfect you can sometimes initiate opportunities to get a job that you can't implement when the job market is great," she went on. "For example, I got my start in a bad recession when I was 21 because I sold an employer on the idea of saving money by merging two jobs into one and letting me do both.

"Somehow I was able to convince him that I could follow through and, from my observations throughout my working life, I'm every bit as convinced today there are winners as well as losers during every kind of crisis.

"If you think and act like a loser, you will be a loser," she continued, "so it's better to take the optimist's view and proceed with initiative and hope, knowing that—somehow, somewhere—there will always be a right job for you."

In good times—and in bad—there's always a job for women who know what's available and what steps to take to get started in the work that is right for them. In fact, I've had that proven again and again in my life while reporting in depth on women and work in newspapers, magazines, and books.

I've interviewed 3,500 of them in lengthy taped dialogues, and as I've talked to go-and-do women who are tuned into women's needs I've probed them for guidelines and sentiments for women of every age who want to look deeper within themselves for a first or second career. From the hundreds of conversations I've recorded and edited, I've chosen 100 for this book because the experiences and insights of these women relate specifically to the hoped-for goals of most contemporary women who want to be go-and-do persons and earn incomes commensurate with their skills.

On the whole, the hundred women who talked about jobs in this book are not "assistants" and "helpers" or the ones who are willing to live out their days in low-paying "women's work." Instead, they're success-story women who are holding the reins and involving themselves in the kind of work that helps them develop and grow. They've proved conclusively that there's more than one way in careers—and in life—to get where you want to be.

They offer a sound perspective and common sense advice on landing and progressing in jobs. They are models to follow as you choose your own right career. Then, along with the personal stories, there are 100 brief pep talks—"Memos"—of the garden-variety "You-can-do-it" approach that, happily, is back in style.

You'll find that your choices in jobs and careers are immensely varied because, as the Alumni Advisory Center, a career-planning association for college women, has pointed out, we now have such new fields as archaeometry, bibliotherapy, community action, and ecology—as well as such jobs as advocacy architect, cross-cultural training expert, environmental systems analyst, and family planning specialist, to mention only a few.

It's obviously an impossible task—in 100 dialogues—to touch upon every field or to look ahead to the many new fields that appear each year. But the detailed resource section in Chapter 10 will give you the addresses for referrals for further information on (1) a breakdown of the variety of jobs available in each field; (2) a rundown on what each job entails; (3) where to obtain training and education; (4) potential places of employment; and (5) general salary scales. In this book I have purposely avoided pinpointing possible earnings because salaries vary geographically and are constantly out of date. Similarly I have also refrained from providing tips and techniques for looking for jobs since a wealth of that material is readily available in many other publications, including my own previous books.

The person-to-person viewpoint is the purpose of *this* book, and the positive statement of hope on each page says "Come on in and do this, too!"

So, as you read these statements of hope—in good times or in bad—let these dialogues with 100 women help you get started or restarted in a job or career that uncovers your special abilities, brings you in contact with others, and provides you with a good living as well as a good life.

Chapter 1

Business

Virginia Miles:
"When I started my career there was a depression. Nevertheless I began working, and I managed to get going in ADVERTISING, *despite the fact the depression went on. When it was over I was established.*

"I'm thoroughly convinced that a woman who has to (or who wants to) work for a living could hardly choose a better career than advertising," said Virginia Miles, a consultant for Young & Rubicam International, and a Ph.D. with the distinction of being the first and only woman in her company to become a senior vice-president.

"Compared to many other businesses, the opportunities are great. There's much less antifeminine prejudice, and there's hardly a department or function that doesn't have women in jobs from top to bottom.

"Account management is still the hardest, and it's practically essential for a woman who hopes to crack that to have an M.B.A. from Harvard Business School or a similarly good school. But, apart from that, there are women in personnel and marketing and, also, women copywriters, supervisors, secretaries, media planners and purchasers, accountants, art buyers, clerical workers, and researchers.

"Granted, when times are tough, the advertising business pulls in its belt. But you have to have courage and persistence if you're going to go into business.

"One way to enter the field is to get into one of the training programs a number of the big agencies run. From that start you can end up as an account executive and move up the ladder from there.

"If you hope to be a copywriter, you can start as a secretary in the copy department. But the *only* place this is true is the copy department, because it's too hard to cross the line in the other areas. As a secretary in the copy department, however, you're surrounded by copywriters. When you're ready you can ask for a chance to show how well you can write. And, if you can deliver the goods, you'll be a copywriter someday."

Dr. Miles began her career with a job as an agency researcher.

"I always wanted to work," she explained, "so I planned to study psychology and, probably, go into teaching. With that in mind, I went to Wellesley College for my B.A. and Columbia University for my M.A. But when I applied for teaching jobs, no work was available. As an alternative I continued my education—not a bad idea when the job market is tight."

Once Dr. Miles had her doctorate, she decided to look beyond teaching and examine other options in the psychology field. After deciding on research (although she knew little about research jobs at the time) she applied for work as a researcher at a small advertising agency.

"There was no opening for a researcher per se," she told me, "but the man in charge was in the market for a person to help with motivation research who could double as both a psychologist and a secretary. When I came along with my Ph.D. plus skills in shorthand and typing I obviously had the job made—especially at $25 a week, a good starting salary at that time."

In the two years she spent at the small agency Virginia Miles became such a qualified researcher that she was ready to move up the ladder when the agency closed on the founder's death.

"To get my next job I sent out 300 letters to employers who used researchers," she stated. "From this mailing I received 40 replies, one of which was from a large department store. After analyzing my options carefully I decided to take that job."

At the end of six years Virginia had progressed to a spot as associate director of the research department. But by this time she also had a small daughter, so she went into teaching temporarily in order to have more time with her child than a job in advertising allowed. Later, when she returned to business, she worked in various capacities in research. Subsequently, she spent 10 years with McCann Erickson, a leading advertising agency. While there she became a vice-president for research.

"I don't think jumping every two years works for women," she advised. "Generally, it's far wiser to stay with a firm and develop a track record there if possible. When you move, do it only for a broader opportunity. I left McCann Erickson to join Young & Rubicam as a non-research person because I had reached the top of my profession as far as research was concerned.

"At Young and Rubicam I began as a vice-president for special planning to help with problem solving (particularly in strategy development on difficult accounts) and with improving the agency's efficiency and the quality of its marketing and advertising output.

"When I was named senior vice-president I was put in charge of all new product development for our clients, and since I've been here I've worked with almost every account—ranging from brassieres to aluminum moldings, from dog food to rubber globes, from puddings to automobiles.

"This is exciting because there's never a moment to be bored. Moreover, the people who are attracted to advertising are generally of a very high caliber—intelligent, alert, well-educated, interesting, stimulating, and involved.

"Equally important is the fact that it doesn't matter what sex you are so long as you do a good job. This, to me, is vital, because women should be able to do anything they want.

"Today we can all pursue more liberated goals and move in one direction or in several directions. And I love being a woman with a chance to do this.

"I also love being a woman in the world of men. It's fun to be the only woman in a conference, and when you make a speech and find you're the only female in a room with 1,000 men—well, I happen to enjoy that, too.

"Naturally, you encounter little putdowns at times. But men are learning, so you take things in your stride. For instance, when they say, 'Gee, you're smart for a woman,' I just smile and accept the compliment, though sometimes I have to laugh at some of the things that go on—like the time I went to Washington and the plaque I got congratulating me on my speech contained the statuette of a man!

"But I still love being a woman, and I've found out from my

, experience that, though you have to be strong and tough-minded, you don't have to be a person who doesn't know how to be nice.

"It pays to have time for people and to ask for and offer help. And a shoulder that others can lean on never hurts anyone."

MEMO 1:

> WHILE YOU ARE PLANNING AND LOOKING AHEAD TRAIN YOUR-
> SELF TO DO AS MANY THINGS AS POSSIBLE WITHIN THE SCOPE
> OF YOUR GOAL. THEN START WITH WHAT IS AVAILABLE AND
> TELL YOURSELF IT DOESN'T REALLY MATTER IF THE JOB WITH
> WHICH YOU HAVE TO BEGIN IS FAR REMOVED FROM YOUR ULTI-
> MATE AIM. THINK OF IT AS A DRESS REHEARSAL FOR THE SPOT
> THAT YOU WILL EVENTUALLY OBTAIN AS YOU GAIN ADDED
> EXPERIENCE—AND AS THE JOB BREAKS FALL.

Eileen Gormley:
"FINANCE *is a challenging field.*"

College economics course started Eileen Gormley on her way to a high-level business career as a vice-president and senior institutional analyst with Thomson & McKinnon, Auchinclos, Kohlmeyer, Inc. in New York.

"I was lucky enough to discover my interest and get on the right track early," she confided. "And I was also fortunate in having parents who encouraged me to follow what appealed to me."

With a B.A. in economics from Trinity College and a M.B.A. in securities investment from New York University Graduate School of Business Administration, Ms. Gormley is one of a small percentage of women who work as financial analysts. In her work she is employed by a brokerage underwriting firm that buys and sells stocks of public-ly-held companies.

"Our customers include banks, insurance companies, pension

funds, and individuals," she informed me. "I'm responsible for the textile, apparel, home furnishing, cosmetics, publishing and printing industries; my job consists of analyzing companies within these industries whose stocks and bonds are for sale to investors at large.

"To do this I start from a very broad field and narrow it down to the specifics that help investors determine if a stock interests them.

"This means I look first at the general economic conditions and expectations and then follow this outlook for specific industries. After assembling these factors I place the industry outlook in the economic framework.

"Next, I evaluate individual prospects for a specific company. I appraise the management of the company, the price of the stock, and its suitability to the potential investor's objectives. Finally, I decide whether I think the stock is a buy, a hold, or a sell.

"My report of this evaluation is distributed by my company to its customers, who use it to help them in their investment decisions.

"Intellectually, this is a very challenging field because it involves so many different things," Eileen Gormley continued. "First, you must do a tremendous amount of reading and studying. For example, you must study a specific company to acquaint yourself with its products, its position within an industry, and the profitability of its various aspects.

"Simultaneously, you must keep up with business journals, government statistics, trade papers, and all the news coverage that keeps you aware of what is going on in the world politically, socially, and economically. Attending and speaking at seminars and conferences is still another involvement.

"Writing my reports is a challenge, too, because an analyst has to be able to communicate ideas and evaluations in a way that sparks interest and provokes action."

Ms. Gormley began her career in this field with a first job in the investment counseling department of a bank. Later she worked as an analyst with the U.S. Securities and Exchange Commission and the American Stock Exchange. During those years she did graduate work at night.

"Education is a continuing thing in this field," she stressed, "so after my graduate work I spent three years studying for the examinations for certification as a Chartered Financial Analyst. I still take courses that increase my qualifications.''

In 1966 Eileen joined the research department of Goodbody & Company as a security analyst. Subsequently, she expanded her experience still further by working with other New York firms before joining her present firm.

''I believe that women with an inquiring mind, a feel for business, good training and experience, and a willingness to work hard can find this field a rewarding one,'' she finished.

''Granted, everybody has seen the stock market go up and down, and its natural to wonder during 'down' times about the job opportunities in the field.

''But on the brighter side a contraction in the number of firms in the industry during the past few years has led to an upgrading of the profession, so that the people who get the jobs in the field today are better qualified than ever before.

''In a sense, it's the old, old story—if you're a little bit better than good. . . .

MEMO 2:

> DEVELOP AN INQUIRING MIND AND A LOVE OF LEARNING BECAUSE WITHOUT MAKING THE BEST USE OF YOUR MIND YOU CANNOT MAKE A WORLD FOR YOURSELF.

Vivian Bruno:
''Market researchers should be people who can see both the forest and the trees.

''MARKET RESEARCH can be defined as the gathering, recording, and analyzing of all facts about problems relating to the transfer and sale of goods and services from producer to consumer,'' said Vivian Bruno, associate director of marketing research at Thomas J. Lipton, Inc.

"In the old days the man who made a cabinet knew the person for whom he was making it. Thus the customer could tell him exactly how he wanted the cabinet made. But today the distance between the producer and consumer is so great that market research is essential.

"Suppose a company wants to run a premium promotion—an offer of an item in return for a box top and a certain amount of money. What should the premium be? What would the consumer like?

"Or imagine a corporation is sponsoring a TV show? Should it continue or drop the show? How does the public feel?"

To learn the answers to problems such as these, independent market research firms and the market research departments of manufacturers, producers, packers, banks, retail outlets, and advertising agencies collect information that will help management make wise decisions.

"Some companies have interviewers on their marketing research staff," explained Vivian Bruno. "But in others—ours, for instance—staff people do not interview or measure the movement of items on store shelves.

"Instead we're here to define the problem and design the methods we'll use to find out what we want to know. To do this, we devise a questionnaire, guide form, or checking sheets. Then we have specialized independent market research firms gather the information, according to our specifications.

"When the raw data is returned we prepare our analyses and reports."

Vivian Bruno got her start after graduating from Douglas College with a major in economics (and a Phi Beta Kappa key which no one ever sees her wear).

"When I was a senior and about to be graduated I heard of an opening at Lipton's," she said, "so I went for an interview and landed it. At that time market research was in its infancy. But business was beginning to boom and everything was upward. It was the perfect example of being in the right place at the right time with the right company."

To take full advantage of this happenstance, Ms. Bruno took courses twice a week at the New School for Social Research and eventually earned a master's degree in sociology.

"In market research today many people put a great deal of emphasis on psychology and social sciences," she commented, "so this background is very helpful. Others stress a marketing and business administration background, so, in many respects, some of both backgrounds is good. Mathematics and statistics are important too.

"Right now we have a prime need for women who can see figures for what they are, for women who view them as symbols that say things. This is important because in analytical work it's often our job to take these symbols and translate—maybe thousands of figures—into two paragraphs.

"One can only do this with experience, of course. But certainly any woman interested in market research should work toward developing this qualification."

MEMO 3:

> PLAN TO GROW WITH YOUR CAREER BY USING EVERY BIT OF POTENTIAL THAT YOU HAVE. THEN REMODEL YOURSELF AS YOU GO AND SEEK EVERY OPPORTUNITY TO ENLARGE YOUR EXPERIENCE.

Bettylou Scandling:
"The longer you're in LIFE INSURANCE *the more money you have coming in.*

"Life insurance is a wide open field," advised energetic Bettylou Scandling, a Chartered Life Underwriter who specializes in estate planning and financial consultation.

"And a woman can decide to enter it at almost any age."

When not making waves selling life insurance in either her New York office or an office nearer her home, Ms. Scandling is flying her airplane on selling trips throughout the country. "I take a trip about every two weeks," she declared, "and often I fly and sell on weekends since clients are free to fly with me then. My flying office makes a wonderful place to talk—and to sell—without any interruptions.

"The biggest problem in pursuing an independent occupation, such as life insurance, is motivating yourself to be a self-disciplined self-starter," she pointed out.

"Your time is your own, so you can talk to the people you want to when you want to. But it's imperative to use your time efficiently and take business to the clients instead of waiting for the clients to come to you. In selling, you're not really doing a thing unless you're in front of people."

On this premise Bettylou Scandling has managed to achieve ever since she switched to life insurance. Earlier she was a mezzo-soprano with the Chicago Opera Company and a singer of popular tunes on radio.

"When I was singing, insurance sold itself to me—I didn't look for it," she revealed. "It all came about when a tenor friend who had entered the life insurance business invited me to lunch and told me I ought to sell insurance.

"At first I thought he was out of his mind. But that night I sold a friend an accident policy for $12. Seven weeks later my friend had an accident and broke her toe; when she collected over $700 I decided I was in business."

From that start Ms. Scandling progressed to more sophisticated selling and eventually moved into her specialty—estate planning and financial consultation. In this specialty she works closely with lawyers, accountants, and trust officers.

"In a career such as mine, you find prospects, make appointments with them, discover the policy best suited to their needs and ability to pay and then help them buy the policy," she commented. "Usually, you represent one company in the beginning. Another alternative is to look for a job in an independent agency.

"College is advisable, since it gives you a base to grow from—but you don't *have* to have a college education for this business. A number of companies and agencies have very good training programs.

"Moreover, if a woman is young or middle-aged—say 40 or under—she can help finance her training period through a plan in which she can draw against future commissions while in training.

"Once you obtain training and experience you can go into joint work with another underwriter and work as an assistant till you gain more knowledge and feeling for the field. Later, you can start out on your own.

"If you decide to enter this field," Ms. Scandling continued, "you need to adopt a professional viewpoint and look ahead to becoming an underwriter who takes her work seriously. You also need a feeling for people and their needs because you can't hope to sell insurance unless you care sincerely.

"As far as money goes, you can earn anything you want," she went on, "because in life insurance you have not only your original sales but also the continuing annuities that are paid over a number of years.

"Fortunately, you can count on selling life insurance in a less than perfect economy, too, because in inflation people need it even more."

MEMO 4:
> WAKE UP IN THE MORNING READY TO USE THE DAY. THEN, DAY BY DAY, BE A FULL-STEAM-AHEAD SELF-STARTER, KNOWING THAT IF YOU DON'T SCHEDULE YOUR DAYS CAREFULLY, THERE WILL ALWAYS BE AT LEAST ONE EXCUSE FOR FAILING TO GET DOWN TO BUSINESS.

Mildred Colon:
"There's romance in BANKING *for versatile women who do their work with feeling."*

Women are now branching out in banking and assuming executive posts, so those who are coming into the field can look ahead to a bright future—*if* they follow Mildred Colon's example and strive to move from their starting jobs right up to the top of the ladder.

"There's *romance* in banking," repeated Ms. Colon, president of a savings and loan association in a New York suburb. "And during the years I've been in it, banking and I have been good for each other."

The climb to her present business career began for Mildred Colon the day that followed her high school graduation.

"I was offered a four-year-college scholarship," she told me. "But money was tight because of the times, so I was unable to take it since it involved the expenses of getting to and from school."

The alternative for the young graduate was a job with a large corporation. "I started in the typing pool," she remembered, "but I liked working from the very beginning, so before I left—after marrying during World War II—I'd advanced to a spot as assistant purchasing agent."

Throughout the war years Mildred traveled as an Army wife. Then when her husband was killed in service she moved to a New York suburb with her infant son and started back to work by doing typing and secretarial work at home.

But her "I like to work" philosophy—plus her need for a regular income—soon pushed her into office work for three different employers each day. "In the morning I worked for an electrical contractor, in the afternoon for a savings and loan association, and in the evening for a physician," she recalled. "Later I remarried and had another child."

Subsequently, Mildred Colon began working full-time for the savings and loan association and devoting her energies to building a career in banking. Through studying and on-the-job training and experience she gradually progressed to the post of secretary to the association. Later she became president.

As president, she administers all banking services, travels, does property appraisals and inspections, and attends a round of meetings. In addition, she generates business, makes decisions, and sees that she is available when and where she is needed.

"In any career, I think women who want to get ahead should face problems with productive thinking and come up with affirmative and helpful answers. Negative thinking is never good. It ends up as an automatic putdown."

For women starting out today with the goal of becoming a bank officer, a college degree in business administration or liberal arts is a good background. Many banks have formal executive training programs, and many offer advanced training through evening courses. Usually after you start in a clerical position you're rotated among different departments to obtain practical experience.

To succeed in getting ahead you must have sound judgment and the ability to make good decisions. You'll also need a constant and current knowledge of such things as the trends of the economy, the status of the stock market, the value of real estate, and the latest developments in state and federal legislation. While building your career, associate yourself actively with business, professional, and community organizations.

"As far as personal qualities go, you require patience and understanding and a sensitivity to the people around you," Mildred Colon stated. "But these are qualities women possess, so as we said at the start of our talk, banking can be good for them.

"And banking is a career field that is going to go on and on!"

MEMO 5:

> GET INTO THE HABIT OF PRODUCING BY FORCING YOURSELF TO ACCOMPLISH A LITTLE MORE THIS WEEK THAN YOU DID LAST WEEK. THEN PUT DOWN IN BLACK AND WHITE AN IMAGINATIVE, HONEST-TO-GOODNESS WORD PICTURE OF WHAT YOU WANT TO BE DOING FIVE YEARS FROM TODAY. START WORKING TOWARD THAT END NOW.

Jacky Hossenlopp:
"TRAVEL *is a wonderful business for women who have a feeling for organizing trips.*

"In many respects I've been involved with travel for most of my life," commented Jacky Hossenlopp, owner of a travel agency and a woman whose interest in traveling goes back to her childhood in France.

"My father worked for hotels, the French Line, and Air France," she said, "and my first travel experience—when I was four—was on an early cross-Channel flight when we went to London for Christmas."

After growing up in France and helping her father manage a theater during World War II, Jacky Hossenlopp transplanted herself to the United States with the husband she'd met during the war.

"While I was raising my children I was always interested in travel, both armchair and actual," she said, "so my husband and I took many trips with our family within the United States and, occasionally, back to Europe.

"But even when we weren't going anywhere I read maps, guides, and newspaper travel sections and planned trips for sheer enjoyment."

Later, when the children were all in school, Jacky Hossenlopp took a job with a weekly newspaper helping out where needed.

This first job gave her a drive to progress, so, eventually, she went into selling advertising for the paper—an experience, incidentally, that was excellent training for a future career in selling travel. Throughout those years she was also active in community organizations—another plus for the travel business since it develops contacts.

"After five years of working for the newspaper, I saw a job advertised for a travel agent with European experience," she said. Though she didn't get the advertised job, the owner of the agency hired her for a starting position. With that as her base she learned the travel business on-the-job.

"Eventually I found that 5 1/2 days a week were too much while the children were all at home," she acknowledged, "so my employer suggested I go into outside sales as I had many friends and contacts and had brought a great deal of business into the agency through them."

The next few years Jacky Hossenlopp sold personalized travel from her home—except for occasional trips to the office for paper work. When she had a good following and substantial experience, she started an agency on a co-ownership basis. Later, she established the Pascack Travel Agency, named for the valley in which she lived.

"In order to open an agency and apply for steamship and domestic and international airlines appointments, you must have a number of years' experience in the business," she stated. "You also need a starting capital in the neighborhood of $20,000 to obtain the necessary bonding."

When you work in a travel agency you plan—or help plan—

itineraries and accommodations for individuals, groups, and businesses. Then you book all kinds of trips, from a bus trip to a flight around the world. You're involved in an unbelievable amount of detail and a great deal of follow-up. But it's interesting talking and planning with people, and after you've been in an office a year you get a discount on airlines and other travel advantages. Usually, you travel extensively yourself. In the years Jacky Hossenlopp has been in business she has been to Russia, Costa Rica, the Virgin Islands, Puerto Rico, Nassau, Freeport, Hawaii, California, Las Vegas, Mexico, Canada, El Salvador, Bermuda, Greece, England, Belgium, Venezuela—and on a number of cruises, of course.

Often the best training for this field comes from working in an agency, though there are a number of travel schools as well as travel courses at community colleges and adult education schools. Once you are in the business you can take seminars and advanced courses that will qualify you to be a Certified Travel Counselor.

The best way to get a job is to watch newspaper advertisements or to apply to agencies for part-time or full-time trainee jobs. If you opt for outside selling—another way to learn the business—you will work on commission. Contact an agency directly if you feel you can bring in business this way.

"When you enter this field you should want to be a professional and work at the highest level," Jacky Hossenlopp advised. "You must know the product you're selling and the people you're selling to.

"All you have to sell is your service," she said when we finished talking. "Since the merchandise is the same everywhere you must understand people and be good at planning their trips."

MEMO 6:

WHEN YOU'RE READY TO MOVE UPWARD MARKET YOURSELF EFFECTIVELY BY MAKING A LIST OF POTENTIAL EMPLOYERS AND WRITING JOB APPLICATION LETTERS BY THE CARLOAD. ONE ANSWER FOR EVERY 20 LETTERS CAN BE PAR FOR THE COURSE. BUT PRACTICE OLD-FASHIONED STICK-TO-IT-TIVENESS AND KNOW THAT A NEW OPPORTUNITY WILL COME.

Therese Fitzhugh:
"Being in charge of OFFICE MANAGEMENT *in a large legal firm is a fairly new type of opportunity.*

"Up until a few years ago office managers in law firms were few and far between," revealed Therese Fitzhugh, office manager for a firm of eight lawyers. "The usual practice was to turn over this responsibility to the managing partner or an associate of the firm.

"In fact, when I first started you could almost count on one hand the number of law office managers in the area in which I work. Now it seems as though every other office has one.

"Actually, an office manager is a middle person who's hired to keep both the attorneys and staff happy," she explained. "In my work I'm responsible for overseeing the work flow and supervising the non-lawyer staff. This keeps me busy recruiting, interviewing, hiring, training, evaluating, scheduling work, purchasing supplies, and, sometimes, dismissing employees.

"I also serve as a sounding board when people on my staff have problems. And when a person is out, I usually try to fill in and handle the job, whether it's a receptionist, administrative assistant, or IBM mag card operator."

Though Therese believes working experience as a legal secretary plus a good business background is one route to a job such as hers, she did not follow this path.

Originally from Indiana, she went to Southern Illinois University and majored in psychology. Later she worked as a secretary and bookkeeper in both a pharmacy and a bank. During those years she was also a dedicated volunteer for the Easter Seal Society, a commitment motivated by a bout with polio which put her in a wheel chair when she was 12 years old.

"Through my work with the Easter Seal Society in Indiana, I obtained a job as secretary to patient services in a rehabilitation center in Connecticut," she said, "so several years ago I came East.

"After working for a while in Connecticut I moved to a spot as an administrative assistant in the New Jersey Easter Seal Society office. Next, I progressed to my present job as our firm's first office manager. At the start I knew nothing about managing a law office. But I got my job on the premise that I was willing to study and learn—and that's exactly what I did.

"For the first six months I used all the reference books at my disposal and burned the candle at both ends, working during the day and studying at night. I still do this to keep up with all that is new."

"Speaking of things that are new," I remarked, "no conversation with the office manager of a legal firm would be complete without requesting a clarification of the fairly recent terms—legal assistant, paralegal, and paraprofessional. They're used so interchangeably that many people who hear them are not sure what each one means."

"I'll have to define them personally," Therese Fitzhugh replied, "but from talking to other people in law I believe my definitions are the general consensus.

"To me, *legal assistants* are very competent legal secretaries. They're usually graduates of secretarial schools, and they have good skills and working experience in a law office. They're also well able to relieve attorneys of many routine duties and to handle parts of the work flow under an attorney's supervision.

"On the other hand, I consider that *paralegals* are college graduates who have pursued their education in the legal field. They can perform many of the ministerial functions of law so long as they're under the supervision of a licensed attorney.

"Usually a good way to distinguish between a *legal assistant* and a *paralegal* is: a *legal assistant* performs secretarial functions; a *paralegal* does not."

When it comes to training for *paralegal* work, Therese explained, there is no one unified requirement, though some community colleges offer a two-year legal associate degree. Another excellent preparation is a three-month intensive course available at some colleges and universities for people who already have bachelor's degrees.

As far as *paraprofessionals* go, Therese, like others with whom I've talked, considers that the term is used loosely. At this writing, there are no formal, established requirements that define the classification, though some states are studying certification requirements.

"My feeling is that whether you're a paralegal or a legal assistant you're actually a paraprofessional if you're specialized in your field and competent in your work," contended Therese.

"But whatever you are specifically," she concluded, "you never stop learning in law. You go home every evening aware that you learned something new that day."

MEMO 7:

KEEP A CHALLENGE IN FRONT OF YOU AND REFUSE TO BACK-TRACK OR GIVE UP. EVEN WHEN SITUATIONS ARE HARD, MAKE YOUR LIFE BETTER BY GROWING WITH EVERY NEW JOB OPPORTUNITY.

Eileen Vergara:
"RETAILING *offers hundreds of jobs and great opportunities to people who want to move ahead—and who prove that they can produce.*

"When I decided to go into interior design I chose to do it within the framework of retailing," said Eileen Vergara, an interior designer at a branch store of Bloomingdale's. "I made this decision because so many things are happening in retailing."

Some of the areas that offer good jobs are selling, buying, advertising, promotion, copywriting, art, display, fashion coordinating, modeling, public relations, administration—and, as Eileen demonstrates, interior design.

"In my job I must be constantly turned on—and I love it," she stated. "One major part of my work is designing for private clients who seek the store's services to discuss floor plans and color schemes, select merchandise, and pick out wall coverings and fabrics. In addition, I work as a floor consultant for customers who need advice on a specific problem—will the sofa they have selected go with what they already have? Planning model rooms or floor changes is also important, as is going to the New York market to shop in fabric and wallpaper houses."

Eileen's interest in design goes back to the age of nine—one of her favorite activities was writing to a newspaper decorating column for advice on window treatments.

"When I wasn't writing for this kind of information I was driving my family crazy by constantly arranging and re-arranging our coffee table," she smiled. "They couldn't see the point of all this, but I had a sense of how things should be—and I was disturbed if they were different."

Despite her interest in design, Eileen didn't go into it when she began her career. Instead she went to Hunter College, majored in psychology, worked for several insurance companies, and obtained her broker's license before she decided to leave insurance and train for her present career at the New York School of Interior Design.

"When I completed my training I looked for ways to enter retailing as an interior designer," she recalled. "But finding a job was difficult because, despite my portfolio, I had no experience. Finally, in responding to a newspaper advertisement I got my start as an interior designer for a small furniture company.

"I enjoyed that job very much," she went on. "But the company was small and I wanted to work for a large store. I answered a newspaper ad for the Bloomingdale's job and landed it."

If jobs in retailing sound good to you, preparation can be a high school diploma, on-the-job training, a training program sponsored by a store, a course of one, two, or three years in a fashion institute or interior design school, or college.

"From my experience I believe it all begins with a good basic education," pointed out Eileen Vergara. "And, for interior design, I think business experience is invaluable.

"The business sense and affinity for detailed work I acquired while working in insurance have been invaluable in my present job, especially when I have to send in orders and think of the many all-important small details.

"I also believe that it's good if you can work part-time while you're in school. It's difficult when you're starting out and have no experience. But if you have worked part-time in the field you can ease yourself in."

MEMO 8:

> YOU CAN'T TAKE A JOB AND SAY TO YOURSELF, "NOW I'VE GOT IT MADE," BECAUSE IN ORDER TO HOLD THAT JOB YOU MUST CONSTANTLY EDUCATE YOURSELF AND STAY ABREAST OF WHAT'S HAPPENING IN YOUR FIELD. WHAT YOU KNEW FIVE YEARS AGO MAY NOT MEAN A THING TODAY.

Dolores Moye:

"You're always meeting people when you're a public accountant."

Not too long ago public ACCOUNTING firms were hesitant to hire women because of the need to travel and work at factory sites.

But women's liberation has changed this, so Dolores Moye, a senior accountant in one of the offices of Haskins & Sells, an international public accounting firm, now travels to a variety of places, usually for several weeks at a time.

While she is on an assignment (she was working at a day school the day I interviewed her) she is the senior person on the job; often she has an assistant working for her. During the assignment she examines the analyzes business records, verifies their accuracy, prepares financial statements, offers suggestions for improving a financial situation, and reports her findings to management.

"But don't think for one moment that this adds up to a sedentary job," Dolores said. "You don't sit down and have things come to you. Instead you run around a great deal.

"Another aspect I like," she went on, "is the fact that in my firm no accountant is assigned to one client for more than three years in a row. Consequently, you're always meeting new people.

"In the years I've worked here I've audited the books at educational institutions, a hospital, a finance company, chemical organizations, a manufacturing firm, a brokerage house, and a bank. So far there has only been one job I've done two years in a row.

"I got started working with figures when I went to business school after high school," Dolores said. "It all came about because I didn't want to be a secretary and bookkeeping was my alternative.

"When I graduated I found a job as an assistant bookkeeper for a small engineering firm and worked there for two-and-a-half years. Subsequently, I switched to a hospital job where I thought the chances for advancement would be greater.

"Later, however, I realized I needed a college education, so I started going to college at night and working during the day."

Eventually, as accounting interested her more and more, Dolores decided to go to college during the day and work part-time in the hours left over. She also went to summer school to obtain additional accounting credits.

"When I received my degree I landed my job with Haskins & Sells through a campus interview. A few months later I began taking my C.P.A. examinations because the Certified Public Accountant title confers privileges and prestige. After a few years I started back to college part-time for courses toward my M.B.A.

"Public accounting is a great field for a woman who is willing to pull her own weight. She can't be turned off by long hours during peak seasons or by the need to travel to different job assignments. In January and February our minimal work week is 50 or 55 hours. Naturally, this is a grind, with work till 7 every evening and Saturdays and, sometimes, Sundays. But we're well compensated for these hours, and when the push is over, we're back to our normal 35-hour week.

"If women can cope with this," Dolores concluded, "the field is wide open for them—though they are only beginning to skim the surface of public accounting.

"A few years ago when we recruited at colleges where most of the accounting classes had 25 students or so, there was a maximum of five girls. But now I would say that approximately one-third of the classes consist of women."

MEMO 9:

THERE'S NO SUBSTITUTE FOR HARD WORK. IT MAKES PEOPLE WHAT THEY ARE AND IT MAKES UP FOR THE LACK OF ALMOST ANYTHING ELSE.

Joyce Loding:
"Consumer affairs specialists are involved in many things.

"CONSUMERISM is a fairly new field—and an extremely important one," stressed consumer affairs consultant Joyce Loding.

"In consumer affairs you are engrossed in anything and everything that relates to the consumer," she went on. "But, unfortunately, many organizations do not yet realize that this type of specialist would be beneficial to them. As a consequence, the best approach to entering this field is to gain the right experience, dig out opportunities, and market yourself accordingly."

Ms. Loding followed her own advice and developed her consumerism career after first training as a home economist and then working for an appliance company in which she represented the consumer viewpoint.

"But to go back to the very beginning—even before my appliance company job—you might say I reached my career by a process of elimination," she said.

"When I was ready to go to college I wasn't quite sure what I wanted to do. But I certainly knew what I *didn't* want to do, so I scratched out such things as teaching, nursing, and secretarial work. Eventually I ended up with home economics because I was interested in things around the house.

"I especially liked appliances, so as I approached my graduation from Penn State I wrote job application letters to a long list of appliance companies. One of the letters landed me a job with a midwestern appliance company where I stayed for 15 years."

But then Joyce wanted a change of scenery. "While thinking broadly of what I'd done in the past I decided to capitalize on my experience representing the consumer viewpoint and market myself as a consumer affairs specialist. I sent out 500 letters.

"One ended up on the desk of the Grand Union Company's director of consumer affairs. She was thinking of expanding her department, so she hired me for the job I wanted. I worked my way up to be director of consumer affairs myself."

As a consumer affairs specialist Joyce Loding and the other members in the department represented the customer. They pointed out to management anything that affected consumers, whether it was deciding on a store program determining what merchandise would be offered, or pinpointing what they believed were future customer concerns.

"We had to keep in touch with everything that went on in the whole ball park of consumerism," she explained, "involving ourselves not only with products and stores, but also with legislative matters and government relations.

"Our second job was to reach out to the customer from the company. We looked for ways to help customers become better shoppers. Direct ways such as having a pamphlet in the store or an ad to read, also indirect subtleties that customers could absorb by osmosis. The latter could be something on a label or a sign in a store that might make customers stop and think about what they are doing.

"Eventually, with this experience behind me, I left the company to work on my own as a consumer affairs consultant.

"When you want a career in this field, you need to aim for training that has a fairly broad application," Joyce declared. "Home economics is a natural, because it trains you to think about the family, consumers, and consumer needs.

"Other potential training grounds are marketing, economics, and business, as they all have flexibility and give you something to offer the retail or manufacturing industry.

"When it comes to advice for job hunting in less than perfect times," she wound up, "I might say that when I was job hunting in 1970 it was a 'bad time.' Today is not the best time either. Neither was the time in between really too good. But no one should hide behind the excuse or rationalization that 'Now is not a good time to be looking for a job, so I won't change jobs or look for work.'

"If you take that approach and attitude you could wait forever!"

MEMO 10:

      BE FAR-SIGHTED INSTEAD OF NEAR-SIGHTED AND CONCENTRATE ON THE BIG-TIME RESULTS OF YOUR DAILY WORK RATHER THAN ITS SMALL-TIME ROUTINE. VISUALIZE WHAT IT CAN MEAN IN THE TOTAL SCHEME OF THINGS.

Susan Rudy:
"RENTAL MANAGEMENT *offers a future and jobs with real potential.*

"Since a current trend in life-style definitely points to multiple-dwelling living, there are growing job opportunities for people in rental management," advises Susan Rudy, rental manager of Horizon House, a six-building luxury apartment complex atop the Palisades in Fort Lee, New Jersey.

As a rental manager, the knowledgeable Ms. Rudy supervises a staff of nine and tries to be available to tenants at all times.

"In many ways, handling a job such as mine is really a question of establishing rapport with people and listening to their needs," she told me. "The key to success is *communication.*

"For example, we deal with quite a few tenants or prospective tenants from foreign countries and there is sometimes a language barrier, so we have to work doubly hard at being patient and understanding. We also rent to many people who are making tremendous changes in their lives—people who are suddenly single because of divorce or a spouse's death; they're in a transitional period and they require special empathy.

"In addition, we work with transplanted New Yorkers who are fed up with the taxes and crime rates in the city. Their move across the Hudson is another challenge.

"But I love these different situations and that's why I love this work."

For the nitty-gritty part of her job, Susan spends a great deal of her time sending tenants invitations to renew rentals, working on leases, listening to tenants' suggestions, checking incoming tenants' qualifications and credit, and talking on the telephone for what seems like hours on end. "We work hard to avoid the old image of the landlord who's the enemy and the tenant who's the good guy," she smiled. "That image is no longer valid."

Susan Rudy got into rental management after graduating from high school and attending the University of Miami. At the time she had no idea what vocational direction she wanted to take. "In high school I liked art,'' she said, ''but I also enjoyed business, so I signed up as a business major.

''When I decided to leave college to get started in a career, I moved from Florida to New York to take a job with a clothing manufacturing firm. After a while I was made credit manager.

''My next job was with Dun & Bradstreet doing credit reporting, and while I was working there a friend who had taken a course in real estate prodded me to join the course and become a licensed real estate salesperson. I began attending classes at night while continuing to work for Dun & Bradstreet.

''The last day of the course I learned of an opening for a rental agent at Horizon House.'' Susan lost no time in investigating and getting the job. After two years, at 31, she was promoted to the rental manager's post.

''Actually, I think women are ideal for rental management because they have patience and tolerance,'' she said. ''They're willing to sit back and listen, and they also understand why women want to check out apartments more thoroughly than men. Moreover, I feel this is a field where women have complete equality with men. When they show what they can do there's a good future ahead.''

MEMO 11:

> BE MORE CONSCIOUS OF THE *QUALITY* OF YOUR WORK THAN THE *QUANTITY* OF HOURS YOU HAVE TO PUT IN TO ACHIEVE YOUR END.

Lore Moser:
"A job as a banquet manager is a wonderful career."

In charge of BANQUET MANAGEMENT for New York's Tavern-on-the-Green restaurant, Lore Moser has been responsible for arranging over 10,000 weddings and more than 25,000 parties, dinners, and luncheons. And in managing these affairs she has cared so much about her job that some of the persons for whom she arranged teen parties have come back for their weddings, named daughters after her, and asked her to be a godmother.

"To make it in this field you have to care about your work," Lore said emphatically, "because otherwise you can't make it mean very much. You have to care so much that sometimes people will ask you if you're the owner's daughter! But if you like people and large-scale planning, a job as a banquet manager can be really great for a woman because, when you're well prepared for it, it's doing on a big scale what many women do in a much smaller way."

Lore prepared herself by working as a waitress, cashier, receptionist, switchboard operator, and dining room hostess in restaurants and hotels part-time and summers while in high school and in Cornell University Hotel School.

"At Cornell I taught myself shorthand and typing so I'd have practical skills to add to my broad general training when I was ready for a job in the industry," she revealed. "If I hadn't had them, I wouldn't have landed my first job as secretary to a manager in one of New York's large hotels."

That job was invaluable to Lore, however, because she made many contacts in the industry. Through one of those contacts, she learned that the banquet manager's job at Tavern-on-the-Green was open. "I applied for it at once and I've been here ever since."

Although some people get into banquet management without any formal preparation, it's advisable to attend a school that specializes in training for the hospitality industry. You should also get on-the-job training through part-time or full-time work while you keep your eye on a banquet manager's post.

Once you land a job your work usually entails making arrangements for cultural events, wedding receptions, fashion shows, dinner-dances, luncheons, business meetings, and other special events. You talk with people planning a function, suggest ways of running it, set up a menu, provide the help needed, and see that the tables are arranged properly. Often you attend the festive occasion to see that all is in order. You also keep busy contacting people on the phone and sending out mailings to introduce your banquet services to organizations and other persons who want party facilities.

During the years Lore has done this at Tavern-on-the-Green, originally built as a shepherd's house in 1870, she has never stopped caring about her job. "This is my world," she told me, as we stood at the restaurant's door and looked out at Central Park where flocks of sheep grazed a century ago. "I work in the park and play in the park," Lore Moser finished. "And I love it and care about it so much that I live right across the street."

MEMO 12:

> GET INTO AREAS WHERE THINGS ARE HAPPENING. THIS PUTS YOU IN A POSITION WHERE YOU WILL BE AVAILABLE WHEN A CHANCE COMES TO MOVE AHEAD. IT ALSO FORCES YOU TO COMPETE ABOVE YOUR OWN LEVEL.

Elizabeth Lyons:
"Women are moving into MANAGEMENT CONSULT-ING*—and the trend is likely to continue.*

"Women were making good progress in management till the 1970s slump in the economy set back many programs and caused lay-offs," declared Elizabeth Lyons, a management consultant and an enthusiastic supporter of women in management. In her own managerial work she heads two firms—Elizabeth T. Lyons and Associates and Elizabeth T. Lyons Placement Services in New Brunswick, New Jersey.

"But as things grow better and we move forward, opportunities will increase—though women who want a management job must prepare themselves to offer something concrete," she stressed. "If they have a liberal arts background they need to combine it with courses that will enable them to work in business and industry. And if they have a degree but have been away from work for several years, they must update themselves and be prepared to start at the bottom of a company and learn about the organization before they can expect to get into a management training program or be promoted to management.

"A few years ago I would not have said that. Instead I would have said, 'Prepare yourself well, hang in there, and try for that management job.' But during the recession, management trainees usually came from college recruiting programs."

Elizabeth Lyons entered management from a broad base of experience and training that included administrative jobs in both business and volunteer work. After growing up in New Brunswick and receiving her education there, she worked in business briefly prior to her marriage. Later, when one of her children had polio at age two, Ms. Lyons was so impressed with the March of Dimes and the National Foundation for Infantile Paralysis that she offered her volunteer services. Soon she was involved in public relations for the Foundation, as well as a weekly radio show on public service time. "During these years as a volunteer I learned a great deal and met some very interesting people," she said. "When I was ready to go back to work, I was hired for a job in the public information office at an arsenal because of these contacts."

While Elizabeth Lyons worked at the arsenal she maintained her on-going interest in the March of Dimes. Subsequently, while attending a conference on rehabilitation, the assistant administrator of a hospital offered her a spot as his public relations director. She spent the next five years serving in many capacities at the hospital until she was made assistant administrator, a post she held for 10 years.

"At that point I had almost every department reporting to me at some time or other," she stated, "so there was a tremendous opportunity for growth and development. I also enrolled in Rutgers University for an evening program in health management. When I finished, I was asked to teach a portion of the program the following year and then revise it into a seminar series. I presented the series for three semesters."

Elizabeth Lyons decided, in 1972, to launch her own management consulting firm. "I work with clients in private companies, public agencies, and other institutions to help them identify and solve problems, evaluate jobs, salary and wage programs, and develop personnel and administrative policies," she explained. "I also present lectures, seminars, and awareness programs.

"One of the things that interests me most is helping women move into the new opportunities that affirmative action programs offer them," she said, "so I have also started a placement service for women seeking professional, scientific, technical, and sales employment. In addition, we place men," she hastened to add. "We don't discriminate in reverse.

"The first move toward a managerial position is an important step," she concluded, "but this initial step is not necessarily a leap into a glorious job. The essential thing is to get into business and industry. Then observe and learn. Make contacts. Pick up necessary courses. And welcome opportunities to take management training seminars.

"Be ready to move and energetic enough to say, 'This is what I want to do.' "

MEMO 13:

> USE RESOURCEFULNESS, INTELLIGENCE AND JUDGMENT IN EVERYTHING YOU DO, AND WHENEVER AND WHEREVER YOU CAN ASSOCIATE YOURSELF WITH TOP ECHELON PERSONS SO THE PEOPLE WHO HAVE THE "SAY" IN YOUR FIRM WILL BE AWARE OF YOU.

Alice Wayne:

"When you're looking for job opportunities the main question to ask—and answer—is 'What have I ever done in my life that would lead to the right work for me?' "

One woman who asked and answered successfully is lively Alice Wayne, SOCIAL DIRECTOR of Kutsher's Country Club in Monticello, New York.

"The story of how I became a social hostess begins when my first marriage broke up, a time when I didn't feel particularly prepared for any type of work," Alice confided. "I didn't know what to do next, so I sold magazines by telephone till I could decide.

"I finally came up with the thought that for the time being, at least, I could use my college degree to work as a substitute teacher. With that as my first step, I enrolled in a round of education courses to refresh my training and obtain certification as a teacher. I continued to sell magazines at night.''

Alice's second step was transplanting herself to California, where, after teaching and taking more courses, she broadened her experience by moving into recreational work for the city of Santa Monica. ''I got that job by telephoning the city officials and asking for a chance to talk with them about the possibility of working in their recreation centers,'' she explained. ''Thanks to that phone call and subsequent interview I was hired as a recreation leader. My initial job was organizing programs for people from 3 to 70. As I worked this field seemed so right for me that I entered a pilot program for recreation directors.

''Eventually a move back East interrupted the start of my new career. But, later, a chance remark in which I was told I'd make an ideal social hostess led me into taking a temporary job at a resort hotel in New York's Catskill Mountains.''

When the temporary job was over, Alice was so anxious to continue in this work that she asked for an opportunity to stay on at the hotel without salary during the off season. She learned how to coordinate social activities, develop ideas for singles and other groups, organize games and activities, introduce guests, and perform on occasion as an entertainer herself.

''From the beginning I moved from post to post to gain experiences and references,'' she said. ''Finally, I landed at Kutsher's, and I've been social director here ever since. Besides, the copious notes I've taken in observing people have yielded two published books. The first was *Love, Anyone* and the second, *Games Singles Play*. A third is in the works. I'm also happily re-married to a maître d'.''

To other women who are interested in being a social hostess Alice suggests making a long list of the steamship and cruise lines, resort hotels, country clubs, group tours, and travel organizations you find listed in local and metropolitan telephone directories. When you're qualified, write to each name on your list.

MEMO 14:

> BRING FRESH IDEAS TO YOUR JOB AND DEVELOP A REPUTATION FOR SEASONING YOUR WORK WITH INNOVATIONS AND PERSONAL TOUCHES.

Chapter 2

Handcrafts, Needlecrafts, Foodcrafts

Florrie Paul:
"FOOD SCULPTURE *is a unique way to make culinary creations more than food.*

"Many talented people who are specialists in a hobby could turn it into a job and share their talent with others," stressed kitchen craftswoman Florrie Paul, who has made an interesting job for herself teaching, lecturing, and demonstrating the art of food sculpture. In addition, she has published a book, *How To Create Incredible Edibles: An Illustrated Guide to Imaginative Food Preparation*.

"Food sculpture is a way of transforming low-cost fruits, vegetables, and meat from supermarkets into table decorations you can eat," she explained. "I make peacocks out of pineapples, whales out of watermelons, Viking boats out of cucumbers, penguins out of hard-boiled eggs, and vegetable bouquets out of cabbages filled with onions that are chrysanthemums, carrots that are tulips, and beets that are roses.

"After teaching this craft in my home and in adult education classes for several years, I now run private workshops limited to nine students each. My students are mostly caterers, restaurant owners, gourmet-cooking teachers, and housewives. And I'm happy to say I'm listed in *The New York Times Cooking School Round-Up*.

"I also make appearances in department stores and on television and give lectures and demonstrations for organizations, conferences, and resort hotels. This takes me traveling quite a bit."

It all began for Florrie Paul in her mother's kitchen, in which, as she describes it, she learned to "play around." "I 'played around' because I liked making food pretty," she said, "so after I married and had three children I continued with this hobby. For instance, as I'd see expensive floral decorations and food garnishments I'd try to duplicate them in my own kitchen working with products from the supermarkets since I couldn't afford to buy truffles!"

Once Florrie Paul perfected her craft she contributed her talent to community organizations on a volunteer basis. "But as the children grew older their college expenses seemed very close," she recalled, "so, like many other couples, my husband and I started thinking of a side business that would bring in extra money.

"Food sculpture never entered my mind. Instead we decided to try a direct selling business which we could work on from our home. The woman who directed it suggested we begin with a demonstration party in which we'd show the products and serve coffee and cake.

"I didn't want to invite people to an ordinary demonstration party, so I added something extra—a lesson in how to use food sculpture to make a cucumber Viking ship and I arranged my refreshment table with food sculpture decorations. That was my start; following that evening, my phone kept ringing with requests for lessons in food sculpture.

"The requests stemming from word-of-mouth advertisement were so frequent that I started teaching in my home. Subsequently, someone suggested I contact the director of adult education at a nearby school, and when I showed him pictures of my food sculpture he hired me to teach.

"From teaching I was asked to lecture and demonstrate for various organizations, so I did that free for a while—to get my name around. Ultimately, I began getting paid for my lectures and receiving invitations to appear at department stores. Then, when people kept saying, 'Give us something in writing,' I wrote my how-to book. In addition, I sell the equipment I use in my demonstrations. My husband, who's now in business with me, takes care of the sales end of our work.

"Sometimes I can scarcely believe that all of this has happened to me," Florrie Paul admitted. "But it proves that there *is* a right job for every woman and that many women can turn their hobbies into profitable careers. All too often women feel that they must have a formal education for a career. In many cases this is true. But particularly in specialties or crafts no formal education or certificate may be needed."

MEMO 15:

> MANY CRAFTSPEOPLE DERIVE GREAT PLEASURE FROM TEACHING THEIR CRAFTS. BUT TO SUCCEED AT SUCH TEACHING YOU NEED A SOLID BACKGROUND OF EXPERIENCE, A SENSE OF ORDER, A KNOWLEDGE OF HOW TO RELATE TO OTHERS, AND THE KIND OF IMAGINATION THAT MAKES THE LEARNING PROCESS STIMULATING AND EXCITING. STUDY, READ, RESEARCH, AND PRACTICE. THEN, WHEN YOU'RE READY TO TEACH, SET UP A PLACE, DEVELOP A LESSON PLAN, ARRANGE SCHEDULES FOR GROUPS OR INDIVIDUALS, AND ESTABLISH FEES BY CHECKING PREVAILING RATES.

"Katie" Samson (Fayne H. Samson):
"The crafts you can teach are unlimited.

"I've always been interested in all arts and crafts," declared Katie Samson, who has had a creative career as owner of a CRAFT STUDIO and director of a large craft school.

"When it was time for me to think about careers, however, I didn't have the money to study art—and a 'crafts career' was not considered a career anyhow. I had to choose something with more security, so I trained to become a teacher. Later that training became the catalyst for my craft school success.

"In the beginning I combined my training, organizational ability, and love of creating with my hands to teach community groups. But all the while I kept thinking that some day I would like to open a studio and do the same thing in a big way.

"At first this was a daydream," she admitted, "but, nevertheless, I found myself collecting and filing any reference material pertinent to my dream—business ideas, teaching materials, and sources—and planning exactly what I would do if ever the opportunity arose to start a craft studio. When our family moved to a New York suburb, the time seemed right, so I launched a small studio near my home.

"A few other teachers and I provided instruction in almost every craft that produced professionally created accessories for the home or as gifts. As the years went on my craft school outgrew that small studio. I knew a couple who operated an art gallery and wanted to combine it with a craft line and school. So we merged our talents, interests, and businesses into a larger art and craft studio.

"We had space for the sale of supplies and three classrooms where teachers introduced students to folk art, decoupage, watercolor, flower beading, gold leafing, dimensional painting on glass, lamp making, flower preserving, and many more crafts. We have nearly outgrown our space.

"I started out as director, but now I limit myself to teaching some advanced courses when I am in the area. I'm taking advantage of this flexibility—a plus in a crafts career—because my husband is in the international office of his company and I travel a lot with him.

"In a few more years we plan to start a new craft venture together. It will be a small one classroom-one teacher studio, and we will sell craft supplies as well."

According to Ms. Samson, the mortality rate in a craft studio career can be great. There are several reasons. First, people believe that if they *do* a craft perfectly, they can *teach* it to others. But in fact you cannot automatically become a teacher without cultivating this skill.

People wrongly assume that craft teaching can be done on a shoe-string, so they start with insufficient capital for a complete stock and without enough money to carry them through the first two years when they are establishing the business.

Moreover, many people are not aware of how much time must be given to "managing the store"—to buying, selling, bookkeeping, store housekeeping, display, and much more. They neglect this basic management and have no way of knowing what their business is really doing. Creative people often do not enjoy "book work," and people who like working with figures may not care about being creative. Even a relatively small business can require several kinds of talent.

"But if you pool your skills with other people's," Ms. Samson warned, "each person should have specific responsibilities spelled out in a written contract drawn up with professional legal and accounting help."

MEMO 16:

> TO MAKE CRAFTS AN INCOME-PRODUCING CAREER, INVESTI-
> GATE THE CRAFT THAT INTERESTS YOU THOROUGHLY AND
> CHECK OUT ITS POTENTIAL. THEN PLAN TO CREATE, SELL, LEC-
> TURE—AND TEACH. ABOVE ALL, DEVELOP YOUR CRAFT INTO
> SOMETHING INGENIOUS, PROFESSIONAL, BEAUTIFUL, USEFUL
> AND NON-RUN-OF-THE-MILL.

Helen Squire:
"I don't think you can sit back and say, 'My idea is not going to work because of the times.' Instead think of ways to make it work in both slow and good periods.

"As a former fashion designer, my working experience has led me into many related fields," Helen Squire said, "and currently I'm using it for my QUILTING business, which I call 'Quilt-In.'"

"I provide a quilting course package to women's clubs, charity organizations, and church groups. The booking has a three-fold purpose.

"First, it offers educational craft lessons to the students. While studying the history of patchwork they also learn to quilt. During the course, they create a pillow front for themselves and a finished quilt, which later becomes a club project for the entire membership.

"The second purpose is to enjoy an old-fashioned quilting bee after the quilt blocks are finished. This is a social event open to all the club members and their friends. On the night of the quilting bee I have the quilt assembled and set up on the frame ready to go. With many women participating, we try to finish it in one sitting.

"The third purpose of the course booking is to raffle off the finished quilt.

"This is the core," Helen said, "but the business has many offshoots. I believe that you have to be flexible and have more than one thing to offer, especially when the economy is tight. You must also revise your programs as you go along and stay tuned in to people's needs. I make this work for me by teaching and department store demonstrations.

"In addition to my quilting packages, I have a one-hour presentation lecture called 'History of Quilting,' which I give when organizations ask me to stop by and explain my quilting course package. Instead of wasting good working time answering questions and talking while organizations decide whether or not they wanted the full program, I worked up a lecture, which I give for $30.

"Another offshoot of my business was a commission from an architect to make a very special quilt for $3,000. I was also involved in designing and working with groups on one of the 1976 Bicentennial quilts for exhibit and loan."

Actually, Ms. Squire's familiarity with quilts goes back to her childhood, when she slept under antique coverings. "But at that time I confess I wasn't aware of what was over me. Nor did I know how strongly quilting would be revived."

When it was time to make plans for working, Helen chose fashion design. After graduating from the Fashion Institute of Technology, she had a thriving fashion career that encompassed designing, production, market research, selling, and purchasing.

"I worked at New York-based jobs till the birth of my youngest daughter," she recalled. "Then I switched to staying home. But almost immediately I involved myself in volunteer work in the schools and teaching patternmaking, design, and sewing in recreation programs. Eventually, the resurgence of interest in quilting led me into doing heavy research on it.''

The time arrived when Helen felt ready to re-enter the job market. As she sorted herself out and thought things over, it seemed that all of her background added up to "Quilt-In."

"I got the ball rolling by thinking of every angle that would make my quilting package useful and interesting to organization,'' she advised. "Then I designed a course that provides everything participants need—a shopping bag for supplies, printed instructions, fabrics, backing for the quilts, and illustrations of various quilting patterns. I also established sources of supply for fabrics and devised the name and logo for the business. I joined the seminar on appliqué and patchwork offered by my alma mater, F.I.T., and picked up new tricks.

"What I didn't realize at the start, however, was that, despite the best planning in the world, you can't control the reception of your program or the time it will take to get it moving. I found that after I sold a booking to an organization it usually took nine or more months before they were ready to schedule it. That meant that if I had had to depend upon those first bookings for a living—or for paying the expenses of starting 'Quilt-In'—I would have been in dire straits.

"But I don't believe in sitting back and saying, 'It's not going to work,' when things are slow. That's when I decided to teach for some day-to-day income. That worked out well, too, because six or eight classes a week publicized my name and more work came my way for store demonstrations, exhibits, library programs, et cetera.

"When you want this kind of career,'' Helen contended, "it's necessary to analyze your strong points, evaluate your weaknesses and set attainable goals. From past experience I knew that I was strong at meeting people, selling, teaching, and organizing. My drawback was that as a mother of young children, I was not yet free for a full-time, 9-to-5 job. I needed employment that would enable me to control the hours I worked.

"And 'Quilt-In' allows just that.''

MEMO 17:

WHEN YOU DECIDE TO WORK FOR PROFIT FOLLOW WHAT

YOU'RE GOOD AT AND DO WHAT YOU CARE ABOUT. PICK UP
POINTERS WHEREVER YOU GO AND GIVE EXPERT WORKMAN-
SHIP AND SERVICE.

Joan Osofsky:
"A PATCHWORK *business seemed right for me.*

"In my business I design and make unique potholders, baby bibs,
tennis racket covers, oven mits, bedspreads, and other patchwork
items," Joan Osofsky informed me. "My customers are better department stores and boutiques across the country, as well as individuals
who hear of my patchwork through word-of-mouth advertising. Since
I have children at home this work is right for me now.

"Although I work alone these days I started out with a partner, and
we began by creating unusual patchwork gifts for friends and relatives
just for fun.

"At the very beginning we never even thought of a business," she
confided. "But as we gave away patchwork items, everyone loved
them, and, almost before we knew it, people were asking, 'Will you
sell them so we can give them as gifts'?"

While Joan and her partner considered this they conducted their
own market research. For example, when they gave a friend a potholder they would ask her to hang it in the kitchen and get comments
from everyone who came in. "Whenever we'd hear anything negative
we'd set about improving the potholder," Joan said. "Eventually we
made so many changes that today the potholders don't even look like
the first ones. When we began, we both lived in small apartments, and
with toddlers, new babies, a small amount of space, and a new
business, we were really crowded for a while. Now I'm established in
a home of my own with space for the business in the basement."

Originally the women sold only to individuals. But one order led to
another and one day someone suggested the names of some stores that
might take the patchwork. "We contacted the stores personally and
made appointments with the buyers," Joan explained. "And when

the buyer in the first store—a well-known store—liked our work he gave us an order.

"This was a big break, because it provided us with an excellent reference. Soon other buyers were happy to see our samples. Some of the stores that became our accounts have branches, so that's how we began selling in different parts of the country. We learned as we worked, and the stores and buyers helped us with advice and taught us many things," Joan added. "I can remember sewing potholders till 4 a.m. some mornings when the business was getting started.

"Now I have several women who sew for me. I cut the fabric into squares and rectangles and put them in the right order. Then I give them to the women, who return the finished items when they're ready to be shipped."

To others who feel that the right job for them might be a home-based craft, Joan suggests these tips: Try various things till you turn what you do best into a very special, different, and professional product or service. Do your own private market research to find out how well it will sell. Don't buy more supplies than you need to fill your initial orders. Aim at placing your product in the best stores and outlets.

MEMO 18:

> WHEN YOU GET AN IDEA FOR A CREATIVE ENTERPRISE ORGANIZE YOURSELF AND YOUR ACTIVITIES SO THERE'S TIME FOR YOUR JOB, TIME FOR YOUR HOME, AND TIME FOR YOU. WITH THIS ORDERLINESS BEHIND YOU, GO AHEAD AND DO WHAT YOU WANT WITHOUT WORRYING ABOUT WHERE YOU'LL GET THE ENERGY AND HOURS TO WORK. INVOLVEMENTS MAKE YOU FORGET ABOUT BEING TIRED.

Marjorie Kubach:
"When craftswomen are professionals there are new opportunities all the time.

"There were no craft classes when I went to art school," said

Marjorie Kubach, an artist-craftswoman who makes STAINED GLASS window hangings and other glass pieces for the home. In addition, she gives equal time to printmaking and painting.

"But today things that were considered strictly crafts at one time are being exhibited side by side with fine arts," she pointed out. "Happily, it follows that the arts and crafts professions are now developing a kinship that is bringing them close together and creating a world of difference between the old and new approach to crafts.

"I approach my stained glass, for example, not totally as a craft but also as another art expression—such as painting or sculpturing. I exhibit whenever I can and sell my work through shops and galleries. I also teach part-time."

Marjorie Kubach has been involved in the arts and crafts world for as long as she can remember. She studied at the Art Institute in Cleveland and the Art Students League in New York. Later she obtained a B.S. and a M.F.A. from New York University. After, she and her husband went to Kansas to teach.

"While teaching I worked in various mediums," she recalled. "When we moved to Chicago I worked as a window display designer for a number of years."

Later, in New York, Marjorie's next step was stained glass. "Up till then I had never really thought of working with glass," she admitted. "But when interest in it was revived in the early Sixties I saw it as an opportunity to learn something new."

Ms. Kubach does not take massive jobs such as church windows. But she does create exciting pieces for the growing field of home decoration. "In the past only wealthy people were patrons of the arts," she noted. "But today the market is much broader and more people are seeking good art.

"If you're interested in stained glass as a career, I suggest you seek a well-rounded art education as a background," she advised. "You need a feeling for what has been done in the past—and for what is being done now. You also need to find out how you, as an artist-craftswoman, can relate to it.

"Once you start producing you can begin building your name by exhibiting in shows, entering competitions, and selling through craft shops.

"As in all arts and crafts endeavors, getting your work known is a basic problem," she acknowledged. "So is earning enough to survive, since the cost of materials and the time involved in producing a work often have very little to do with the price at which you are able to market it. This is *realism!* It's also a problem that women do not always recognize when they think of something like stained glass as a career field.

"But the arts and crafts field is a great way of life and the kind of career experience that brings satisfaction and joy."

MEMO 18:

>TODAY, AS ALWAYS, WHEN YOU WANT A GOOD JOB YOU FIND AND DEVELOP IT BY USING VISION, COMMON SENSE, AND INITIATIVE.

Suzi Schroeder Lifschitz:
"If you're willing to put in plenty of time and take the proper steps you can make a career of potting.

As a worker in POTTERY Suzi Lifschitz creates such visual delights as casseroles, wall hangings, planters, pitchers, mugs, Christmas wreaths, vases, sculptures, ash trays, and plates. Some of her work is for sale in her studio, and some is made on commission for decorators and individuals.

"I produce all of the articles that I sell," she told me, "and my studio with its potter's wheels and kiln is also home base for the potting classes I teach."

Suzi took the school teaching route to her present career.

"I always had a drive for art," she disclosed. "But when I finished high school, it was important to go to a college where I could get a scholarship. When I received one to Davis and Elkins in West Virginia, I majored in education—and took the art courses offered. After graduating, I taught elementary school. I also enrolled in art courses at neighboring colleges, so I could become an art teacher.

"While teaching I discovered potting," she went on, "so I started studying with a potter and taking courses at the New School and the Greenwich House Pottery in New York."

Suzi Lifschitz also spent many hours in museums, attended potters' exhibits, subscribed to potters' magazines, and studied other publications in her field. She also worked as a volunteer tour guide for children's groups at the Museum of the City of New York.

"I try to travel," she went on, "and wherever I go I visit museums and carry a sketch pad. After I visited England, for example, I created pottery based on ideas I found there. On a visit to Pompeii I became fascinated by the pottery remains I saw.

"The great thing about pottery is that it's an art form any one can learn," Suzi continued. "It takes perseverance and accepting casualties in the beginning. But that's part of learning. I have some lovely collapsed pots around my house today. But in a way that gives you incentive. You see exactly how far you've come—and realize how far you can go."

A few years after establishing her studio Suzi decided to open a gallery in an art and antiques area where she would continually show and sell her work—much like a one-woman show.

"For the benefit of other women, I should add that I had an interesting revelation during the six months I ran the gallery with the help of two salespersons. I found that money and recognition are not my only goals. Emotional fulfillment is important too, and as time went on, I found myself becoming too fragmented between two business establishments and my home. The right answer was to terminate the gallery.

"You don't necessarily need a college education for this career, but you do have to be willing to train yourself," Suzi Lifschitz pointed out. "As part of this training you must be critical of yourself and place your work in an environment where people who are good judges will criticize it in a constructive manner.

"It also helps to expose yourself to craft schools, where you have the opportunity to study with the best teachers. There are some excellent summer schools. One is in Haystack in Deer Isle, Maine.

Another is Penland School of Crafts in Penland, North Carolina. Attendance at one can give you a preview of how well you'd like a crafts career.''

MEMO 20:

> KNOW YOU WILL HAVE TO BE PERSISTENT—SOMETIMES IN THE FACE OF DISCOURAGEMENT—IN BUILDING UP MARKETS FOR YOUR WORK. SOME SHOPS OR GALLERIES WILL BUY YOUR HANDCRAFTED ITEMS OUTRIGHT. OTHERS WILL TAKE THEM ON A CONSIGNMENT BASIS.

Floss Perisho:
"Determination plus daily involvement put my CANDLEMAKING *on the road.*

"My family has always been closely associated with crafts," said Floss Perisho, whose candles have been exhibited in the American Embassy in Rome and sold in such places as Georg Jensen's in New York. "In fact, my mother, a weaver, was one of the first instructors at Penland School of Crafts. Eventually, I taught graphic arts there myself."

While Floss Perisho was teaching, her husband suffered a disabling heart attack. "In addition to having to stay home with him, I needed something new to do," she informed me, "so a former Penland instructor suggested candlemaking. My first molds were milk cartons and food containers, and the entire Penland community helped me collect them.

"In the beginning I made solid color candles, but they seemed to lack creativity. To overcome my dissatisfaction, I developed my own methods for mixing the colors by pouring the candles into molds with a separate layer for each color. I believe that the color combinations are what made my candles so salable."

Floss's first sales were through the Penland School of Crafts Gift Shop and through shops owned by fellow craftsmen and friends. Later she became a member of the Southern Highland Handicraft Guild and sold to its shops through its wholesale warehouse program. This established her and gave her a steady income.

"When I'm making candles my first job is preparing the molds," she explained. "Next, I melt and color the waxes and start pouring. After the candles harden, they're removed from the molds. Next they're checked, cleaned, wrapped in cellophane and packed for delivery. Though I've made thousands of candles," Floss confided, "I feel very personally involved with each one. In fact, I almost want to tell each candle to go out and do *its* best, since I've done *my* best in preparing it. The recognition my candles have brought me has been most rewarding.

"If I have any advice for women," Floss finished, "it's be determined to do your best, have faith and confidence in what you're doing, and work hard to make the craft you produce a part of you."

MEMO 21:

> WHEN YOU WANT TO CREATE A PRODUCT FROM YOUR CRAFT ASK YOURSELF: "IS IT FUNCTIONAL?" "IS IT A GOOD DESIGN?" "ARE THE COLORS ATTRACTIVE?" "IS IT IN DEMAND?" "WILL PEOPLE WANT TO BUY IT?"

Ruth Brandrup:
"If you can read, you can do anything.

"No one is born knowing how to do things," maintained Ruth Brandrup, whose initial career in the RUGBRAIDING field laid out the carpet, so to speak, for working in antiques too.

"Rugbraiding is easy to learn and through the years has led me in interesting directions," she said.

Ruth's memories of making rugs go back to her Midwestern childhood, when her family and other farm people sewed cotton strips together and wove them into rugs. Later, after marrying and moving away, she began braiding rugs with wool.

"I wanted to make a living room rug that would be an expression of my own taste and imagination," she confided, "so I began assembling wool strips. When I had enough I took them to a man with a loom and had a rug woven from them."

In the beginning Ruth felt great pride in her woven rug. But when it began to wear out too soon she realized that there was a defect in the weaving. To improve wear, Ruth took lessons in rugbraiding, sent for every publication she could find on the craft, and researched other people's methods. Combining all she learned with her own practical experience, she devised her own technique and began braiding outstandingly beautiful rugs which she exhibited at craft and antiques shows. She-began selling the simple tools required for her craft and taught rugbraiding, both in her filled-with-antiques studio and in adult education classes. Occasionally, she gives special rugbraiding courses for county historical societies and similar organizations.

"People who came to my studio for rugbraiding classes kept asking to buy my antiques, so I went into that business too," she said. To be as successful with antiques as she was with rugbraiding, Ruth again studied and learned all she could. Ultimately she became so knowledgeable that she was approached by a community college to teach a course in American antiques. Opportunities to lecture followed. While teaching she continued to expand her own knowledge by enrolling in Fairleigh Dickinson University for courses in American history and the history of art. She looks forward to a time when a college credit course on American artifacts can be offered.

"No one is born knowing how to do things," she emphasized. "It's sitting down and patiently learning what makes it possible for us to create what we want—be it rugbraiding or anything else."

MEMO 22:
DON'T BE A DILETTANTE AND PURSUE SOMETHING JUST TO FILL

UP YOUR AFTERNOONS. GET OUT IN THE WORLD AND PROVE
THE SERIOUSNESS OF YOUR COMMITMENTS AND GOALS.

Irene Preston Miller:

*"When you want to develop a business from a hobby you
have no idea how far even the smallest start can take you.*

"I've always loved to create with my hands, so SPINNING AND
WEAVING was a natural for me," said Irene Preston Miller. She
greeted me from behind her spinning wheel in "The Niddy Noddy" in
Croton-on-Hudson, New York.

"Before I had my family I taught art history," she continued.
"Then I married a photographer and began learning about his profession. When I had children I started working in crafts because I wanted
to keep busy in their growing years. Actually I began with our first
case of measles. To get through it I made figures of carrots, potatoes,
and raisins to entertain my child. I became so interested in the figures
we created that I researched puppetry in our local library and learned
enough about it to put on community shows as a volunteer.

"A few years later I got into spinning and weaving when my son
acquired a pet sheep. I was hooked by that sheep from the first," Irene
admitted. "Every time I looked at its wool, I couldn't help thinking
what fun it would be to weave thread into fabrics."

After fabrics Irene's challenge was embroidery. Then came teaching, stitchery, and writing *The Stitchery Book* with Winifred Lubell,
another creative woman Irene met while working as a volunteer in
school and community organizations. "But all the while I was working at assorted crafts I had no idea whatsoever that someday I'd be
involved in a business in a four-story studio and teaching center like
this," she declared.

It all came together when—very unexpectedly—Irene was offered
a chance to rent space for her first shop. "I had so many involvements

I didn't think for a moment that I could put a shop together," she told me. "But the more I thought things over, the more I realized a business that offered classes and supplies in all the textile crafts could be the culmination of all my interests."

In the nearly 10 years since Irene has moved from her original spot to the picturesque studio where adults and children congregate for instruction in spinning, dyeing and weaving; macrame; simple and advanced knitting; crocheting; tatting; lacemaking; beading; and all other kinds of stitchery. Books are available for sale or rent, and colorful shelves house supplies. A staff of experts teaches and occasionally outstanding craftspeople present seminars. Irene teaches, lectures, and demonstrates extensively at the center and in other parts of the country.

"With automation and jet-paced activities surrounding us, I see again and again that many people want to return to simple things, at least in some area of their lives," said Irene, as she patiently showed me how to spin a thread.

"And when you come right down to it, what is simpler than sitting and spinning?"

MEMO 23:

> MOST OF US CAN DO ANYTHING WE REALLY WANT IF WE MAKE A START. THAT START MAY BE VOLUNTEER WORK IF YOU CHOOSE IT CAREFULLY AND USE IT TO STIMULATE YOUR MIND AND TO GIVE YOU SOMETHING PRODUCTIVE IN WHICH TO INVEST YOUR TIME.

Adelma Grenier Simmons:
"There are many opportunities for free enterprise and small business in the creative crafts.

"To make the most of them I always try to avoid wasting time," said Adelma Grenier Simmons, who specializes in HERBS AND HERB GARDENS at Caprilands, her large eighteenth-century farmhouse in Coventry, Connecticut.

Ms. Simmons' business is varied. She plans and plants special herb gardens for colonial homes and antique shows; designs and makes pomander balls, potpourris, and other items for her farmhouse herb shop; devises recipes that use her herbs in delightful and imaginative ways; and holds open house for groups who come to tour her gardens, taste her dips, dunks and, breads, and attend special lecture-luncheons from April through December. She has 14 complete gardens and 26 different plantings. The garden plans are available in her shop. In addition, she lectures on herbs and herb products before garden clubs and horticultural groups; exhibits and sells at shows and expositions; carries on an ever-growing mail-order business; and compiles booklets on gardening and herbs in the scattered moments she has to sit down at her Caprilands desk. She is also the author of five books on herbs.

"My only free time is in January and February," she told me; "I use it to study the fine library I have amassed, with its material on food, folklore, and festivals that I need as background for my enterprises.

"Herb work—my own strange combination of the things I like to do—first interested me when, as a former department store buyer and stylist, I went in search of herbs for the store's gourmet shops. As I traveled for the store, I found that people knew very little about the fascination of herbs. On buying tours in Europe, I found that foods based on herbal cooking were so interesting that I began to dream of developing my own recipes.

"I gradually worked out a plan for starting my business with garden tours and lecture-luncheons for 50 people. Originally I worked alone. But now that all aspects of my business have grown, I naturally have people helping me.

"The secret of making a 'go' of it," Adelma Simmons advised, "is to live each day to the fullest, never waste a moment, go about your job with calm persistence, and make your pleasure and work such a happy unity that you never know where one begins and the other ends."

MEMO 24:

> YOU CAN FULFILL YOUR FINANCIAL AND PSYCHOLOGICAL
> NEEDS BEST IF YOU'LL FORCE YOURSELF TO TAKE SOME
> ACTION, INVOLVE YOURSELF ENTHUSIASTICALLY IN WHAT-
> EVER YOU DECIDE TO DO, AND ACCOMPLISH AT LEAST ONE
> WORTHWHILE THING EACH DAY.

Chapter 3

Professions

Linda Winikow:
"POLITICS *and government are open fields for women.*

"I feel very strongly about the need for more women in politics," asserted New York state senator Linda Winikow. "And I say this because women's sensitivity is an added and important ingredient."

The senator's own interest in government began when a high school history teacher was influential in helping her decide that teaching was the right career for her. To prepare she began college at the University of Rochester and then—when she married—finished at Hofstra University with a major in history and political science.

"When I obtained my degree I went back to my former high school to teach history," she continued, "and, as I taught, my all-consuming interest was giving my students an awareness of what they should derive from education.

"As I look back I imagine that I was also thinking of getting into politics sometime, even though I may not have actually said, 'Someday I'm going to run for office.' But, somewhere in the back of my mind, I knew even than that I wanted some kind of input."

While teaching, Linda Winikow also commuted to Columbia University to work toward her master's degree. Later, she transferred to Queens College.

"When we moved to a young, developing community, I had a new baby and a master's thesis to prepare," she said. "I wanted to start working in the community at once. For a time I debated whether to let my thesis ride or get right to work and complete it. I'm glad I decided to finish it, since I might not have had the opportunity later. To make completing it possible, my husband brought me into the New York Public Library on Saturdays and Sundays, and my parents cared for our baby."

Ms. Winikow's first step in politics was joining a campaign committee that a cousin chaired. Later she moved to a spot as a Democratic committeewoman. "I also associated myself with other community activities and eventually led the fight against certain zone changes," she disclosed. "Service on the local zoning board of appeals followed. I was pregnant with my second son at the time—and I always say I gave birth to him between two meetings."

Seeing government at work on the zoning board brought Linda Winikow to a realization that politics and government added up to the right career for her.

"My next step was the town council," she reported. "As a member I established the first local consumer protection board in the state of New York. Later I helped set up other local boards. Now consumer protection is one of my greatest strengths."

Approximately nine years after Linda Winikow joined her first campaign committee she ran for the county legislature and became the first woman ever elected to that body. Next, she sought the senate post, because she saw more and more that many of the things she felt should be accomplished had to be done on a state level. She took the oath for her senatorial post at a high school since her interest in government had begun in a classroom.

"As a state senator I go to Albany Monday morning after seeing my sons off to school," she told me. "While there I attend sessions and committee meetings. Late Wednesday night I leave to work in my office at home and meet with the people I represent for the rest of the week and the weekend.

"While at home I try to be with my family as much as possible," she went on. "When I'm away my husband takes over. This was a family decision, and I couldn't manage my career without his help.

"The basic qualification for women who want a career in politics and government is capability and a background of preparation," added the senator. "If you lack the desire to communicate, running for office is not for you. I found teaching an excellent background, because communicating in the classroom gives you the ability to communicate in other areas too. Another plus is my history education, because—through the ages—we make the same mistakes.

"We just change the time scene."

MEMO 25:
> REALIZE THAT YOU CAN'T GET AHEAD ON A HIT-OR-MISS PLAN. BUILD TENACITY INTO YOUR PERSONALITY AND STICK WITH WHAT YOU START.

Edith Balt:
"There's tremendous hope for women in LAW, *and the earlier they're made aware of all the possibilities, the larger their job horizons can be.*

"Today every woman of every age should be guided into thinking of *all* job possibilities," stressed Edith Balt, a practicing lawyer who covers the gamut of legal work from early morning till late at night.

"I'm so interested in the women's movement and in helping women make lives for themselves that I work fourteen hours a day," she declared. "I devote much of my time and practice to matrimonial and family law, and I do a great deal of consultation work in this area. For example, women who are contemplating divorce or separation (or who have had it thrust upon them) come to the office for guidance and advice on their rights. Outside of the office I spend a great deal of time speaking to women's groups and participating on panels on women and the law.

"I always knew I wanted to go into law," Ms. Balt disclosed. "But when I was attending high school and looking toward the immediate business of earning a living most girls were being steered into commercial subjects rather than college preparatory courses. The general assumption was that typing and shorthand were their be-all's and end-all's.

"I was aware then—and I'm *much* more aware now—that, along with shorthand and typing, girls could be learning other subjects that would open more doors to them. Proper guidance would have shown me this."

The typing and shorthand, however, led Edith Balt to several jobs—always in a lawyer's office. She hoped to continue studying but was rejected for college for lack of some high school courses.

She wasn't about to give up. She learned in New York at that time you did not have to go to college to prepare for a law career. With diligence and perseverance you could learn your profession in the tradition of Lincoln by studying, working in a law office, and filing for college equivalency credits. So she made up her college equivalencies and obtained a law student qualifying certificate, all while working in an office. The lawyer for whom she worked became her husband.

"I was unable to continue with my legal clerkship," she recalled. "However, to keep my hand in the business of law I worked on a publication which digested material from law journals. Later, since I'd moved to another state which did not recognize my college equivalency credits, I had to enroll in college to fulfill my pre-law and law school requirements. Upon graduation from New York Law School and passing the bar examinations, I was admitted to the bar and joined a law firm as an associate.

"I love it, and I'm glad I'm a lawyer," she said. "It's a tremendously exciting field—especially when you're interested in people. Some of the problems can pretty much drain you, because you're always so responsible for crucial decisions in other people's lives. And you're always so pressed for time that sometimes you feel you can't do the reading and studying needed to keep up in your field. But when you do a good job and overcome a big hurdle you get a rewarding feeling of confidence and satisfaction.

"As far as opportunities go, I think women who want to enter law have a wide-open, well-paying field. They can make their choice and go into individual practice, group practice, government employment, or corporate work.

"Though you shouldn't necessarily see yourself as a 'woman going into law,' I do think that in many areas you're better equipped because you *are* a woman. You often have an innate understanding when a case involves money management, relationships between people, or matrimonial and child care problems. In fact, if you're a mother you have *special* feelings for the last type of case.

"Don't think for one moment, however, that prejudice against women has completely died out in the profession. You *still* have to work harder and be better prepared because women are coming in from behind. In my office, though, I've never encountered any kind of prejudice. I'm treated as an equal in every respect.

"I'm so up to my ears in work that I feel about 40 years younger than when I began. When my time is up they'll have to put extra nails in my coffin to keep me down!"

MEMO 26:

> WE'D ALL BE BETTER OFF IF WE NEVER THOUGHT ABOUT AGE— IF WE NEVER REACHED THE POINT WHERE WE SAY: "WELL, NOW THAT I'M THUS AND SO I OUGHT TO BE DOING THIS," OR "NOW THAT I'VE PASSED—WHATEVER MILESTONE—I OUGHT NOT TO BE DOING THAT." DO WHAT YOU WANT TO WITHOUT THINKING ABOUT HOW LONG IT WILL TAKE OR HOW OLD YOU WILL BE WHEN YOU REACH YOUR GOAL.

Virginia Brown:
"You need a broad outlook on living and learning when you're a public school MEDIA SPECIALIST.

"The school librarian's role has changed, and we're now called media specialists," explained Virginia Brown. "It's a great challenge to be in this field because of the revolution in the way that libraries are run.

"With computer technology we're into all kinds of interesting new things," she said, "while simultaneously we're also involved in such traditional activities as selecting books, reference materials, and other publications. Now we're responsible for selecting and keeping up audiovisual equipment and materials. This keeps us on a constant search for new aids to teachers and students.

"Part of my job is to work closely with teachers to see what supplemental audiovisual material will help them most," she went on. "I spend a great deal of time going through many catalogues to find out what's available. When a teacher is interested in something new we get it on approval. If we didn't buy with care, we'd soon have obsolete materials."

Quite understandably a job as a media specialist calls for continuous course-taking. "If librarians cannot use all the new materials to their fullest to help teachers and students, the purpose of the equipment is defeated," Virginia Brown pointed out.

Education for a media specialist's career begins with a bachelor's degree and then a fifth year of specialized study in library science, usually leading to a master's. Teacher certification enables a school librarian to teach use-of-the-library and other classes.

"I obtained both my bachelor's and master's degrees at Syracuse University," Ms. Brown informed me. "Then I taught high school English while working as a part-time school librarian. In a subsequent job, I worked as a guidance director and reading teacher. All of this contributes to my foundation for this job."

After interrupting her career while her children were small, Virginia Brown returned to work when they entered junior high school. Eventually the family moved to a new community and she applied for a job in the school system where she now works.

"At that time we had never had a school librarian here," she recalled. "But now we have five librarians, five paraprofessionals, and five clerks. When I started my home base was in the junior high school and, when I could, I went to the other schools to help with the libraries that were then set up in the classrooms. When the librarian's role began its changeover to media specialist status, I began preparing by taking college courses and in-service workshops.

"I'd go to any campus where a course was being offered and I'm still doing that. In this field you can never say 'I've done all that I can do.' But I love this work, and I wouldn't do anything differently from the way that I have.

"And, looking at your job in retrospect, that's a wonderful way to feel."

MEMO 27:
> TALK WITH YOUR FRIENDS ABOUT YOUR HOPES, ASPIRATIONS, AND FUTURE WORKING PLANS BECAUSE FRIENDS CAN PLAY A MAJOR PART IN TELLING YOU ABOUT POTENTIALS OR IN TELLING PEOPLE ABOUT YOU.

Joan Greentree:
"LANDSCAPE ARCHITECTURE includes design and planning for every type and every scale of environment."

Landscape architect Joan Greentree is the first to say—emphatically—that the way to achieve her career goal is *not* the way she did it!

Nevertheless, Ms. Greentree, who is entirely self-taught, is accomplishing so much with her style and thrust that, after several years in her field, she has gained a notable reputation for working within the ecology of an area. She has also received merit certificates from the National Landscape Association.

Besides her private practice, she has worked as a designer and plant consultant for Lawrence Halprin & Associates, a San Francisco firm in environmental planning and design.

"The work of a landscape architect encompasses urban and regional planning, site development, design of urban and rural places, the design of new cities, the re-development of existing ones, landscape architecture, and the input of numerous disciplines that go toward creating better environments for human life," she said.

"Part of my work for Halprin was to conceptualize dreams for a new town for 60,000 people in Illinois," she told me as we talked in her plant-filled studio.

"In this project the goal was to lay out the downtown in a more human way than has been done in the past 25 years. We were challenged to make the 'ideal' of suburbia work, so our provisions for services, recreation, and employment included a multi-use shopping center complex and a planned industrial zone. I also conceived ideas for an environmental center in which children can make the exhibits instead of merely coming to look at them. This helps teach the importance of stopping the destruction of nature and our environment.

"My own interest in nature began as a child—actually, when I was taken to the Brooklyn Children's Museum in a baby carriage," remembered Joan Greentree. "And my sense of design came from inside, I believe, because all of the women in my father's family are artists. As I visited museums and botanical gardens, summered in the Adirondacks, and went to camp my love of natural surroundings grew."

At 16 Joan Greentree was graduated from high school with top honors and an award in biology. The next move was Alfred University, with plans for a major in animal husbandry because of its emphasis on soil chemistry and livestock.

"But I couldn't work within the system and accept the trivia I had to go through to get the courses I wanted," she admitted, "so I soon became one of the original college dropouts. When I finally decided landscape architecture would be the right career for me I spent the next 16 years educating myself."

Ms. Greentree took courses wherever she found one she wanted and needed—practical things at the State University of New York, botany at Fairleigh Dickinson University, philosophy at New York University, and architectural rendering at a trade school, to cite a few examples. "I also took almost every course given at the New York and Brooklyn botanical gardens, studied a great deal on my own while bringing up my children, used my large-sized yard to propagate and experiment with plants, and went to Japan to study landscape architecture," she revealed. "As a volunteer I did some landscape designing for my temple and for friends."

Gradually people became aware of Joan Greentree's work, and her first professional job—after starting a private practice—was the land-scape design for an apartment house. The first year she was in practice there were a few gardens. Every year since there have been more.

"My thrust has always been to work within the ecosystem," she pointed out. "I want to continue the natural environment as it includes not only rocks, plants, and land forms but also the birds and other creatures that—with men—inhabit the earth."

A few years ago Joan Greentree was accepted as a member by the American Society of Landscape Architects. Her assignment with the San Francisco firm followed when a prominent architect insisted that she show it a presentation of her work.

"My way of developing a career as a landscape architect has been most unusual and innovative," she advised. "I'm an anomaly—a deviation from the rule. And my way was the hard way to do it.

"To others who want this career I definitely recommend formal training from a college that gives a degree in landscape architecture after a four- or five-year program.

"While in school get summer or part-time jobs with landscape architects, drafting firms, or nurseries. You can pick up knowledge by osmosis."

MEMO 28:

> LEARN FROM PEOPLE IN ALL WALKS OF LIFE AND INCORPORATE
> WHAT YOU LEARN IN YOUR WORK WHENEVER IT'S PERTINENT.
> KEEP A NOTEBOOK WITH YOU AND, AS YOU RUN INTO PLACES
> TO VISIT AND PEOPLE TO CONTACT, JOT DOWN THE NAMES AT
> ONCE.

Dr. Laura E. Morrow:

"MEDICINE *is a favorable profession for women—and it bothers me that, too often, women thinking of medical careers are discouraged from entering the field.*

"Even though it takes a lot of work to be a doctor, a woman doesn't have to give up living," stressed Dr. Laura Morrow, a psychiatrist in private practice and, also, director of psychiatry at a general hospital.

"Because of the demand for physicians," she went on, "a woman in medicine today can set her personal time schedule and allow for flexible hours to be shared by family and patients in a way that's most helpful to both and least disruptive to her home life."

Dr. Morrow is living proof that this premise is the truth. As the wife of Dr. Lloyd Morrow, also a psychiatrist, she's the mother of three grown sons and a daughter. Over and above her family life, practice, and hospital work she's past president of both the American Medical Women's Association, Inc. and the New Jersey Neuropsychiatric Association. She is former Chairman of the Special Committee on Drug Abuse for the Medical Society of New Jersey, and she was instrumental in the issuance of a postal stamp honoring Elizabeth Blackwell, the first woman to receive an M.D. in America. In the time left over her interests run to sketching, painting, photography, and embroidery.

"In high school and college I always liked science and studying," said Dr. Morrow. "Then once I started working with patients at the University of Pennsylvania School of Medicine I was hooked on medicine for good." After completing medical school, Dr. Morrow interned in Pennsylvania and had a psychiatric residency in Washington, D.C. In Washington she met her husband, and they were married while they were both staff physicians at a state hospital.

"When my husband went into service during World War II, I started my private practice," Dr. Morrow informed me. "After the war, we bought our present home, set up joint offices on the ground floor, and began combining our medical practice with family living. While the children were small, I often scheduled patients in the evening—or during nap or school time. Naturally, household help is a most desirable adjunct when you're a woman in medicine. Today women are in every medical specialty, but the specialties that appeal to them most are pediatrics, psychiatry, general practice, internal medicine, anesthesia, obstetrics, gynecology, and pathology.

"I feel that psychiatry is a good specialty because women by nature are sympathetic, empathetic, nurturing, and comforting."

Everone knows that a medical education is a highly expensive undertaking. But Dr. Morrow believes no good student who is truly interested should decide against a medical career because of lack of funds. "Any woman who really and truly wants to, who has the ability, and who can get herself admitted to a medical school will be able to get scholarships and loans and finance her education with a small amount of help from her family," she contended. "Whenever possible most physicians believe it is advisable to try and complete your training without any interruption."

Once college, medical school, internship, and hospital residency are completed, you can go into private practice independently or in a group practice. Other options are work in industry, in schools, in laboratory research, in administrative positions, or in advisory and consulting capacities.

"Besides the pleasure of working with colleagues and getting to know them, doctors are able to serve their fellow men as physicians in clinics—and as leaders in providing sponsorship of educational, health, and preventive disease programs," Dr. Morrow concluded.

"There's a great deal of joy in this service, and the longer you're in it the more rewarding and fulfilling it becomes."

MEMO 29:
> APPRECIATE YOUR ABILITIES AND DECIDE WHAT YOU CAN DO BEST. THEN DON'T BE AFRAID TO WORK TILL IT HURTS AND DON'T EVER COUNT THE HOURS.

Kathleen O'Driscoll Ryan:
"Today there is a growing number of jobs in SOCIAL GERONTOLOGY, *the field of aging."*

Kathleen O'Driscoll Ryan has an unusual job—but one with a

growing future when, in the year 2000, 28 million Americans will be over 65.

"I'm a social gerontologist," explained Ms. Ryan. "My specialty is pre-retirement education, and I work as a consultant on pre-retirement programs. One aspect of my work is lecturing and giving courses on pre-retirement for management and educational groups. Gerontology is the study of aging," she added, "and a social gerontologist is one who works with the aging population from the social or psychological approach.

"Retirement is part of today's life cycle. We have to get people to realize the importance of getting ready for it and preparing to depend on themselves."

Ms. Ryan's courses, lectures, seminars, and workshops include discussions in four areas: Income (evaluation of sources, budgeting, stretching money); Housing (planning, family status, retirement communities, mobile homes, low-income projects); Health (physical and mental); Leisure (recreation, hobbies, travel, community service).

"I chose social gerontology because I'd seen some sad situations among old people," Kathleen told me. "Some of the members of my own family were older people who had stopped working and living, so after I had three children I enrolled in the University of Washington to get a degree in this new field."

When Kathleen Ryan completed her undergraduate studies, there was nothing set up on a graduate level. Consequently, she went to the University of Chicago's Industrial Relations Center to get some special courses in pre-retirement education. "As you might expect there were not too many jobs in the field at that time," she recalled, "so, in addition to having to look for training, I also had to hunt for places to work. Usually, I had to make my first jobs by going to people and selling myself and my ideas."

Through this approach Ms. Ryan worked her way into the field on the West Coast by teaching courses in Seattle on radio and television and through corporate and educational institutions. Eventually she launched a tour program for senior citizens. When she moved East she was hired as a consultant for a state leadership-discussion training program in pre-retirement.

"The participants who signed up for the 10 all-day sessions in this program were representatives from business, labor, industry, government, and adult education," she reported. "They took their training back to their organizations, and I helped them devise programs for their employees or students. Through the contacts I made in this program I began giving other seminars and speeches on retirement.

"Not all of the jobs in the aging field require college training," advised Ms. Ryan. "With or without it, there is work to be done in agencies, environmental planning, community-based care facilities, education, housing, library service, health, nutrition, research, and rehabilitation—to name some possibilities.

"And when you choose this work you'll find, as I have, that as you learn more about aging, you also learn more about yourself."

MEMO 30:
> BUILDING CONFIDENCE IS ESSENTIAL. IT GETS YOU OUT WHERE THINGS CAN HAPPEN.

Selma Rossen:
"I'd like to encourage more women to go into ENGINEERING.

"Engineering is great for women," asserted Selma Rossen, manager for four major programs for ADT Security Systems, headquartered in New York.

"Granted, there have been problems in the past with some engineers being out of work, just as there has been unemployment in many fields," she acknowledged. "But no situation lasts forever, so if you're terribly interested in a field and capable of working in it you shouldn't hesitate to enter it. The rewards in engineering are considerable, and if you're good you'll do all right."

Selma, who has proven she is good (and who also does *all right*) was always interested in mathematics and physics. "But on the other hand I was also interested in men,'' she confided. ''I knew I wanted to marry and have a family, and I realized that if I went into physics I'd have to have my Ph.D. before I could really get started. As I thought it over it seemed that engineering would be more feasible for me.''

With this goal in mind, Selma started college at Barnard, married between her freshman and sophomore year, and had her first child before her junior year. Following that, she switched to Fairleigh Dickinson University and earned her bachelor's degree in electrical engineering. By working during the day and attending school at night, she obtained her master's from Stevens Institute of Technology.

''My first job was with an electronics company and when I got into microwave component design I found that specialty exceedingly interesting. In college you receive general training. Then, when you start to work, your specialty seems to choose you. At least that's what happened to me.''

After several years of working in microwave component design Selma Rossen switched to another corporation and became a project engineer specializing in microwaves. ''While working there I was involved in everything—from writing proposals to obtain jobs to designing systems to fulfill jobs,'' she revealed. ''I work primarily with men, and I've never had any discrimination problem, though on second thought maybe there was one exception when I took my first job and soon became pregnant with my second child. I was told I had to quit after four months. There were no if's, and's, or but's and my boss refused to listen to any arguments I advanced.

''But when I had my third child and was more valuable to the company because of length of service, my boss's reaction was, 'What day will you have to go to the hospital?' I worked till three weeks before that time.

''In general, I think one problem women face in engineering is the lack of part-time work,'' Selma Rossen continued. ''You have to deal with this realistically and recognize it before you go into the field. You also have to realize that in management most engineers are absolutely crazy. They seem to stay till midnight and work Saturdays and Sundays. If you're interested in management you must be able to match those hours and put in the extra time. Management can also involve traveling, and that's a problem when you have a family.

"In my situation, however, I've been most fortunate, because when I started with ADT the company was extremely open to permitting me to set up a working schedule that was well adapted to my needs. I obtained my present job when I was recommended as a consultant because of my microwave work," she disclosed. "For two years I worked in that capacity on a yearly contract in which I was guaranteed work three days a week. This allowed me some time at home in a period in which I wanted that arrangement, so I think the company deserves a great deal of credit for its open-mindedness and flexibility.

"While I worked under this arrangement I became involved in management and that led to my current spot as program manager.

"A plus for women in engineering is the fact that there's a tremendous amount of intuition in this work," Selma Rossen concluded. "And since you often need a hunch to help work out a problem, a woman's time-honored intuition can sometimes have real value."

MEMO 31:

PROGRAM YOUR MIND WITH AN UNDERSTANDING OF THE BUSINESS YOU'RE IN. TRAIN YOURSELF TO THINK QUICKLY AND WORK UNDER CONSTANT PRESSURE DURING OCCASIONAL LONG HOURS. WORK HARD AT PLEASING EMPLOYERS, AND SHOW ENTHUSIASM FOR WHAT YOU DO.

Eleanore Pettersen:
"In ARCHITECTURE it's a person's ability and what he or she accomplishes that counts.

"If an able woman has a feeling and talent for architecture it's no harder for her to be accepted than it is for a man," emphasized Eleanore K. Pettersen, a five-star example of genuine success in designing such structures as the Living-Learning Center at Nasson College in Maine, a large resort complex in Puerto Rico, and a Christian Reformed church in New Jersey.

"Admittedly, architecture is often on the cliff of depression in hard times, so work from former clients is what maintains your practice, *if* you are established," she said. "On the other hand, women who are unestablished usually have a difficult time because they must compete with unemployed persons who have more experience. This is the spot I was in in the last big depression.

"When I chose architecture I had no idea about where or how I would find employment," she confessed. "It was a shrinking field because of the times and, when I started, it was not receptive to women. I believe that you can always find reasons not to do things, and if you dwell too long on them you'll never get anything done. Consequently, the best way to deal with supposedly formidable obstacles is to ignore them. If women pursue the work for which they have the aptitude and enthusiastic interest they are bound to be successful.

"When your interest and aptitude point to architecture you'll find extensive opportunities for broad creative expression, public service, a substantial income, a durable achievement, and significant influence upon the appearance of our times. And, to my way of thinking, this is more lasting than sitting home and cooking every day of your life, just to have it go down people's stomachs."

Eleanore Pettersen chose architecture after discovering her aptitude for it as an art student at Cooper Union. Upon graduation, she applied for an apprenticeship with Frank Lloyd Wright and was the only woman among the 50 architects who were accepted.

"It was a great experience," she remembered. "I was motivated before I went with him. But my period of learning from him strengthened my motivation and gave me the courage to go on.

"Subsequently, I worked at a variety of other jobs so my background would be as broad as possible. It's wise to do this; new architects should not spend more than two years in any one office while they're accumulating experience."

After gaining sufficient expertise Ms. Pettersen launched her own firm in a barn built in 1752 that she converted into a home and office. Again, she turned her back on negatives when people tried to tell her that no sane person opened a practice and built an office in the same year.

"When you have a leaning for architecture you can work with clients, financiers, builders, and suppliers of building materials to design homes, housing projects, office buildings, factories, health centers, shopping centers, airports, banks, and restaurants," she said. "And because the field is so complex there is also a wide range of jobs outside the area of architectural design.

"Except when the economy hits a slump, there are chances for jobs in administration, construction, land use planning, urban planning, interior design, manufacture of building products, and architectural research."

Besides five years of college and a period of internship, prospective architects must be able to use their hands, have a penchant for putting things together, a deep dedication, a willingness to work long, hard hours, and an ability to visualize in three dimensions.

"It's also vital to develop an awareness of everything around you and have a broad life experience," she added. "That's what you'll work from later on. You can't design a ballroom, for instance, unless you've danced. You can't design a boathouse unless you've maneuvered a boat.

"I also feel that an architect should be a bit of a rebel—someone who's not willing to take things for granted. It's terribly important to realize there's more than one way to do things."

It can take quite a while to become established in architecture because there's so much to learn, digest, and bring together. For some time the rewards can seem harder to reach than in many businesses and professions. But, always, the goals are visible and the rewards—when they come—are great.

"In the final analysis, the future is constantly present when you're an architect," put in Ms. Pettersen. "And you're only limited by yourself in what you can achieve."

MEMO 32:

> THE MORE YOU DO THE BETTER YOU BECOME—AND UNTIL YOU ACTUALLY DO THINGS YOU OFTEN DON'T REALIZE HOW MUCH YOU CAN ACCOMPLISH AND ACHIEVE.

Dr. Donna Cosulich:

"Today's rapid technological changes and developments require constant retraining, so anyone contemplating a career in SCIENCE *should be prepared to be flexible and make such changes as needed.*

"I began my career in pharmaceutical research," reported Dr. Donna Cosulich, a chemist for American Cyanamid Company. "But as new techniques came along I moved into X-ray crystallography. This is the definitive way to determine the structure of organic compounds—in my work, drugs. Crystallography is becoming increasingly useful as a research technique.

"I chose and prepared suitable crystals and aligned them on an automatic X-ray diffractometer," explained Dr. Cosulich. "Once the computer was set, it collected data needed for analysis. This allowed me to work on a number of structures at a time.

"With this technique it typically takes about three to six weeks for analysis of an organic compound. Earlier it required teams of scientists two years to make similar determinations.

"The more scientists know about the structure of drugs, the more responsible manufacturers can be about what they are selling," continued Donna Cosulich.

After working in X-ray crystallography, Dr. Cosulich was transferred by American Cyanamid to the drug metabolism department, where her experience in structure determination, use of automated equipment, and chemical isolation was important.

"Since this is an entirely new field of endeavor for me, it will require more retraining and learning of new techniques," she told me, shortly after making the move. "The importance of drug metabolism studies is also increasing rapidly," she went on. "This work is useful in the design of new drugs and is essential in the study of pharmacological effects, absorption-excretion, and safety."

Looking back, Donna Cosulich cannot remember when she didn't have an intense curiosity about science. She narrowed it down to chemistry in high school. She went to the University of Arizona for her B.S. and M.S. degrees and to Stanford University for her Ph.D.

The young scientist obtained her first job in pharmaceutical research through a professor of veterinary medicine at the University of Arizona. He was testing drugs for American Cyanamid, and, at his suggestion, she came East and began her work with that company.

Her outstanding job performance earned her a year's leave of absence to go to the University of Geneva to study new scientific developments. For her work on folic acid, Methotrexate, and Leucovorin she received the Iota Sigma Pi Research Award given triennially to a young woman scientist for outstanding contribution to chemical research problems.

If your interest lies in a chemistry career, you can work with the composition and chemical properties of substances and processes of chemical change, not only for drugs and medicines, but also for consumer products and scientific materials. Educationally, you need a bachelor's degree and —ideally— a M.S. and Ph.D.

You may do basic and applied research, analysis, testing, teaching, selling, or management and administrative work. Employment opportunities exist in manufacturing or processing industries in the fields of chemicals, drugs, plastics, soaps, and metals, and in universities, government agencies, and research institutions. Dr. Cosulich chose the pharmaceutical field because she was interested in medicine.

"One of the biggest problems and challenges in a chemist's career is keeping up and catching up with today's information explosion," she advised. "You need to know what is happening, so the reading you must do can be endless. My own greatest pleasure has been having compounds I have worked on become useful drugs. This is a happy throwback to my reasons for choosing the pharmaceutical field in the beginning.

"From a realistic viewpoint, however, you have to recognize the fact that the tools a chemist needs are so expensive you're dependent for your career on a large corporation or institution.

"There's not much opportunity today to be a loner scientist or to work as the Curies did."

MEMO 33:

> MAKE EDUCATION YOUR CONTINUOUS AFFAIR. LEARN ALL THAT YOU CAN ABOUT AS MUCH AS YOU CAN.

Marianne McNair:
"I don't see how you can miss when you choose HOME ECONOMICS.

"The varied aspects of this career give people who select it the multiple choice of teaching, doing research, entering business or industry, working in the home service field, associating themselves with hospitals and social agencies, or starting a business of their own," stated Marianne McNair. "And the specialties include food and nutrition, housing and household appliances, home furnishings, home management, child development, education, and clothing and textiles.

"My speciality is clothing and textiles," continued Marianne, who started her career with teaching and followed that with nine years in business working for a pattern firm.

Her present business—named "And Sew Forth"—is housed in a 200-year-old farmhouse. On the first floor there are fabrics, notions, trimmings, patterns, and sewing machines. On the second, classrooms for basic dressmaking, couturier dressmaking, tailoring, and pattern-making. The courses are taught by Ms. McNair and her staff.

"Many things added up to my decision to choose home economics," disclosed Ms. McNair. "In the first place, I had a home background that fostered a great interest in sewing, since my mother made everything we owned. In addition, a tremendously dynamic sewing teacher nurtured my career interest."

To prepare herself, Marianne majored in home economics education at Pennsylvania State University. Her first job was teaching seventh- through twelfth-grade daytime classes and evening adult sewing classes. After four years she answered an advertisement for a home economist with teaching experience and obtained a job in New York as a traveling educational representative for a pattern company.

"I was one of seven economists who traveled across the country to present assembly programs and fashion shows in junior and senior high schools," she informed me. "Since this was an incentive program for sewing, we had the girls from various schools model clothes that had been made by the pattern company. I lectured and commentated. Three years at this job gave me the background to switch to a spot as assistant to the director of the company's educational office," she recalled. "This put me in charge of adult educational service. While I did this I also took courses at the French Fashion Academy and the Traphagen School of Fashion."

During that period Marianne married, and she and her husband—who was working in sales at the time—often talked of putting their backgrounds together and starting a business of their own in which people could buy choice fabrics and learn to sew under trained teachers. "When we decided to go ahead with this idea we looked for a good location, moved in on a Memorial Day weekend, painted and got the house ready during the summer, and opened for business in August. In one week, 300 people signed up for sewing classes.

"We attribute our present success (which we consider phenomenal considering our lowly, undercapitalized start) to our high standards in selecting stock and to the quality performance we demand from our employees.

"While many businesses were hurting because of the sagging economy in the early Seventies, we had our best time. Business was so brisk we were often at 'And Sew Forth' 12 hours a day. We were thrilled to see customers turning more and more to our specific services. And I was particularly pleased to see my convictions on 'good' fabric and superior service pay off.

"From my experience I recommend that all people who are interested in home economics take education courses in college so they'll be able to teach," Marianne advised. "This is a credential that can lead to other jobs and prepares you for something specific.

"As everyone knows, teaching jobs have been limited, so women need to equip themselves with skills that are needed and marketable in far more places than public schools and college classrooms. But with consumerism emerging as a whole new field, education graduates can look ahead to countless jobs that demand interaction with consumers of all ages.

"For example, I have four women working on our staff with credentials to teach in high schools. With us they teach about three hours a day and do a variety of other things.

"When you are starting out, it's often wise to be willing to begin with a small salary," she suggested. "Then once you're in, home economists' salaries are good.

"But the way to begin is to get a desk to sit behind, so you can prove you're a willing, resourceful worker who is able to do many jobs. This can be particularly true when you're looking for a start with a pattern company.''

MEMO 34:
> ONCE YOU GET A JOB—EVEN A SMALL JOB—PROGRESS IS UP TO YOU. IF YOU HAVE EXTRA ABILITIES THEY WILL SOON BE NOTICED, SO DON'T UNDERESTIMATE YOUR ULTIMATE CHANCES IN A FOOT-IN-THE-DOOR JOB.

Dr. Doris Marshall Harris:
"Women are not the weaker sex when it comes to careers in DENTISTRY.

"The strength women can exert in a tooth extraction is as great as anyone needs," declared Dr. Doris Marshall Harris, a general practitioner. "I would definitely encourage interested women to become dentists because they have patience, manual dexterity, and a feeling for fine details. These are assets as far as dentistry is concerned.

"Often women elect to specialize in pedodontics, or children's dentistry, because many children seem to relate to a female dentist."

Dr. Harris, who is in solo private practice, cares for patients of all ages and does a bit of everything—including fillings, extractions, root canal therapy, periodontal treatment, and prosthetics.

"I was brought up in Halifax, Nova Scotia," she revealed, "and I didn't decide to become a dentist immediately after high school. In fact, I started out as a secretary. But after a couple of years I wasn't satisfied with secretarial work, and I knew I wanted a college education."

With that as an immediate goal the future dentist enrolled in McGill University in a liberal arts course. But along the way she found that many of the students in liberal arts later took a secretarial course and went to work as secretaries. She made up her mind to study a profession.

"I chose dentistry for several reasons," she pointed out. "To begin with, I liked the idea that it was a health profession through which I could render a service. I also liked working with my hands—and, certainly, dentistry provides the opportunity for that.

"Another motivating force was the fact that as a young adult I had a great deal of dental treatment myself. As a result, my family dentist was able to save all of my teeth without a single extraction. That in itself is a tribute to dental science and I credit that dentist (who later became one of my teachers at dental school) to a great extent for my career. My mother and father also gave me tremendous support and encouraged me to go to the top of the profession, even though the proportion of women in dental school was very low. I couldn't have succeeded without their help."

After obtaining her D.D.S. from Dalhousie University, Dr. Harris began her career in a school. Subsequently, when she married and moved to the United States, she received a fellowship in pedodontics at the former Guggenheim Dental Clinic in New York. She also worked for the Children's Aid Society till she was able to obtain her license and go into private practice.

"Like all fields, dentistry has both its joys and problems," she confided. "One problem can be long working hours to accommodate the business people who are only available Saturdays and evenings—though dentists do have the option of controlling their hours fairly well when they wish. This is an asset for a woman who wants a profession that's compatible with married life.

"Another problem is broken appointments—and any dentist will tell you how much this throws things off! Still a third is the fact that it's sometimes stressful to work in one position all day long in a rather small circumscribed area. Sometimes you feel this at the end of the day. But to compensate for these small problems is the great joy of restoring a badly diseased mouth and bringing it back to good health. It's also rewarding to overcome a patient's fear of dentistry and see someone who hasn't been to a dentist for years be so pleased and thrilled with your work that he or she becomes a patient on a regular maintenance schedule.

"All in all, there are many opportunities and many joys in this field," concluded Dr. Harris. "People who choose it can be general practitioners in a solo or group practice or they can specialize and be orthodontists, oral surgeons, periodontists, prosthodontists, or oral pathologists.

"The majority of work is in private practice. But there are also openings for dentists in clinics, institutions, hospitals, and government services.

"And with more and more people demanding more health care I can only foresee a good future."

MEMO 35:

> INOCULATE YOURSELF WITH INCENTIVE—AND MAKE THAT INCENTIVE A PICTURE OF YOURSELF AS AN ACCOMPLISHED, SATISFIED WOMAN WHO HAS ACHIEVED HER GOALS.

Fay Ellison:

"I would encourage both young women and women going back to work to prepare for a career in the MINISTRY *if that's what they really want.*

"We are going through a period of transition in which things are opening up for women in the churches," announced Fay Ellison, minister of the Palisades Presbyterian Church in Palisades, New York.

"And even though women in the clergy still have to count on entering from the outside and then becoming an integral part of the profession, things are likely to be different in the future.

"As far as older women go," she added, "some of the best women in the church now are those who have gone back to school and work after raising families, participating in volunteer and civic activities, and living through the experiences that most people in congregations face.

"These women are mature and confident and a seminary education on top of that really puts them in a good position to start."

Ms. Ellison (in the "young women" category) is the first woman Presbyterian minister with her own parish in the area in which she lives and works. As the parish's religious leader she prepares a worship service each week, preaches every Sunday, performs religious rites, works on administrative duties and the Christian education program, makes hospital visits, and keeps in touch with older people and convalescents.

"We're always involved in a series of projects too," she said, "and all of them entail extensive planning and many meetings. For example, we took youth and adult volunteers on a mobile health fair to an Appalachian town in southeastern Ohio for a week."

Ms. Ellison, who was born in Phoenix, Arizona, majored in religion at Wellesley College.

"When I was required to take a religion course I became interested in the subject from an intellectual point of view," she told me. "Consequently, when I went on to graduate school at the University of Chicago my plans were all made to be a professor of religion."

But a great deal happened at graduate school, Ms. Ellison went on to say. First, she met her husband Marvin, who was planning to pursue a career in teaching and obtain a professorship. Next, she realized that she herself wanted to preach instead of teach.

"Actually, it took me less than a year in graduate school to decide that, rather than being a commentator on religion, I wanted to be the leader of a worshiping community," she revealed. "And I stuck with that decision, because of the way the church was starting to open up for women.

"Admittedly, the real crunch is yet to come—maybe in another two or three years. But women are making up a significant part of the student body in Protestant seminaries today. In Presbyterian seminaries I'd say it's about 40 percent."

After obtaining a master's degree from Chicago, Fay Ellison enrolled in the Union Theological Seminary in Manhattan. "The training for a career in the ministry requires four years of college and three years of seminary," she pointed out. "I wouldn't have needed the graduate study at University of Chicago. At the seminary you do both practical and academic work," she explained. "For my practical work I was a student minister in Dobbs Ferry, New York.

"I obtained my master's degree from Union in January 1974," she said, "and from that point it took me a year and a half to be called to my parish in Palisades. Even though things are starting to open up for women, you're still limited to churches where there's a warm welcome for you. Because of this some women take jobs in diversified ministries—administration, counseling, working with the aging or other activities that were thought of traditionally as social work.

"When you want a full-time ministry in a parish, you often have to wait till you find someone willing to give you a try. While I was waiting and taking short-term jobs, I sent out my qualifications to about 50 churches. Most did not want to check out the possibility of having a woman. The two interviews I obtained were token ones forced by someone who wanted to talk to at least one woman. Palisades was the first serious interview.

"But even though it took me a while to get started, I'd still say to women 'Do it—if this is the work you want,' " Fay Ellison urged in conclusion. "By the time you're actually prepared for ordination things will be entirely different."

MEMO 36:
>   DO WHAT YOU CAN WITH WHAT YOU HAVE AND MAKE THAT .
>   THE THING THAT COUNTS.

Chapter 4

The Arts and Arts-Related Careers

Lillian Kornbluth:
"If you like surrounding yourself with art and associating with artists, owning or running an ART GALLERY *might be the right work for you.*

"But first you should know that collecting and selling art requires much physical and creative energy," warned gallery owner Lillian Kornbluth.

"In fact, the most important thing is to have a lot of energy and make things happen," she said. "When you're busy with a project or show it's routine to work on Sundays, as well as the rest of the week, often without a break.

"On one side, running an art gallery is a very personal activity," Lillian went on; "but besides creating an environment and shows that you respect artistically, you must make the business pay for itself. This demands a real knowledge of what art patrons like."

Lillian Kornbluth entered this business after training at the New York School of Interior Design and marrying and having a family. "Following our marriage, my husband and I became interested in collecting art," she explained. "And as we began buying fine reproductions I gradually grew more interested in arranging paintings on a wall than in any other aspect of interior design.

81

"One night at a party I made the statement, 'The only thing I really want to do is walls!'

"The next day my husband, who's an accountant, handed me $500 and his blessing. I said then and there that I would never come back to him for another cent if I lost that and couldn't make something of my ambition from that beginning."

Ms. Kornbluth invested the bulk of the $500 in lighting and turning the basement of her home into a gallery. Next, she mailed out announcements of its opening—and waited two weeks for her first phone call in response.

"I chose to have my first gallery in my home because my children were in school and I wanted to keep all my involvements under one roof. Besides I could establish roots without the financial pressure of paying extra rent.

"This is important, because in my more than 15 years in the business I've observed that many galleries don't survive two years, often because of overspending before enough income comes in.

"When you start out you should expect merely to survive while you feel your way," she warned.

To obtain work for her first gallery, Ms. Kornbluth contacted artists she knew and offered to show and—hopefully—sell their output. Her criterion was to buy as a collector and never purchase anything she could not include in her own collection. Many who began their careers with her have since succeeded as artists in New York, an achievement that's satisfying to her.

"One of the great rewards in this work is seeing artists grow and watching people's taste in art develop," she commented.

After seven years of running the business in her basement, Lillian opened a gallery away from her home. Today she puts on art shows several times a year and keeps busy with framing.

"I started framing at my patrons' request," she said, "and these days I also hang the paintings if I'm asked to. While I'm in my patrons' homes I often re-arrange the room around the paintings if they wish.

"So in many ways my decorating background has run the whole cycle after all."

MEMO 37:

> YOU CAN'T STAMP YOUR FOOT AND SAY, "I WANT IT NOW!"
> YOU HAVE TO MAKE LONG-RANGE PLANS.

Phoebe Berger:
"For me the way to be completely liberated and fulfilled is to be a mother and wife —and, also, have a career.

"I've been a liberated woman since the day that I was born," declared FOLK SINGER Phoebe Berger, who's now engrossed in a career that is—literally—a family affair.

"I always wanted a career," she said, "but I also hoped for children, and I wanted to stay home with them. So I didn't want to work full-time while my family was growing up."

Attaining this goal isn't easy, as many women know. For Phoebe, the resolution lay in developing her love for music and in passing it on so that today she and her husband—plus their daughters and son—perform professionally here and abroad as a folk singing group.

Known as the Bergerfolk, Phoebe, Jennifer, Margaret, Jonathan, Emily-Kate, and Dr. Stephen Berger are all accomplished instrumentalists as well as folk singers. Their array of instruments includes guitars, ukuleles, tambourines, banjos, bongos, kazoos, dulcimers, autoharps, mouthbows, mandolins, flutes, fiddles, and drums. Interesting arrangements of instruments decorate their living room.

"Since my husband practices dentistry and the children go to school, we rehearse in our A-frame home and perform primarily on weekends and during summer vacations," Phoebe told me. "When we're not performing I keep busy with teaching. I also take care of our bookings and business."

In the years the family has sung together they have appeared on local and national radio and television and have given concerts at Lincoln Center, Town Hall, the New York Historical Society, the

Brooklyn Museum, and at folk festivals around the country. In Europe they have performed in France, Italy, Switzerland, Holland and Norway. They have also recorded several albums.

For Phoebe the struggle to find a career that would mix and match with motherhood began in Brooklyn, where she started studying the piano seriously and performing in plays at school.

"I knew that I was really oriented to performing," she revealed, "but I felt in my heart that being an actress or a concert pianist would not allow me to be as much of a mother as I wanted to be.

"Consequently, without knowing where I was going career-wise, I worked as a model to support myself after high school. Simultaneously, I took music courses at New York University, the New School, and the City College of New York.

"When I met and married my husband he was a dental student, so I continued modeling and fashion commentating till I stopped work to have our first baby.

"Two weeks after she was born, however, I realized that though I loved the baby and my home I needed something else right away. To satisfy that part of me, I made arrangements for the baby's care and started working three days a week modeling for illustrators."

When Dr. Berger began his practice the family moved to a suburb and Phoebe continued her part-time job till the traveling became too hard.

"The work was very unpredictable," she pointed out, "since I often get a call at 8 a.m. for a booking the same day, and that made it very difficult for me with commuting and arranging for the baby.

"So I gave up modeling and switched to a local part-time job as a Welcome Wagon hostess. This wasn't really a career, of course. But it served as an interim activity, and it got me out with people. In fact, I went from a Welcome Wagon call to the hospital for my second baby."

It was after the Bergers' third child arrived that Dr. Berger purchased a stringless guitar at a Mitch Miller auction.

"He had always wanted to study music," Phoebe said, "so after the instrument was repaired we both began lessons in classical guitar. A year later our fourth child arrived. I decided then to study folk music and develop the natural singing talent my bathtub renditions convinced me I had.

"After a very short period of study, I applied for work as a folk singer at a club—and no one was more surprised than I when I got the job! I sang my heart out, and other engagements followed—first at birthday parties and old age homes and, later, at one-woman concerts."

Though Phoebe sang alone at first, her oldest daughter began singing and harmonizing with her when she was 10. Next her husband started accompanying the duo. Eventually, the other children joined in, and the Bergerfolk was born. When the Bergers' fifth child was six weeks old, the family sang its way to Europe on an ocean liner.

Concluded Ms. Berger, "I believe that women can be totally happy and fulfilled with a career *and* a family.

"But you must have energy and health. And you have to keep moving all the time."

MEMO 38:

> BEING A WIFE AND MOTHER DOESN'T HAVE TO MEAN SITTING AROUND ALL DAY TILL THE CHILDREN COME HOME FROM SCHOOL, WITH TIME OUT FOR LAUNDRY, DISHES, AND BEDS— PLUS PLANNING AND FIXING DINNER. WHEN YOU WANT TO DO SOMETHING CREATIVE BESIDES, THESE TASKS CAN BE SQUEEZED INTO SEGMENTS OF YOUR DAY.

Juliette Koka:

"I've found that—in both the arts and as an ENTERTAINER—*women can keep up with their profession while raising a family.*

"As an entertainer, I've discovered it's completely possible to continue a career in the child-raising years if you shift your priorities around and compromise here and there," stressed vivacious Juliette Koka, who maintains a normal family life while working as an entertainer. "Despite my love for my career it was very important to me to be at home with my children while they were small, so I took jobs in my area but not in Timbuktoo.''

In these jobs, Juliette uses her professional training and experience as a Continental actress to entertain at supper clubs with her 45-minute program of songs, dances, and chatter in English, Spanish, Italian, French, Finnish, and Hebrew. She also performs at social and civic functions and in industrial shows and promotions.

"My parents and grandparents were all entertainers in Finland," said Juliette, "and since my mother was a dancer my first training was in a dancing school. As I danced I began singing, too, so I got an early start traveling and performing with my parents.''

In her late teens, however, Juliette struck out for herself. "When you're young you feel you can go anywhere and be anything," she remembered, "and I was no exception. Because of my confidence I got my first break when I went to a restaurant in Helsinki that specialized in gypsy music. I was 15 and knew only three songs of that type. Still I told the owner how wonderful I would be for his place. The members of the gypsy orchestra wanted me. Fortunately, the audience liked me too, so I gained great experience there.

"My second break came when I approached the producer of a Helsinki theater famous for its satiric revues,'' she disclosed. "In much the same manner I told him I'd be perfect for his theater. For three days, the producer put me off by saying the pianist was too tired to audition me. On the third day, however—when the cast had an unexpected break during rehearsals—I took matters in my own hands, ran up to the pianist, and said the producer would like me to audition.''

That audition led to a job. While Juliette worked she also attended the graduate school of dramatic arts in Helsinki. Eventually, the combination of study and performances brought her starring roles in dramatic, comedy, and musical productions. She also made films, appeared on radio and TV, and performed in clubs in Paris, Milan, Zurich, and Brussels.

"Through some of my contacts I obtained a booking for a job in New York,'' she informed me, "and since I wanted to study in America I came here, expecting to go back and continue my career in Finland. But fate intervened, so instead of returning I married and moved to Baltimore. There I had my two sons and continued my career as a performer on a television show.

"When we moved to the New York area my children were still small," she said, "so I involved myself in a great deal of study and kept my finger on the pulse of show business by working close to my home. This has turned out well for me. Women can stay ready to resume their careers while they're raising families if they use the time to study and grow. When they want to go all-out again, they can step into a second career that can even be better than the first.

"In show business there's a variety of facets, and a job as an entertainer is well worth pursuing by a woman with some degree of talent for it.

"It's important to realize, though, that not everyone has to be known in New York or Hollywood. There are many spots in between, and if you really want one you can find what's right for you.

"Speaking personally, I'm the happiest and luckiest person in the world to have a place in the field I adore. It's wonderful to hear the applause when the stage lights are on. But I also think you should keep in mind that it's great to have someone to come home to also.

"That's the same all over the world."

MEMO 39:

> COME TO TERMS WITH WHAT YOU CAN DO, ACCORDING TO YOUR OWN SITUATION AND TALENT. THEN REALIZE THAT THERE'S A PLACE BETWEEN THE TOP AND BOTTOM OF THE LADDER THAT CAN PROVIDE *YOU* WITH A VERY GOOD LIFE. AS THE OLD SAYING GOES, IT'S SOMETIMES BETTER TO BE A BIG FISH IN A SMALL POND.

Kathryn Naumann:
"A penny pack of seeds from grammar school and encouragement from my father introduced me to my love of FLOWER ARRANGING AND HORTICULTURE.

"When I brought that penny pack of seeds home," she said, "my father dug a garden and I planted them in the spring.

"In the fall I showed marigolds in the school flower show. And the prize I received—a little brown card with a pasted-on blue star—was my first blue ribbon award."

Now a great many blue ribbons later, Kathryn Naumann has a national reputation for expertise, lecturing, and judging. For example, as a member of the Horticultural School of New York she is on the board of flower exhibitors. She has taught flower composition at the National Arts Club of Gramercy Park in New York. And she's an active member of the National Chrysanthemum Society and the New York Flower Show Committee.

"For my kind of work," she advised, "you need to invest many years in study before you're professional. You can't expect to take a few courses and have an instant career."

To prepare for her diversified work, Ms. Naumann studied flower arranging (*ikebana*) in Japan with some of the leading masters. After eleven years with the Ikenobo School, five with the Sogetsu, and several with the Ohara, she holds professorships in the Sogetsu and Ikenobo schools and a master's degree fourth grade at the Ohara School. For other phases of her work she studied at Cornell University and the Boyce Thompson Institute for Plant Research.

As a background for judging she holds six accredited judges certifications, the highest of which is master judge from the National Council of State Garden Clubs. "Working up to the latter took me almost 15 years," she revealed.

For a career in flower arranging you need a thorough knowledge of flowers plus training in special schools. To teach, you must acquire a diversified background in the major styles of arranging from traditional to abstract to Oriental.

When horticulture is on your mind your main interest will be the development of new kinds of garden flowers, fruits, and vegetables. A college background with a major in botany is the desirable training for this. In addition, attend every lecture that you can on better methods of breeding, growing, harvesting, and storage. While you're studying and learning, jobs with florists or horticulturists help give you a feel for the field.

"Municipal park departments are also good places to work," added Kathryn Naumann, "and if there's a little lake near by, you can learn about aquatic plants too."

Once you're a qualified horticulturist there are jobs with colleges, universities, state and federal governments, nurseries, conservatories, and parks. Like Kathryn Naumann, you can also lecture, judge shows, teach, and write articles on your subject.

"In all," pointed out Ms. Naumann, "your knowledge of growing things can take you in many directions. The trick is to put your mind to it and—literally and figuratively—grow!"

MEMO 40:

> LEARN FROM OTHER PEOPLE. BUT TO COPY THEM LIMITS YOUR FREEDOM TO USE YOUR OWN NATURAL ABILITIES.

Joan Wolf:
"BALLET *dancing is a career in which you can express yourself in a profoundly fulfilling way.*

"If you're determined to be a dancer, there will always be a place for you, despite intense competition," commented Joan Wolf. "Besides, when you are well-trained, you can look ahead to other opportunities, such as teaching and choreography."

Joan Wolf began in ballet in her native Virginia, where she studied and performed throughout her school years while training under a teacher who was one of the original members of the National Academy of Ballet. At William and Mary College she continued dancing. After moving to New York she enrolled in the National Academy of Ballet to study dance pedagogy.

"I fell in love with teaching while I was still in Virginia," she said. "At the time I was dancing in a civic ballet company, performing on television and concertizing for an opera company. From teaching in the ballet company I learned a good ballet teacher was like a good craftsperson carving a musical instrument such as a violin. But in ballet the instrument is the human body.''

With a teaching future on her mind, Joan reacted instantly when she saw a "For Rent" sign in a suburban store window. ''I looked over the available space and made up my mind immediately to make it the first 'Joan Wolf School of Ballet,' '' she recalled.

Since that day—over 15 years ago—Ms. Wolf has launched a second school, moved the original one to larger quarters, and begun the Joan Wolf Ballet Ensemble, a semiprofessional group composed of her teaching staff and advanced teenage students.

Although finding your niche as a ballet dancer is admittedly difficult, opportunities have increased with new ballet groups throughout the country. Other opportunities exist, in this country and abroad, in classical ballet companies, music and stage shows, opera, television, and motion pictures. Teaching goes well with dancing, too, as Joan Wolf's experience shows. If choreography appeals to you, you can look ahead to that work too, and, along with dancing, express yourself by creating dances.

To succeed in ballet you need, along with dance training, talent, good health, a graceful and symmetrical body, strong legs, perfect feet, sensitivity, discipline, determination, perseverance, and patience.

''And for teaching you must communicate well and see others, first, as human beings and, second, as dancers,'' Joan Wolf concluded.

MEMO 41:

> WHEN A JOB FIELD IS COMPETITIVE—ESPECIALLY WHEN IT'S COMPETITIVE—YOU HAVE TO USE THE POSITIVE APPROACH IN GOING AFTER WHAT YOU WANT.

Barbara Anton:
''If your idea of a gem of a job is working with glamorous

jewels, consider a career as a ⌐ signer, goldsmith, silver-smith, or model maker.

"In JEWELRY DESIGN you can create work at every possible price range," stated award-winning Barbara Anton, who enjoys a worldwide reputation.

"As a goldsmith or silversmith you will work with metals," she went on, "and as a modelmaker with wax.

"In my salon I use diamonds, cultured pearls, emeralds, topazes, and fine metals. My first step in creating a design is to talk with the client and discuss what she or he wants. Then I make sketches and when the clients make their selection, I quote an approximate price.

"After I create the final design on paper, a modelmaker casts it in wax. Eventually, when the wax model is perfected, the finished jewelry is re-created from it in gems and metals."

Barbara Anton's preparation for this career was in fine arts. "For some years I worked as a painter," she said. "But after I married a salesman of precious gems one of his customers suggested I apply my artistic ability to jewelry and design an unusual ring for him. That, and other requests, led me into jewelry design. Working with gems and metals taught me that jewelry design could become a permanent medium of expression," she went on.

Once her career decision was made, Barbara took courses in forging, goldsmithing, metal work, wax model making, and gem stones and their properties. She studied design at the Gemological Institute of America, for which an art background is necessary. Later, she and her husband Albert began working together in the elegant salon they established.

"Courses in goldsmithing and model making are relatively inexpensive," she reported. "From them you learn techniques, but after that it's the practice on your own that counts. For model making, your equipment can be as simple as a small alcohol lamp, one or two metal dental tools, and jewelers' casting wax.

"If you're interested in design, you need a good background in art," Ms. Anton stressed. "A college education isn't necessary, but you should take as many specialized courses as you can to give you thorough preparation and knowledge."

Once you obtain sufficient background, employment opportunities will exist with jewelry manufacturers; in shops that make, repair, and sell jewelry; and, in a business of your own if you design and are a goldsmith and model-maker. It goes without saying that top jewelry designers do extremely well, because people who order custom-designed jewels expect to pay high prices for them.

To succeed in this career field you need patience, good eyesight, artistic ability, manual dexterity, and a capacity for exacting work.

"Obviously, parts of the work are very glamorous because you're handling precious materials," concluded Barbara Anton. "But, because of its exacting demands, it's a hard and grueling profession. Women should think of that aspect, too."

MEMO 42:

> WHEN YOU DECIDE ON A JOB GOAL, ADJUST TO THE FACT THAT SOME OF YOUR FRIENDS WILL HAVE TO GO. IN RETURN, YOU'LL GAIN THE REWARDING FEELING THAT YOU ARE PART OF THE WORK OF THE WORLD AND NOT ON THE SIDELINES OF LIVING.

Judith Insler:
"Traditionally those who could draw were labelled artists and those who couldn't non-artists. But, today, the art field has opened up tremendously.

"I wasn't an art major myself," admitted Judith Insler, a SCULPTOR who entered her job field accidentally. "But now there are many areas in art that don't deal with drawing at all and the field attracts people with diverse backgrounds and points of view. Sculpture is part design, part art, and part construction. You have to get involved in all its aspects.

"As my medium, I combine stone, steel, and wood into abstract sculptures which deal with positive and negative form relationships," she went on. "To carve stone I use pneumatic tools and other power equipment. To create color gradations, I laminate thin layers of slate or different types of wood.

"As for my studio, my whole house is filled with my work. The kitchen table is piled high with tools. The bedroom is ceiling-to-floor with art magazines and folders. My basement holds much of my equipment. In fact, wherever you look my environment shows very clearly what I'm committed to."

From the time Judith Insler finished high school she wanted a serious commitment—something that would last her for 20 or 30 years. "But I had a very traditional kind of upbringing, and I didn't know what I wanted or what was right for me," she said. "Consequently, I went to Brooklyn College but dropped out after two years, mainly because I didn't find just going to school and then coming home very exciting. As an alternative I tried secretarial work."

But office work wasn't right either, so after Judith married an engineer she entered Lehman College to major in psychology. That work turned her on to the point that she considered obtaining a master's degree in social work. First, however, she did some volunteer social work to make sure it was right for her.

"It wasn't," she confided, "so I switched to education and enrolled in Fairleigh Dickinson University to obtain the credits I needed for teaching. After I received my credits I worked on a reading program and again found out that this was not the commitment I was looking for either."

In the meantime, however, Judith had started stone carving courses at an art center in her area. "I grew very much involved," she declared. "I loved it so much I continued taking courses. I also began studying sculpture. When I learned about carving with power tools, working with marble opened up to me. This was a terrific experience, because I'm five feet tall and weigh just a hundred pounds."

As Judith began perfecting her art she exhibited in museums and started teaching in adult education programs. "In an art such as mine it's important to exhibit non-commercially first in order for the galleries to feel you are a productive artist," she explained. "And women, especially, must hustle and get into good shows to prove the seriousness of their commitments and long-range goals.

"The long-range goal," she continued, "is to sell through galleries and get sufficiently well-known so that people seek you out and commission work. But this takes a long time. It is not an immediate gratification.''

If you have a non-art background and want to enter some area of the art field, Judith Insler suggests as much as possible exposing yourself to the phase that interests you and acquiring technical know-how.

''For esthetics, you have to read, visit museums and galleries, keep your eyes open, and ask a lot of questions,'' she advised. ''Sensitize yourself, because understanding is a means to seeing. Get to know craftsmen and artists who have been in the field for 10 or 15 years. If you can establish a good rapport they will impart much of their knowledge and skills.

''Finally, find your own approaches. It's exciting when you do.''

MEMO 43:

> HAVE REGULAR SET TIMES FOR ATTENDING TO THE THINGS THAT SHOULD HAVE PRIORITY. ONCE THAT BECOMES YOUR HABIT SECONDARY MATTERS WILL FALL INTO PLACE.

Monica Anagnostaras:
''COMMERCIAL ART *has been good for me.*''

Many women dream of the free-lance life and a chance to work on their own as the way to bypass the schedule of 9-to-5 and a boxed-in day at an office. And for Monica Anagnostaras, a commercial artist, this way has been very good, since she enthusiastically combines the life of a mother and homemaker with a bustling business.

''I believe in the saying, 'To everything there is a season, and a time to every purpose,' '' she said, ''so I feel particularly happy that, as a free-lance commercial artist, I can be quite flexible with time and successfully adapt to my husband and my three children's active family interests.''

Monica's work in her home studio includes book illustrations, wall paper and textile designs, color separations, film strips, motifs for children's items, and layouts for books and brochures.

"While vacationing in Greece, I discovered batik—a method of creating designs on fabric using wax and dyes," she told me. "By implementing this ancient technique with experimental methods of my own I came up with a style of batik painting that caught the eye of many publishers. In the creative art field, it's wise to have an individual style," she advised. "For example, one artist my agent handles illustrates only in bread sculpture; for me the agent handles only batiks.

"When you have your own style you stand out from the many artists who are all alike. Once, formerly, when I was hired for part of a book, even I found it difficult to distinguish between my work and that of the three other artists."

On the other hand, there is a lot of non-creative artwork, Monica went on to say. All that is needed is a steady hand and the appropriate knowledge. Color separation and paste-up and mechanicals (the placement of type and photos) for printing, publishing, and advertising fit into this category. Layouts and book design are another category. Here the artist does not necessarily have to know how to draw or paint, but must have good ideas and a sense of design and color.

Monica Anagnostaras was brought up in an artistic family. Her mother was an artist and commercial photographer, and her grandfather was a high-style hat designer who also had paintings in the Museum of Modern Art.

"Actually, I was surrounded by so much art and so many artistic people that, at first, I thought I'd like to go into another field," she admitted. "I even took an aptitude test, hoping to be something other than an artist. But all the results said, 'You're an artist.' "

Once she made her career decision Monica began working part-time and holidays for an advertising agency. "In the beginning I worked for nothing in order to learn. After my high school graduation I chose college and a major in art rather than art school, because I wanted a broad educational background."

Following graduation from the City College of New York, Monica continued in advertising for a large New York retail store. Later she joined the staff of Grolier Incorporated and designed and illustrated material for *The Book of Knowledge* and their annuals.

"At that point my education came in handy," she pointed out. "Since that publisher does a large business in Canada, the knowledge of French I gained at college gave me an edge over other capable applicants."

With the advent of her first child Monica left the 9-to-5 routine to devote time to her family and free-lance. "I obtain jobs from former contacts and from following newspaper advertisements," she explained. "For example, when I see an advertisement for 'Artist-Designer-Art Director' I call and tell them I'm available on a free-lance basis. The knowledge gained on one job leads to the next.

"As your skill grows you leave behind work that bores you or pays less than other jobs," she commented. "A free-lance artist has only so much time and sometimes one or two clients are enough."

Despite the fact that you free yourself from a 9-to-5 routine when you're a free-lance artist, you do need a personal schedule that you stick to. You also need a hefty supply of self-discipline and sufficient push to work long hours when deadlines hang over your head.

But in return for the discipline you have the wonderful freedom of juggling your own time, since before-breakfast stints and midnight hours can make up for 9-to-5. The obvious disadvantage is that free-lancers don't know just how much money they will make in a year. But this is balanced by the promise that your earnings can reflect your abilities more directly than in many other jobs. And there's no financial limit on how high your year's earnings can go.

MEMO 44:

> THINK EACH DAY ABOUT WHAT YOU MUST DO THAT DAY AND PUT EVERYTHING ELSE OUT OF YOUR MIND.

Helen Hartje:
"I've always been interested in objects d'art and other antiques and collectibles.

"Actually, there's a collector for everything—from anti-macassars to zithers," commented Helen Hartje, a collector, dealer, lecturer, and teacher who created a full-time job for herself with a commitment to *every* aspect of COLLECTING.

"My background is in art," she explained, "and my interest in antiques and collectibles started when a friend and I began making candles for a business we called 'The Candle Loft.' Through candles I became interested in early lights, so I started a collection which has grown over the years from some of the earliest pieces known to man, Victorian objects. An important stimulus was the questions people coming into the candle shop asked. To find the answers I started a round of research in libraries and museums. I decided to become an authority on the subject of candles and early lights. Since I like to talk I began guest lecturing for adult school classes and women's organizations.

"Currently I lecture on lighting, the uncommon collectibles of the 19th and 20th centuries, and 'Facts, Fakes, and Frauds,' which is an introduction to antiquing with its hazards, pitfalls, and fabulous finds. In addition, I teach in adult schools and a community college, and as a dealer, I do a few shows each year myself.

"Plus my lamps I collect baskets, miniatures, crafts, glass, china, covered animal dishes, early games, brass pieces, and old clay smoking items. Many of the objects are set up in my living room. I also have a room for an office and display area.

"Once you start collecting seriously, a business often evolves, because as your tastes and interests change you find that in order to afford new things and make room for them, you must sell others. In this business there is room for all levels of collectors," Ms. Hartje added, "and the cost can range from practically zero up. You can also collect *anything* that you choose, but from a practical point of view pick an interest with your purse and the availability of your field of collectibles in mind. As a starter, I'd suggest collecting privately and for the fun of it. Then study and learn as you go. Read extensively. Visit museums. Attend classes that will broaden your knowledge. As your knowledge expands, increase your collection by keeping your eyes open for announcements of flea markets and antique shows. Contact dealers and leave a notation of what you're interested in with them. Garage sales are not a great source, but they are fun and you might find something. When you go to an auction set a price for whatever you're interested in—and don't go above it.

"The fun-and-games element of collecting is like Russian roulette," Helen Hartje finished. "You never know what you're going to find, and the search for things is endless. Moreover, whatever you collect today will be something someone will want tomorrow. Even if you collect toothbrushes, a collector may say—50 years from now—'Look at these great plastic brushes!' "

MEMO 45:
>   BE WILLING TO TAKE THE TIME TO LAY THE GROUNDWORK YOU
>   NEED FOR THE WORK YOU WANT. THEN BUILD YOURSELF FROM
>   THE GROUND UP.

Lori Colligan:
"One of the interesting facets of a THEATER MANAGE-MENT *job is meeting the performers."*

When Lori Colligan was in her teens she and her twin sister founded a little theater group that performed in the Boston area.

"And in between that time and now I've held a variety of jobs—in summer stock, modeling, advertising, management, selling, and personnel work," she stated. "I've also written a shopping column and served as an associate executive director for the United Fund. All this background has helped me put things together for my present job as manager of the 'Playhouse on the Mall' in the Bergen Mall suburban shopping center in New Jersey. As a theater manager my department is the administrative or front-of-the-house business. The people on my staff include box office persons, ushers, the house manager, assistant house manager, and other non-production personnel. Sales is a big part of my work, so I spend a great deal of time selling and booking theater parties and benefit and fund-raising performances. I devise all kinds of plans—student and senior-citizen discounts, subscriptions, et cetera—so that everyone can come to the legitimate theater. Another part of my job is deciding, with the producer, what shows will appeal to our audience and when we should produce them.

"Since I attend all benefit performances and try to be at all the openings, this Bergen Mall theater is really my home away from home. And it's wonderfully exciting to meet the celebrities."

Lori, who believes that enthusiasm is the key to making the grade in careers, has been enthusiastic about everything she has done from that first little theater group on. "I was still in high school then," she reminisced, "and we used to take the group to veterans' hospitals. After high school I worked at a summer theater in every sort of capacity and obtained first-hand knowledge that's still helpful to me.

"A subsequent stint at modeling led to a job in an advertising agency—another invaluable work experience. Then work as assistant manager and manager of a slenderizing salon provided excellent background in management."

In the New York suburbs Lori acquired expertise in interviewing and hiring people (jobs in two employment agencies), in selling (mutual funds), and in administration (four years with the United Fund).

"I was also coming to all the opening nights at this theater," she said, "and because I was here so often I got to know the manager well. When that manager left, I was asked by the owners of the theater if I would be interested in the job. I knew my experience was right for it, and I knew the job was right for me. So, several years later, here I am."

Today the best opportunities for such management work are in the regional, community, summer, and dinner theaters springing up over the country.

"I would certainly advise those interested to learn everything possible about the theater and to obtain strong experience in business and expertise in publicity and promotion," she emphasized. "The woman who goes into this work needs to be calm, patient, level-headed. And enthuasiam and business acumen are both keywords for success."

MEMO 46:

> WHEN YOU WANT TO PROGRESS YOU NEED DRIVE AND AN
> INTEREST IN EVERY AREA OF THE BUSINESS IN WHICH YOU'RE
> INVOLVED. BESIDES, YOU NEED LUCK, WIDELY VARIED EXPERI-
> ENCE, AND THE ABILITY TO DO A BETTER JOB THAN ANY OF
> YOUR PEERS.

Anita Kaufhold:
"Teaching music privately has been a rewarding life.

"When you're a private PIANO TEACHER you educate both
audiences and performers," declared Anita Kaufhold, whose two-
piano home rings with music every day. "Most of the people I teach
attain an increased understanding and appreciation of music whether
they actually do anything professionally with it or not."

Anita Kaufhold has 35 elementary, intermediate, and advanced
students all told. Each person is a different sort of challenge to her.
"You don't teach any two alike because each student's need is
different," she put in. "I feel that the students need goals, so I like to
have performance classes every six or eight weeks in which they play
for each other. In addition, I enter my students in state auditions.

"Besides this, I hold a week of annual auditions in my home,
sponsored by the National Guild of Piano Teachers. This is very
exciting, since other teachers bring their students here too. An out-of-
state judge assigned by the Guild's headquarters in Texas listens to a
hundred students."

Ms. Kaufhold's love of music goes back to lessons in Havana,
Cuba, where her family lived for a time. "By my teenage years I knew
I wanted to be a private music teacher," she went on, "so when I
returned to the United States I continued studying toward that goal.
After high school I studied privately under artist-teachers. As part of
my training I'd do practice teaching and would bring my own students

to my teacher every three or four weeks. Today, however, you must go to college to prepare for work such as mine.''

Following Anita's marriage, she taught for three years in a private music school. Then she struck out on her own, starting with six students. "From the first this work has been right for me," she contended, "because I can teach in the hours that fit my life-style and pursue my work at home.

"But women who want to be private piano teachers owe it to themselves and their students to be highly qualified and professional," she pointed out. "Take an active part in professional organizations. This adds to your credentials, gives you a way to exchange ideas, and provides on-going training. To keep on top of everything, I study with an artist-teacher every few years.

"Another great plus in teaching piano privately is the fact that you can continue working for as long as you want to without worrying about retirement," she concluded. "One teacher I know 'retired' several years ago. But now that she's living in Florida I hear she's as busy as she ever was in her former music studio.''

MEMO 47:
> WHEN YOU MAKE A PLAN FOLLOW THROUGH ON IT AND GIVE YOURSELF THE SATISFACTION OF KNOWING YOU'RE A DOER INSTEAD OF A DREAMER.

Elizabeth Case:
"When you practice the FINE ARTS, *the wise use of time is one of the best talents you can have.*

"I was brought up to create—always to create," observed painter Elizabeth Case. "I now live the life of an artist and incorporate painting into my life at home raising children and running a household. A United States Navy art program commissions marine paintings from me. I go on assignments to pain naval events and operations. I have also worked on a national touring exhibition called 'Caravan of American Freedom' for the Bicentennial.''

In between these and similar projects Elizabeth Case fills her studio with paintings of people, riverscapes, and the history of submarines. Occasionally she teaches.

''My work week is a tapestry in which I take out the various threads and weave them together again,'' she told me. ''Sometimes I put in red, sometimes orange. But I get the colors, or the activities, all together, and the texture begins to take form and I develop my own special life-style. A strong way of life is very important to a fine artist.

''Except when I'm traveling I worked mostly in my home, and my entire home is my studio. Right now I have five easels in the living room supporting canvases from five feet to eight feet. Every wall is hung with pictures, and the desks and tables are covered with work. In the fine arts you must have the work on hand. It's crippling to get it out and put it away.''

Elizabeth developed her creative penchant when she was a child of 10 living in California. ''I started drawing,'' she recalled, ''but all through my childhood I had no formal lessons in art because my teachers told my mother just to let me draw. After high school, I went to the Art Students League in New York.

''Later I studied at Elmira College and Syracuse University because I wanted to learn more than just painting. It's important for any aspiring fine artist to build a varied background. My next move was a return to California to take a job in the animation department of the Disney Studios,'' she went on. ''That was a tremendous experience and discipline for me. I worked on the movie *Sleeping Beauty* and drew birds and running animals in perfect detail at least for eight hours a day and sometimes for fourteen. Happily for me, the people at the studios grew interested in my fine art too and exhibited my paintings in the research department.''

After California came a move to rural Pennsylvania, where Elizabeth spent four years painting and exhibiting. She then returned to New York and, finally, to Edgewater, New Jersey on the banks of the Hudson River.

"I'm overwhelmed by the beauty of the Hudson and entranced by Edgewater,'' she said, "so as soon as I moved down here I started marine painting and got into the Navy art program.

"My first work for it was a test assignment to paint the U.S. Submarine *Ling.* My second was the Submarine *Whale.* I've also painted a midshipmen's ball in Tallahassee, Florida and worked on the history of submarines for a mural.

"In the future I hope to paint every element of Edgewater—the people, the houses, the schools, the children, and the boats. Nothing stands still, so I must paint all that I see.

"As a fine artist, the use of time is one of my best talents,'' Elizabeth Case pointed out. "So I don't venture forth from my studio too much except for meetings connected with my work or for the physical fitness that I think is so important to an artist's health and vitality. I make sure everything I need to get or do is included in the one expedition.

"It takes a while to develop a profitable career,'' she stressed, when I asked about the compatability of the fine arts with making a living. "In most instances at first you need some form of patronage or means of earning. But people find all kinds of ways—teaching, working in galleries, even unrelated jobs.

"Apprenticeship is eternal, and for most of us it takes years to get where we want to be. But when you start setting high standards and developing at each stage it all comes together after a while.''

MEMO 48:

YOU HAVE TO KEEP LOOKING FOR NEW DIRECTIONS, BECAUSE IF YOU'RE SET IN ONLY ONE THERE'S NO WAY YOU CAN GROW IN THESE CHANGING TIMES.

Chapter 5

Education

Dr. Jacqueline Holland:
"Women going into education with their eyes on administrative posts should get the best training possible and keep their sights on their goal, regardless of the times."

What about telling women to set their sights on administrative posts in the education world, such as SCHOOL PRINCIPAL, when the start toward that goal—a teaching job—is so hard to come by now?

That was my lead-in question when I interviewed Dr. Jacqueline Holland, principal of two elementary schools. "First, I'd say that no one should sacrifice her goals because of the times," answered Dr. Holland, who has had a long haul to her own post in school administration. "But I'd also add immediately that the goal must be realistic and based on what women can bring to the job.

"If you believe in something and have ability, training, dedication, and mobility, then you should certainly aim for administration. Good administrators are always needed.

"Men have always had greater mobility, and I could have been a principal sooner if I had been able to move around. I didn't want to because of family considerations. But if you are willing and able to be mobile there should be something for you."

Dr. Holland's dedication to education began in Boston in second grade when she fell in love with school. "I admired my teachers so much that I wanted to be one myself," she said, "so after high school I went to Salem Teachers College."

After 2¹/₂ years the future educator transferred to Boston University on scholarship. After receiving her bachelor's degree she was given a fellowship for graduate work at Howard University in Washington. "I obtained my master's degree in history there," she told me. "Then I taught in a small town in Maryland till I married a year and a half later."

Following her marriage to a lawyer she moved to New York state, where her two children were born. "When my son was 2¹/₂ I took a job working with a psychiatrist and setting up a school for emotionally disturbed girls at a state hospital," she continued. "After my daughter was born I stayed home for a while. Then I went back to the state hospital to work in the emotionally disturbed boys' school. After I joined the staff of a public grammar school and taught there for 10 years."

She pursued her next goal of a principalship during a sabbatical at a special program in instructional administration at Fordham University and then interned at an elementary school in her area. However, there were no openings for Jacqueline Holland in principal's jobs in the county where she had taught. "But you don't have experience," she was told.

"Rather than go back to teaching when I was ready for a principalship, I took a leave of absence to return to Fordham to work as an administrator-teacher in a teacher-training program," she told me. "But I kept my eye on my goal and began to work for my doctorate.

"When another try for a principalship yielded nothing I continued my leave, kept on with my doctoral work, and taught at Brooklyn College for a year. Then I had to come back to my school district and teach for two years in the fifth grade in order not to be dropped from the roll," she explained. "With this as my only real choice, I taught full-time and worked on my doctoral dissertation in my spare hours. But since I was dedicated and qualified it was admittedly disappointing not to be able to fulfill my role in a way that was commensurate with what I had put into my profession."

After the necessary two years of teaching—and getting her doctorate—Dr. Holland tried again for a principalship and, once more, was unsuccessful. Consequently, she took an administrative position with a community college.

"But I continued to let my school district know my goal was still a principal's job," she said. "Finally, while vacationing at Martha's Vineyard one summer I received a telephone call offering me the long-awaited principalship.

"In a way I suppose the final step to reaching this long-sought goal was a meshing of different kinds of pressures all at one point," she admitted. "I'd been an area teacher for many years. In addition, the Office of Equal Opportunity and the Human Rights Commission were helping people take a different view of a person's skin color and sex. As a black woman, I was at the right place at the right time with the right qualifications.

"To get back to your starting question," Dr. Holland concluded, "let me repeat that women going into education with their eyes on administrative posts should get the best training possible and keep their sights on their goal, regardless of the times. Even though the opportunities in education may not always be in the form you wish for, *your* opportunity will eventually come if you are qualified.

"I waited for years, and I didn't give up. So I hope other women won't either."

MEMO 49:

FROM EMBARKATION TO ARRIVAL YOU NEED SINGLE PURPOSE AND PERSEVERANCE.

Lois Marshall:
"Women should be administrators and women should aim high.

"It's still somewhat rare for women to be school administrators beyond the elementary level," acknowledged Lois Marshall, herself a COMMUNITY COLLEGE DEAN. Her position is Dean of Community Services at New Jersey's Bergen Community College. "In fact, while I worked for my master's degree I was the only woman for two years in the administrative program. Now I've almost completed my Ph.D. at Columbia University.

"But even though we're a rarity, I believe women who want to be administrators should prepare—*if* they're wholly cognizant about the number of jobs that exist," she continued.

Lois Marshall is responsible for managing all non-credit programs. This includes the design, development, implementation, and evaluation of a wide range of learning experiences for adults. Essentially these experiences consist of cultural offerings, continuing professional education programs, education within industry, education for women, consultant services, workshops, seminars, and similar specialized projects. She is on the National Advisory Council for Adult Education and the New Jersey State Advisory Council for Adult and Continuing Education.

"My position is particularly interesting because I get to know so many stimulating people and because my activities span such a great gamut," Dean Marshall added. "At 8 a.m. I may be at a drug meeting. In the evening I may be working with a cultural council helping encourage arts activities in areas not reached before. In between, I may be involved with our Adult Learning Center, a very rewarding program that enables adults to obtain a high school equivalency certificate without cost."

Dean Marshall arrived at her interesting job after starting a second round of college when her daughter was in elementary school—and when she was president of the P.T.A.

"When I graduated from high school I had one year of college before I dropped out to work and get married," she confided. "But I kept very active in various associations. This increased my interest in returning to school, and when I started my second round I decided to major in English and minor in speech and dramatics. I went into teaching after receiving my degree.

"But after about a year I thought I'd like to get involved in more than classroom work," she stated. "As I evaluated the possibilities I decided on administration. I took my master's by going to school nights and summers. My interests were secondary school administration, continuing education, and community colleges."

While she was teaching and going to school, Lois Marshall was given a year to plan and launch an adult education program in the town where she taught. While traveling around the state learning about other programs and getting to know many people, she was offered a job as a full-time director of another already-established adult school.

"It was a good opportunity," she explained, "so I moved to that full-time job instead of launching the new program in the system where I taught. Through my interest in continuing education, I eventually became acquainted with Dr. Sidney Silverman, President of Bergen Community College. My present job developed from that contact.

"The field of education has many positions in it," she advised, "and right now, as everyone knows, teaching jobs are competitive.

"But, if you're interested in education there are teaching-related fields and alternatives to consider. Look to special areas and special fields. A few examples might be nursery and pre-nursery education, adult education, high school equivalency programs, vocational education, technical schools, and education for the handicapped. There are also jobs in day care, educational research, educational materials and equipment, and audio-visual education.

"From my experience I'd say that when you want a career in education (and especially in administration) volunteer work and activity in many professional associations can be extremely valuable," Dean Marshall concluded. "So is getting to know many people, being aware of what's happening in the field, and constantly setting new goals."

MEMO 50:

GO IN THE DIRECTION OF THINGS THAT ARE HAPPENING AND DON'T BE SATISFIED TO GIVE ANYTHING LESS THAN YOUR *ALL* TO YOUR GOAL.

Harriet Lefkowith:
"There's a great deal women can do if they'll build up their confidence and learn to use their potential.

"Moving outside of myself and my home to find out what I wanted to do led me to a fascinating career helping others recognize their potential," pointed out Harriet Lefkowith, who works with Lois Marshall [see previous interview] and, like her, found the right job in a community college.

"I'm Assistant to the Dean of Community Services and WOMEN'S INSTITUTE AND WOMEN'S CENTER COORDINATOR," she explained. "A few years ago when I was with Catalyst, the national organization devoted to part-time employment for educated women, Lois Marshall asked me to talk at a 'Women Speak' forum. When she asked me to be program coordinator of the Women's Institute she had envisioned for some time, I was absolutely delighted.

"Essentially, the Women's Institute was developed to answer the needs of women who were discovering that changing life-styles often require support and information. It is a non-credit educational program that provides a wide variety of educational experiences, including career planning workshops, enrichment courses, training programs, refresher courses, conferences, and seminars.

"The Women's Center grew out of it," she continued. "It offers programs geared to suburban women who have come to feel they are part of the women's movement even though they don't always identify with it through membership in feminist organizations. The Women's Center answers their needs for informal information programs. And once their eyes are open there is much that they can do."

Harriet Lefkowith herself has found there is much that she can do ever since she married a fellow student while majoring in sociology and English at Penn State University.

"My first child was born nine months after I graduated," she recalled. "Our other two were born while my husband was in the Navy. While I was home I loved raising my children since I believe very strongly that there is a time in a woman's life for child rearing if that is what she wants," she declared. "But even then it doesn't seem to me that you have to sacrifice yourself. I went to school when my children were young, and I was always able to read three books a week, whether I was stirring the chocolate pudding or minding babies.

"When my youngest child was in first grade, I returned to college for my master's degree in English. When I finished and was wondering what to do next my mother—a buyer for a department store in Pennsylvania—became terminally ill. It seemed right to help by buying for her in New York. When she passed away I continued as a resident buyer. But after a while it grew ridiculous to run to Pennsylvania one day a week and New York two days. I gave up that rat race to work for my husband, who had become a communications consultant."

About that time Ms. Lefkowith began to hear many of her peers asking, "What will we do?" And when solving this problem became her interest, she answered an advertisement for a job with Catalyst. While there she led a course in career planning for women at the Saturday College of Fairleigh Dickinson University, taught adult school classes appropriately titled "For Women Only" and "Developing Your Potential," and, for a large pharmaceutical house, prepared an in-house training program to upgrade female employees through the use of career counseling.

"This work took me right up to the time I was asked to become program coordinator for the Women's Institute," she recalled. "I'm now so enthusiastic about adult and continuing education that I'm enrolled in Columbia University working toward my doctorate in it.

"As you can obviously see from my story, I've found that one thing feeds another if your mind keeps going all the time.

"So when women who want a chance seek advice my words are always the same. 'If you don't like where you are get some place else, whatever you have to do to get there. Dare to be. Dare to try. And don't put yourself in your own way!'"

MEMO 51:

> IF A JOB IS RIGHT FOR YOU SEE IT THROUGH TO THE END AND FOCUS ALL OF YOUR ENERGY ON GETTING A SOLID GRASP ON IT.

Kathryn Stilwell:
"Involvement is the name of the game for the HIGH SCHOOL GUIDANCE COUNSELOR.

"The main reason for going into guidance is because you like to work with kids," maintained Kathryn Stilwell, who's deeply involved not only with students but also with administrators, classroom teachers, special teachers, parents, psychologists, social workers, and referral agencies.

In fact, her involvement has been so great that for two school years she was on leave of absence from her job to serve as the first full-time president of the New Jersey Education Association. In the time left over from professional activities she's equally engrossed with such hobbies as travel, cars, coins, stamps, and dogs.

"As a guidance counselor I have found that many interests help me get through to students by providing another frame of reference from which to deal with them," she emphasized. "For example, more than once my interest in coins has helped me communicate. And once when I was working with a boy from Angola the fact that I had traveled in Africa made him open up immediately.

"In high school guidance you work with students on a day-to-day basis as well as on long-range plans," said Ms. Stilwell.

"You sit down with your students, listen to them, and help them by tests and other means to learn more about themselves and to evaluate their assets, interests, and values. You can then try to indicate what education and career choice might be right for them and what they need to know to make a wise selection. Right now much of the emphasis has swung to career counseling rather than the college counseling because of the job market and economic factors."

If helping young people find their potential is the job that seems right for you, you will need a college degree in education or psychology. In addition, a master's degree or one year of graduate work in psychology, sociology, or education is usually required. Teaching experience is an asset. In some instances it is a must.

Kay Stilwell, who strongly recommends experience as a teacher before you become a guidance counselor, began her career as a high school history teacher. While teaching she went to Columbia University at night to obtain her master's degree. Later, after more than 20 years of teaching, she switched to guidance upon the completion of required courses from Montclair State College, New York University, and Rutgers University.

The personal qualities you need for this work are patience, understanding, tact, emotional stability, warmth, friendliness, and empathy. In addition, you must know and understand developmental psychology, be well attuned to the job world, and be deeply implicated in education. Kay Stilwell, whose commitments in all these respects have earned her a spot in *Who's Who In American Education* is a prime example of filling this role.

"Salary in this field varies with degree level and years of experience," Kay Stilwell said in conclusion. "But even greater than the financial rewards is the huge satisfaction of work that you know to some degree at least constantly helps people make better use of their abilities and contribute more to society."

MEMO 52:

START AT THE BEGINNING AND PRODUCE. WHILE YOU'RE PRODUCING, HUSTLE. AND WHEN IT'S NECESSARY, FIGHT TO SURVIVE.

Sandra Sabatini:
"The ELEMENTARY SCHOOL GUIDANCE COUNSELOR *is a wonderfully challenging means to a very worthwhile end.*

"Counselors in the elementary school see themselves primarily as developmental educator-counselors who work with children, teachers, and parents," declared Sandra Sabatini. "For maximum effectiveness, we hold teacher in-service education and parent discussion groups, because we can't reach everyone ourselves.

"Much of the work in my school is in preventive mental health education, because we have discovered how necessary it is to identify children with special learning needs, whether they're gifted or disabled," she went on. "I share this responsibility with the reading-learning disabilities teacher and the classroom teacher.

"We work to help children realize their fullest potential, not only in terms of emotional adjustment but in career education also. This means helping children learn a little bit about the world of work and training them to think about making choices and decisions for themselves. We talk about developing responsibility and finding out more about the things that interest them. Group discussion counseling in the classrooms is one type of work.

"My small group activities are really play groups where children can learn social skills while being creative with crafts, drama, and puppets," Sandra continued. "The idea is to have their natural learning environment—the play group—act as an energizing force for life-coping skills. The children love the play groups, and getting picked for one is a real status symbol. Playing together in an imaginary and creative way seems to be related to academic school success."

Sandra Sabatini came to elementary school guidance after majoring in elementary education at the City College of New York.

"At college I became a freshman advisor in the House Plan organization," she told me. "In this plan, which is somewhat like a fraternity or sorority (but open to everyone) I helped a small number of freshmen over their hurdles. The work was group-oriented, and I found it very enjoyable. I also met my husband and married him in a House Plan center—which, naturally, added to the pleasure."

After graduating from college, Sandra was a teaching fellow at City College in the House Plan organization. Simultaneously, she took courses at Columbia University Teachers College. Eventually, she left the college counseling field to enter elementary school guidance.

"I found out almost immediately that I loved to work with small children," she stated. "So I went back to school at night to take courses in elementary school guidance.

"Subsequently, I began a program in a school where I taught. Later, I worked in a ghetto school, which gave me experiences I'm never going to forget."

After a move to the suburbs—and time out to have four children—Ms. Sabatini returned to the counseling field through a part-time job at a guidance center for women. "I counseled women for several years," she remembered. "Then a friend who worked in a nearby community told me of an opening for an elementary school guidance counselor here.

"I'm finding this job fantastic," she declared, "and there's so much potential in the field, I went back to school for my doctorate and have now completed four long hard years of graduate study—an interesting combination of neurology, behavioral psychology, statistics, child development, and child lore.''

According to Sandra Sabatini, women seeking a job in elementary school guidance should have warmth, sensitivity, and a desire to help others. It's a smart idea first to test your interest and talent in working with people by holding a variety of part-time jobs, such as camp counseling and volunteer work with children. If your interest warrants going ahead, write to the state departments of education where you would like to work before enrolling for college courses and find out the requirements for certification. Generally, they include basic courses in psychology, child and growth development, and counseling techniques.

"At the moment the outlook for jobs could be brighter," admitted Sandra Sabatini, "because most school districts are not adding extra staff members. However, there's hope for the future because many spokesmen for this field believe more preventive mental health programs for children are just around the corner. It's vitally important to have them too," Sandra Sabatini stressed, "since so many people get the feeling of failure in their early lives. By third grade this pattern can be set.

"And if you don't get to its crux in time and help children see some value in themselves, this sense of failure becomes ineradicable.''

MEMO 53:
> WHILE YOU CULTIVATE A WIDE RANGE OF SKILLS AND ABILITIES, PREPARE FOR GOOD JOB OPPORTUNITIES BY PLANNING TOWARD A SPECIFIC AREA OF CONCENTRATION. THEN FOCUS YOUR TALENT ON THAT CONCENTRATION.

Joan Schuster:
"The wonderful world where a MUSEUM DIRECTOR *operates is a wide-open education field.*

"Admittedly, the field can be hard to get into because some of the jobs are so specialized and because news of openings isn't always directed to spots where potential candidates hear of them," advised Joan Schuster, executive director of a community museum of science, art, history, and photography.

"I must also point out that most women in museums are volunteers or highly-specialized curators. Few are full-time paid directors in major museums, and these are rarely paid at the same rate as a man, even though the expectations of a woman are usually far higher.

"I got into this work because I've been in administration and management for a long time, and my background is a peculiarly suitable combination of personal interests. I'm involved primarily in fund raising, planning, implementating plans, cataloging, registering, and indexing material.

"I plan programs, workshops, art and photography shows, and other activities. Our art shows change each month, though we have a permanent exhibit too. We also have changing photography exhibits. Our science hall and history collections are somewhat permanent.

"One of our popular events is a 'Sundays At Six' wine and cheese series in which we have featured speakers and programs. We also hold many classes—for instance, woodcutting, photography, and drawing."

Before she assumed her present job, Ms. Schuster's background was varied. Growing up in her native California, she had a strong interest in galleries and museums. After graduating from Ohio Wesleyan University, she taught high school in Georgia. She later took a job as a multimedia coordinator and area supervisor with the New York City Board of Education. Simultaneously she began her graduate work and eventually got her present job through the employment service at Columbia University while working for her doctorate.

"While in education I became involved as a volunteer in a county museum," she informed me. "I was a founder and member of the board of trustees and served on the science committee. In addition, I obtained gallery experience organizing shows when I worked as the assistant to the director of a New York art and sculpture gallery. Though I didn't realize it at the time, these jobs were apprenticeships for my present work."

There are several ways to approach the museum field, according to Joan Schuster, and there's every possible position one could think of in a museum. In small museums you do many things; in large museums all the jobs are specialized.

Among the job opportunities are spots for photographers, curators, directors, assistants to directors, registrants who take in monthly exhibits, exhibition specialists, fund-raisers, writers and publicists, secretaries, guides, lecturers, and class instructors.

"Art history or a very good basic education in history is useful," suggested Ms. Schuster. "So are some of the science fields. Advanced degrees are often necessary for curators or administrators. Another way to get into the field is to follow a museum-oriented interest and make a specialty of it. As examples, paleontology, ornithology, and 20th-century American paintings can be developed into fine careers.

"An excellent approach to a future career is a part-time job in a museum while obtaining your education," concluded Ms. Schuster. "Many museums have programs in which you can obtain academic credit for museum work. This gives you an excellent means of obtaining a practical apprenticeship and a behind-the-scenes view."

MEMO 54:
>SEE THE WORLD WITH AN OPEN MIND AND BE RECEPTIVE TO THE IDEAS OF OTHER PEOPLE.

Thelma Schoonmaker:
"I truly feel that my work as a DAY CARE PROGRAM DIRECTOR *takes me into the most important facet of early childhood education today.*

"But work in this field is demanding, so those who enter it must be loving, understanding, and, above all, stable," stressed Thelma

Schoonmaker, director of a school and center for early childhood education.

"In between a director's post and a volunteer's job, there are many challenging spots for head teachers, group teachers, and assistants or aides," she went on to say. "Admittedly, the field of teaching has been glutted for a while, so many people seeking careers in early childhood education have had problems. But when you find a job you will spend rewarding hours providing supervised learning experience for pre-school children. You introduce social skills and attitudes, language, numbers, and health and safety habits and teach stories, games, and songs.

"It's important to give the children a wide range of experiences that will help them build from the concrete to the abstract," explained Ms. Schoonmaker.

"Often mornings are devoted to group programs, the established curriculum, and weekly projects involving such things as shapes, puzzles, seasons, and colors. Afternoons can be geared to individual work, tailored to each child's needs."

Ms. Schoonmaker's dedication to education began while she was in Europe attending the University of Berlin or taking courses at the Sorbonne. "As I studied, I developed an interest in childhood development that I maintained in the early years of my marriage right through the birth of my three children—one in Paris, one in Algiers, and one in Aruba. Since my husband worked for an oil company, we moved a great deal. But in our 14 years in Aruba I put my training to use and ran a nursery school for the children of the employees of my husband's company."

When the Schoonmakers returned to the United States, Thelma worked as head teacher in a suburban nursery school. She enrolled in college to obtain a degree in early childhood education. Subsequently she became director of a cooperative nursery school and of another child care center before assuming her present post.

Educational requirements for the personnel of child and day care centers vary from state to state. In some areas the laws and standards for the centers—be they private, federally-funded, or cooperative—are in a state of flux chiefly centering around two main areas: teacher certification and teacher-child ratio.

"Until things work out in the long run," said Thelma Schoonmaker, "it's imperative that teachers, directors, and aides be equipped to deal with increasing numbers of children who come from environments of stress. These days we see many children from one-parent homes, foster homes, or homes where they've been subjected to abuse or desertion.

"Early childhood education is indeed a demanding and exhausting career field. But when you have a liking for children and find them fascinating it brings you the gratification of knowing you're filling a need."

MEMO 55:

> ONE WAY TO GET AHEAD IS TO HAVE THE KIND OF PERSONALITY THAT INDICATES YOU ARE NOT ONLY COMPETENT TO DO YOUR JOB BUT ALSO *WILLING* TO DO IT. THIS APPROACH TO WORKING IS IMPORTANT AT EVERY LEVEL AND IN EVERY CAREER.

Dr. Dorothea Hubin:
"College teaching permits you to delve very deeply into the field that appeals to you most.

"As a COLLEGE PROFESSOR you think of yourself, first of all, as part of your own discipline—whether sociologist, political scientist, musician, or whatever," said Dr. Dorothea Hubin, a specialist in criminology and a member of the sociology department at the Center for Social Work at Fairleigh Dickinson University.

"So if you want to be a professor it's vital to pick a special interest that's absolutely fascinating to you. I love my specialty—and I love college students, the sense of freedom of the university, and the feeling that I'm doing something meaningful."

Dr. Hubin prepares lectures, instructs students, gives assignments, plans exams, grades papers, conducts research, and keeps up with her field. Her activities have included working on training volunteers in a probation program; consulting for the Institute for Social Research at Fordham University on local action and delinquency prevention programs and on a project in Puerto Rico sponsored by the Puerto Rican crime committee; and teaching a course in "Women." She has also been extremely active in the American Association of University Professors, serving first as president of the faculty union at Fairleigh Dickinson and then as president of the state conference of the national organization. Much of her energy has gone into contract negotiations.

"I had parents who were very much engaged in social issues," she told me, "and it never occurred to either of them that I wouldn't follow in their steps. The die was cast long before I became a professor."

Along the way Dr. Hubin went to Smith College for 1½ years, married, took various jobs, and eventually enrolled in New York University at night to obtain a bachelor's degree. "I took some very stimulating courses in criminology," she said. "As I grew more and more interested, one side of me kept saying, 'This is ridiculous, you can't be a criminologist if you're a woman.' But the other side replied, 'Why not? I'll study it anyhow.' "

After finishing her studies at N.Y.U. Dr. Hubin took a position with the New York City Welfare Department. As she worked toward advanced degrees, she tried other jobs. "I had an internship in an institution for boys," she recalled. "Then I became director of admissions for Mills College of Education and taught a class here and there on a part-time basis. I kept wanting to go back to the classroom, however, so I embraced an opportunity to conduct research on delinquent problems, along with part-time teaching. Later I was director of research of the Association of Junior Leagues of America. But all the while an urge to get involved in a university kept gnawing at me."

So when N.Y.U. asked her to be the first women on the faculty of its University College in the Bronx she switched there for six years. "I worked my way up to administrative positions and found myself working 18 hours a day. I decided once again that what I really wanted was to be in the classroom and do the research that I loved. Consequently, I came to Fairleigh Dickinson to be an associate professor. Later I became a full professor.

"When you want to be a college professor it's important to enjoy being a student too," added Dr. Hubin, "because you'll always be studying. And for most jobs you'll need a Ph.D.

"The one negative is that awful chore—grading papers," she warned. "Most college teachers worry whether they graded properly. They don't think of marks as punishing or rewarding people. But the rest of college teaching can be the best job in the world. You'll find yourself saying to colleagues, 'Isn't it marvelous the way we get paid for doing what we would do anyhow?'

"It's enormously sentimental of me to say it, I know, but I love the college age group. They have maturity as well as hope, and some of them catch fire. Each generation gives you new perspective by the kind of questions it asks and by the way it deals with your approach. It's a marvelous back-and-forth exchange."

MEMO 56:

> IF YOU'RE QUALIFIED TO IMPROVE YOUR JOB STATUS, SPEAK UP AND LOOK FOR WHAT YOU WANT. QUALIFIED WOMEN HAVE DONE THIS—AND QUALIFIED WOMEN HAVE ACHIEVED!

Carolyn Kohn:
"Special education teachers need a great reserve of knowledge and experience."

It has been said that people who work in the special education field have the deep satisfaction of feeling that they have enriched their lives and the lives of the children whom they help.

That was the feeling I got during an interview with Carolyn Kohn, a SPECIAL EDUCATION SCHOOL DIRECTOR. At the private, non-profit, state-certified day school program for emotionally disturbed children where she works, Ms. Kohn and her certified and assistant teachers take a child from the developmental point reached and attempt to help further social, intellectual, emotional, and physical growth.

"This is our general goal," explained Carolyn Kohn. "Our specific goals differ because each child's program is individualized and tailor-made. For example, if we have a child who is unable to take care of any of his own needs, our immediate, specific goal is to aid him in developing self-help skills. With another child our immediate specific goal may be to help him relate to other people.

"Since our emotionally disturbed children have many learning disabilities, we are interested in helping the total child develop," she went on. "Our multi-faceted approach is humanistic, and every small success calls for great praise."

The children, who range in age from 5 to 16, mostly are referred through other schools. They attend from 10 to 2:30. In addition to an informal, ungraded classroom program that stresses social adjustment, self-care, arts, crafts, games, physical and language development, and health, safety, and arithmetic, there are many field trips and activities to satisfy the children's need for movement. Each class has one male and one female teacher.

"As we work with the children's learning problems we draw from their experiences and interests," Carolyn Kohn explained. "Our lesson plans are broad and our teachers flexible. We must all be able to change directions according to what comes up each day and what special problems must be faced."

Carolyn Kohn arrived at her career after initially training for work in early childhood and elementary education. Upon graduating from Hunter College, her first job was as a kindergarten teacher. But she soon exhibited such a talent and feeling for working with children with problems that school administrators started sending them to her classroom. She began hearing more and more, "You ought to go into special education."

"I left kindergarten teaching for a while to become an airline stewardess and see more of the world," she told me. "But I missed teaching so much that I soon worked my way back into the field as a substitute teacher. Eventually I worked with troubled children in a public school program. Summers I worked in New York in Head Start, both as a teacher and a director."

Her colleagues continued to urge her to go into special education. Then one day her principal confronted her with an application blank for a master's degree program in the field and ordered bluntly, "Fill it out."

After Ms. Kohn received her master's from New York University, she worked in Cincinnati as a teacher therapist at the Children's Psychiatric Center and also held a staff appointment as assistant clinical instructor in the Department of Psychiatry at the University of Cincinnati School of Medicine.

"At the end of a year I returned to the New York area to take a job as assistant to a former colleague who had started a school for disturbed children," she recalled. "After two years there, a co-founder and I began this center several years ago.

"People in the special education field need to be giving individuals with a great reserve of knowledge and experience themselves," she advised. "They require a delicate balance and sense of when to move in and help and when to step back. They need strength and stamina since the job admittedly takes a lot out of you.

"It's also important to point out that persons considering this field need to plan for an outside life that brings them immediate satisfaction because on the job you wait a long time to see progress and success."

MEMO 57:

> REMIND YOURSELF ON A DAILY BASIS THAT ALL OF US HAVE OPPORTUNITIES TO FIND A JOB THAT IS RIGHT WHEN WE TURN IN OUR HOPELESSNESS FOR HOPE AND CHANGE DESPAIR TO DRIVE.

Chapter 6

Publishing and Communications

Helen Bottel:
"I prefer being a NEWSPAPER COLUMNIST to all other forms of writing. It's great fun, allows me to stay home and earn, and gets me involved with all sorts of people."

"Syndicate" is a magic word in the minds of most hopeful writers—so how does a woman achieve a career as a syndicated newspaper columnist?

For another view to complement my own, I talked to columnist Helen Bottel, whose columns, "Helen Help Us" and "Generation Rap" appear in 200 newspapers from coast to coast. Three days a week she writes "Helen Help Us" solo. On Tuesdays, Thursdays, and weekends she's joined by her daughter Sue in a feature aimed at solving the mutual problems confronting young people and their parents.

"The way Sue and I work is a little unusual," said Helen. "I give her a batch of letters and she answers them her way. Then she brings them to me and I answer them my way. Afterwards we discuss them. But we don't change our viewpoints unless we're really convinced."

The rest of Helen's work day is filled with her mail: reading it, answering it when possible, researching questions it raises, getting help for the correspondents, directing them to nearby agencies and counselors, studying new approaches in psychology and human relationships, tearing her hair—besides, of course, writing the column. In addition, she occasionally lectures and writes magazine articles and books.

"In this job deadlines are a problem, as you know," she pointed out. "So is never having a real vacation. You have to work twice as hard before and after so you can take off in between.

"You're never really free either because you're always thinking of what to write and are always looking for good ideas. But that's a plus, I guess, because it keeps you alert and alive.

"As a result of my work, I'm proud of the happy endings in my files and constantly amazed at the vast number of readers who go all out to help people they only know through our letters or columns."

The empathy that readers recognize in Helen's columns undoubtedly stems from her own childhood, which was, to put it mildly, disadvantaged.

"I was an orphan and had no family life, so I feel very strongly about the importance of home ties in the lives of others," she confided. "A high school English teacher took an interest in my writing and encouraged me to develop that skill."

In college Helen majored in journalism and psychology and joined the staff of the campus newspaper—only because young Bob Bottel was editor. When he graduated she succeeded him as editor and later married him. Once out of college she worked for various newspapers and produced four children, her apprenticeship, so to speak, for the syndicated columns she does today.

" 'Helen Help Us' obtained its start seventeen years ago when my husband was reading aloud to me from a syndicated advice column while I was washing the dishes," she said.

"I told him anyone could do better than that, and he replied that *I* couldn't. On account of that challenge I knocked off a little question-and-answer column for the Oregon paper on which I worked as a stringer.

"After it appeared in print four times I mailed it to King Features Syndicate with a letter which began, 'Being a veteran of the P.T.A., four kinds of scouts, and a number of other kid-and-parent-beamed activities, I figure I've got the same kind of *I was there* approach that appeals to those on the same merry-go-round.' "

It was a 10,000 to 1 shot, of course. But it landed Helen at one of the pinnacles of journalism overnight. At the time Sue was four years old. Today she is married and a communications major in California State University at Sacramento.

"Obviously Sue was a cart-before-the-horse in her career since she got the job collaborating on a column with me before she began her communications major," admitted Helen.

"But when she was a teenager, she used to assist me with 'Helen Help Us' teen questions, and her contributions did not go unnoticed by my editors at King. Eventually they suggested she join me in an adult-and-teen view column, so a few years ago we started 'Generation Rap.' "

Helen's advice to others who would like a syndicated columnist's career is: "Try! But back yourself up with a regular job at a newspaper or in publishing, because getting syndicated is rough, especially in depression or recession times. First, make your name in a newspaper, then progress to syndication with the same or a similar column. Today a college degree is pretty necessary. But sometimes, if you're a natural writer, you can get along without it.

"And to my way of thinking one of the best ways to learn the writing craft is to enroll in an inexpensive class."

MEMO 58:
>   VALUE YOUR TIME AND INVEST IT IN YOUR GOALS.

Lucie Kirylak:
"The ability to communicate in more than one language led me to a career as a TECHNICAL PUBLICATIONS EDITOR.*"*

What can you do with a language major if you don't want to be a teacher?

Lucie Kirylak, a bilingual technical editor, writer, and translator in the service publications department of Volkswagen of America, has the answer. "I have a mission to show that people can pursue various careers with a language proficiency," she asserted. "But you must obtain language training in conjunction with a career-oriented subject that will prepare you for a position in journalism, industry, business, or the like.

"My objective was a career in international business, and I've always felt fortunate that my training prepared me so well for a position in industry.

"Now I'm mainly responsible for the English publication of owner's manuals, maintenance records, and emission control brochures for Volkswagen, Porsche, and Audi vehicles. I also write the VW Campmobile brochure and do 20 brochures or manuals twice a year.

"I talk to many people and obtain information on new models each year from Germany. Then I coordinate all that information with our marketing, advertising, product development, safety, emission, and legal departments. Once everything has been clarified for the United States market I write the bilingual text."

Lucie Kirylak's multilanguage skill began in Poland with her childhood home, where German and Polish were spoken.

"In addition I started to learn English at age 10, Latin at 11, and French at 12," she reminisced. "When we left Poland for Germany after going through bad times under Russian occupation, I continued studying languages so that I could enter the University of Mainz to prepare for an international business career. In addition to my majors, I took courses in technical areas and the sciences. I was required to write the thesis for my degree in an area of economics involving a foreign language. I chose English. During my student years I traveled to France and England and studied one semester at the Sorbonne in Paris."

While still at Mainz Lucie Kirylak married and had a son. In 1959 she and her family came to the United States, where she began working in bilingual positions and earned an M.S. in German literature at New York University.

"Before moving into my present position I worked in other spots in this company," she told me, "and I attended service advisors' and mechanics' courses to deepen my knowledge of automative matters.

"There are opportunities in many international companies for people who know a language *plus* a career subject area," Lucie emphasized. "This applies not only to publishing and communications but to other job fields as well.

"For example, there are such opportunities in chemical and pharmaceutical companies, international accounting, banking, buying, finance, engineering, law, marketing, research, and science. In addition, the international airlines need a variety of languages in practically all areas of their operations."

If you're interested in a language career with a communications or business orientation, when it's job-hunting time study the advertisements in the business and finance pages of metropolitan newspapers. Often you'll find somewhere at the end a reference to international operations. Whenever you see "international" you know the job usually involves language skills.

"At the starting level you're far away from the high-echelon jobs," Lucie Kirylak reported. "But one day, if you keep working, you'll find that you are there."

MEMO 59:
> ADVERTISE YOURSELF FOR GETTING AHEAD BY REMEMBERING THAT EVERYTHING YOU DO, SAY, WRITE, AND PRODUCE CONTRIBUTES TO THE IMAGE THAT WILL HELP YOU PROGRESS.

Karin Davison:
"Translating, interpreting, and writing were my entrees to television journalism.

"I began my career in the United States in the translation department of a bank," disclosed German-born Karin Davison, who's now an on-the-go TELEVISION JOURNALIST for a German studio in New York.

"Next, I went to *Time* magazine as a contributing editor. I translated material on cultural events and world politics for the German edition. When I had the first of my two children, I decided to work in free-lance interpreting and translating out of my home."

On one assignment during this period Karin was hired by the German Consul General to accompany and interpret for a delegation from the German Congress in America to study legalized abortion. On another, she worked for delegates from Germany in the United States to learn about urban planning.

"I was also on call for the State Department, Department of Agriculture, Immigration Bureau, and the criminal courts in New York," she added. "And often I would go on study tours in which I might accompany, say, a group of architects from another country to San Francisco for two weeks. I took daily assignments at an embassy or to help a businessman from overseas negotiate an agreement. I ran into a great deal of interesting material—so interesting that one day I decided to try developing some of it into magazine articles. I was off on a journalism career when German's largest magazine bought one of my pieces and asked me to let it know if I ever had anything else."

Karin's magazine writing on a wide range of subjects attracted a journalist from the German Television Network in New York who told her of an opening there. "When I went for an interview I landed the job," she smiled, "so that's how my television career began. I started off as a researcher and now I do the research and the interviews. I also travel extensively and continue with my other writing.

"I'm still getting calls for translating and interpreting too, particularly from the government, and handle them when I can. I see every day that my background and interest in languages has helped me tremendously. I knew by the time I was 14 that I wanted a career in which I could use languages, so I set about preparing myself while I was growing up in Germany. When I was 16 I went to England, where I attended classes at a boarding school in the morning, at a commercial college in the afternoon, and at a university in the evening."

Back in Germany, Karin Davison continued her university education; English, French, and Spanish and American social science were her subjects. She built up a background in the legal and economics fields and in architecture, agriculture, and animal and plant genetics.

"I also studied at the interpreters' college at Göttingen, went to

Spain for two semesters of Spanish, and attended the Alliance Fran-
caise in Paris.

"While at Göttingen I worked at the International Trade Fair. There
I met a group of Americans at whose suggestion I came to America to
translate and interpret. The banking job I mentioned launched me
here.

"To build a good career you need luck—and you need to know
when to move along," acknowledged Karin. "But I believe in giving
yourself a little time to get ready for the upward steps you want to take.
Do it when you're ready but not before.

"I also believe in being interested in everything. Even though it
might be boring in the beginning you eventually find yourself knowing a little bit more than the person next door—and I say that without
any arrogance.

"As for the question of landing a job in post-recession periods, I
think the reason women hold back and say there are no jobs is that
they've always felt they were in Number Two spot anyhow. They've
assumed men were more important in the job market, so when times
are less than perfect they almost expect to stand back and let the man
have the cake. Psychologically that's easy to understand if you've
followed the women's movement through the years.

"But it's a totally wrong approach. And it's setting back the
women's movement after we've come a long way."

MEMO 60:

> TOO MANY WOMEN FEEL SORRY FOR THEMSELVES. THEY'RE
> AFRAID TO FIGHT BECAUSE THEY'VE NEVER LEARNED HOW.
> BUT IN THE JOB WORLD IT'S THE SURVIVAL OF THE FITTEST. SO
> WHY NOT PREPARE TO BE THE FITTEST?

Mary Clark:
"A career in BROADCASTING COMMUNICATIONS
calls for creativity and a constant flow of fresh ideas."

Mary Clark cracked the broadcasting field several years ago when she wrote a series of radio scripts while substituting for a friend. Now she's vice-president and one of two partners in Aerial Communications, Inc., a New York firm that creates and produces radio programs. Mary's job also involves planning, selling, and developing good relations with clients and with the celebrities who star in the packaged shows.

"After we sell a client the concept of using radio to advertise a product, we create a proposed series and then go back to the client with a format, a sample script, a suggested 'star,' and a list of radio stations all over the country on which we would place the show," she explained. "Later we hold auditions.

"Some of the shows we produce are *The Wonderful World of Food* with Betsy Palmer, *Women Today* with Lee Meriwether, *Up To The Minute* with Bess Myerson, *Travel Today* with Frances Kolton, and *Hometalk* with Fred Gwynne.

"Broadcasting communications is *not* easy to get into," Mary advised, "and it demands great discipline because there are always deadlines and commitments.

"One way to start (and, again, it's not easy) is to land a job as a scriptwriter. But if you hope to break in that way you should plan on accumulating some writing credits first. If you're serious about scriptwriting, check *Writer's Market,* published by *Writer's Digest* magazine, for its lists of over 5,000 markets. Among these small, medium, and large markets, there should be something for everyone who wants to show his or her kudos as a writer.

"I had published short stories in *Redbook, McCall's,* and *The Saturday Evening Post* and had several of the stories in anthologies before I entered broadcasting as a scriptwriter.

"My background also includes night school at New York University, while during the day I worked in advertising as an 'assistant to the assistant advertising manager' of a Manhattan firm," Mary said. "Later I was an airline stewardess. After marrying and starting a family, I began the serious business of developing myself as a writer by writing short stories."

Following five children—and five years of rejection slips—Mary sold her first story for $100. Other magazine pieces saw publication. It was then that she substituted writing radio scripts for a friend.

"I was not in a position to tie myself down to a regular job," recalled Mary. "But after I finished the substitute work my friend suggested I let her know if I ever wanted free-lance assignments.

"When my husband suffered the heart attack that eventually caused his death, I knew I had to make some plans for the future, so I said I would like some script writing. The firm in which my friend worked on a show called *Portrait of a Patriot* gave me a job of research and writing that I could do at home. Shortly after I was widowed and started commuting to New York on a full-time job with the firm."

As Mary's script-writing position developed, she began interviewing celebrities and writing the programs in which they were featured and branched out into sales and public relations. A few years later she opened her own broadcasting firm with a partner.

Since establishing her own business the energetic Ms. Clark has enrolled in Fordham University two evenings a week to work toward a bachelor's degree. Moreover, through stints of before-breakfast writing and eight-hour-per-day dedication in her time away from the office, she has become a successful novelist. Her first suspense novel, *Where Are The Children?* was hailed as "the debut of a major mystery writer." Two other novels are in the works.

"Women who get into broadcasting communications can look ahead to excitement and really great challenges," Mary concluded, "because with a future that's full of promise for electronic miracles job opportunities should be good for those who have something to offer. But I can't emphasize enough that people who are interested in the field must prepare first to be good writers. In radio broadcasting the thing to remember is that you're writing for the ear and not the eye. This means the material you produce must be short and to the point."

MEMO 61:

> WHEN YOU SAY, "I'D LOVE TO DO THAT BUT I DON'T HAVE THE TIME," YOU'RE REALLY SAYING, "I'D LOVE TO DO THAT BUT I WON'T MAKE THE TIME." LIFE IS A SERIES OF CHOICES, SO WHEN YOU'D *REALLY* "LOVE TO DO SOMETHING" YOU PUT IT AHEAD OF THINGS YOU CAN BYPASS.

Roberta Smoler:
"When you want to be a COOKBOOK WRITER *the obvious prerequisite is a strong penchant for cooking."*

Now that the buying of cookbooks is almost a national pastime, more and more women think seriously of careers as cookbook writers, especially since the economy has caused people to eat in each others' homes more frequently than in the past.

One person making a career of this with great collections of treats is Roberta Smoler, who writes her best-selling recipes on individual, washable cards that are patterned after an oversized deck of playing cards. Her three collections of 52 recipes each are *French Recipe Cards, Italian Recipe Cards,* and *American Recipe Cards.* She has also written *The Passionate Palate* with co-author Jeanine Larmoth.

"Writing cookbooks wasn't anything I planned or studied for," admitted Roberta, when I visited in her kitchen with its restaurant stove, espresso machine, and adjacent herb garden. But I've been interested in cooking for as long as I can remember.

"When I looked ahead to a career, I went to art school in California and, later, came to New York to work in an advertising agency."

It was while she was in advertising—and cooking for pleasure on the side—that she met Albert Haman, a writer who also loved to cook and who had a cookbook on his mind.

"As Albert and I collaborated on agency accounts we put our heads together on cookbooks and came up with an idea for recipes on cards," she informed me. "Since French cooking has always come naturally to me, we started with that. I designed the cards for our presentation and Albert went out and sold the idea.

"Once we had a contract we worked out recipes and spent about a year testing and re-testing them. When the recipes were ready I made the illustrations. Later I prepared the other recipe cards on my own."

If you're a prospective cookbook writer, Roberta advises that an excellent way to get the feel of it is the method she followed of making up handwritten books of prized recipes for friends.

"You need a strong theme and original recipes for each book," she stressed. "In *The Passionate Palate* Jeanine Larmoth wrote essays to accompany the recipes and establish the theme.

"Admittedly, there are certain basic things that you can't change too much. A cream sauce is a cream sauce. Mayonnaise is mayonnaise. But though the names may be the same in every book, your own touch makes them different.''

In addition to Roberta's suggestions, here are the other main ingredients.

Study the cookbook field and find out what has already been done. Ask yourself if there is a need for the type of cookbook you'd like to start a career with. If so, can you write a steady stream of books in a new way? (One writer with a novel approach has written nearly 50 commercially successful cookbooks.)

If you get over this hurdle—and into cookbook writing—collect and arrange a good presentation of recipes to show an editor. As Roberta emphasized, you'll need an angle to hang them on, because a collection of recipes that has no reason for being will get you exactly nowhere in today's competitive cookbook world.

Make sure your presentation is well organized, neatly typed, and written with skill, personality, sparkle, and charm. Many would-be cookbook writers ruin the opportunity to get the material read simply because their manuscripts are carelessly typed and difficult to decipher.

When you have sold your idea to an editor, test each of your recipes more than once. Be sure no ingredients are left out. Check proportions for accuracy.

When you plan on cookbook writing as a career, combine it with an allied skill. Roberta, for example, is still a free-lance artist in advertising.

MEMO 62:

> THE WILLINGNESS TO ADOPT AN ACCEPTIVE ATTITUDE IS OFTEN AS IMPORTANT IN ACHIEVING SUCCESS AS HARD WORK AND GOOD LUCK.

Teri Martini:
"When you want to write for children realize that, more than likely, it won't be the only thing you do.

"If you wish to make a full-time job as a CHILDREN'S AUTHOR, you certainly can," declared Teri Martini, who combines a career writing children's books with teaching in elementary school.

"Children's books usually don't make as much money as successful adult books. So even though you can earn a reasonably good income from writing them, it's good to have other financial security. Once you establish yourself with a list of titles, you can leave the other job if you wish. However, some established writers prefer to keep it, because it provides contacts with people."

For Teri, writing and teaching has led to impressive publishing credits. Among her books are *Patrick Henry, Patriot, The True Book of Indians, The True Book of Cowboys, The Fisherman's Ring, Treasure of the Mohawk, Sandals on the Golden Highway, What A Frog Can Do, The Mystery of the Hard Luck House,* and *The Lucky Ghost Shirt.*

"When I won an essay contest in school I was hooked on writing," she reminisced, "so with teaching and writing for children as my goal I went to a state college and then Columbia University."

While in college an expanded writing assignment led to the publication of her first book. She then went into elementary teaching combined with writing children's books and magazine stories.

"Some of the church publications can be good beginning spots for children's writing," stated Teri. "Writing workshops and courses led by professional writers can also offer very practical help. A storehouse of knowledge as broad and general as possible is necessary. So is talent for reporting, perseverance, and self-discipline. Learn all the techniques of research. College training and extensive reading are advisable."

If you choose to (or must) combine writing with a job, opportunities to consider besides teaching are editing, preparing educational books and pamphlets, producing television scripts, and providing material for audio-visual presentations. In the future, cartridge TV will also offer expanding opportunities.

"To succeed in children's writing, you should make as many contacts with editors as possible," advised Teri Martini. "Put yourself on a schedule and plan to produce a specific number of books per year and stories per month.

"Many people dream of huge advances and royalties when they read of the sums paid out for best-sellers," she commented. "However, children's books don't bring in that kind of money.

"As a conservative estimate, a good children's book might earn $5,000 to $10,000 over 10 years, unless it's the winner of an award—and most children's books are not award winners. But children's books sell for a long period of time. And often the editors of children's books and stories are much more approachable when you start out than the editors of adult publications."

MEMO 63:

> WHEN YOU'RE HOPING TO ACCOMPLISH A GOAL, YOUR BEST OPPORTUNITY IS NOT IN THE HOURLY SCHEDULE YOU SET UP. INSTEAD IT'S IN THE PACE YOU SET—AND THE WAY YOU STICK TO IT—TO PRODUCE ACTUAL RESULTS WITHIN THAT TIME-TABLE.

Arlene Eisenberg:
"I married my way into becoming a FREE-LANCE MAGAZINE WRITER."

On their honeymoon in Sarasota, Arlene Eisenberg's husband went inside a lion's den to cover an action story while she stood outside with her camera nervously taking pictures.

After the birth of their baby they side-tracked the usual "first baby carriage ride" and made the newcomer's initial outing a jet trip to where they were assignment-bound. Later, when they went to Europe, Arlene typed her way through Holland while her husband drove their car, so they could meet a deadline for a *Reader's Digest* piece.

Since then Howard and Arlene Eisenberg have worked as a writing team producing magazine articles for *Good Housekeeping, McCall's,*

Reader's Digest, Holiday, Woman's Day, and many other publications. Howard is also a magazine editor, and both Eisenbergs have books to their credit.

"We write on nearly every subject," said Arlene, "but a favorite is family articles, since we have three children. Another is travel, as our writing has taken us on assignment in this country and abroad. We also write about medicine—because of Howard's interest—and education—because of our involvement with our children and school.

"When I met Howard," explained Arlene, "he was a press agent for Eddie Fisher, and I was Fisher's secretary.

"After we married and left Fisher I found out very quickly what it's like to be married to a free-lance writer. So I soon got into the act with picture taking, typing, research, and, eventually, interviewing and writing. Through the years we've both agreed that two writers in the house can be better than one."

In a free-lance magazine writer's career, you write articles full- or part-time for men's, women's, and general interest magazines; trade and business papers; house organs; specialized publications, such as juvenile, religious, and travel magazines; and other diversified outlets.

You'll often find it's to your advantage—financially and in other ways—to combine magazine writing with another job—editing, teaching, advertising, public relations, television, radio, or film work.

In order to consider this demanding career you need a great desire to write, much persistence and self-discipline, physical stamina, an awareness of the meaning of every experience, a penchant for getting people to talk, an enthusiasm for reporting accurately and turning out good work quickly, a tough attitude toward rebuffs and disappointments, skill in researching, a willingness to work long hours, and a certain amount of talent.

"It's good to be something of a generalist at the same time that you have a specialty," reported Arlene. "If you're a specialist in science, for example, editors often come to you when they want a piece in that field.

"You have to know how to juggle budgets and live without a dependable, regular income," she added. "It's often a feast-orfamine existence. For example, when Howard and I hit New Orleans on our honeymoon we had just $2 between us, but, luckily, a $400 check from our agent at the post office averted the crisis.''

The training for a magazine writing career comes from a good education—and a nonstop reading program. Some magazine writers have not gone to college; others have a degree. Attending college provides a broader background—you might major in English literature, journalism, or communications. Simultaneously gain some knowledge in a subject you can make a specialty. Typing is a must. Shorthand can be an asset, even when you tape interviews.

Once you embark on a free-lance career, you work at the hardest job in the world. But you'll also be saying what you want to and getting your message across.

"If you have a crusading bone in your body," Arlene concluded, "you can work and write for a cause that might help change the world."

MEMO 64:

>IN THE LONG RUN, DOING SOMETHING INTERESTING COMES FROM STARTING WHERE YOU ARE TODAY AND BECOMING WHAT YOU WANT TO BE BY A SERIES OF LITTLE STEPS AND ACTS.

Susan Howatch:
"Developing a career as a NOVELIST *takes time.*

"You only learn to write by writing, so the longer you keep at it the more you increase your chances for a writing career—*if* you do it right," said Susan Howatch, one of today's major novelists and author of *Cashelmara* and *Penmarric*.

As we talked in Ms. Howatch's studio on the 26th floor of a

building facing the Hudson River, I took in the breathtaking panorama.

"I've worked at writing for a long time," she noted. "At age six I made a short story collection. At 12 I began writing seriously and steadily."

At 17—while still in her native England—Susan Howatch began submitting her work to publishers and collecting a big batch of rejection slips for her efforts. At 24—and in America—her first book, a mystery novel, was accepted. "Even though I was quite young," she reminisced, "it took me all that time, so I felt that I was also old in terms of rejections and experience in writing."

Before coming to America Ms. Howatch went to King's College, London University, where she won a degree in law. This, according to her family, would prepare her to earn a living, since they felt there was no money in writing. "I worked in a law office for a year," she told me, "but I soon found that it did not combine well with the writing I was determined to do. It was too much of a career in itself and the writing had to come first."

So Ms. Howatch took a shorthand and typing course and used those skills for her bread and butter while her main effort went into writing. Still unpublished in England, she boarded a plane for New York.

"English secretaries were very much in vogue when I arrived," she said, "so I used my secretarial skills for over two years until I settled down to write full-time. My first novel was published after I saw the name of a publisher who was interested in mysteries in a writers' magazine. I'd been in America for about 10 months and I sent it in cold."

After that breakthrough Susan Howatch wrote a mystery a year for the next five years. She also began working on her labor of love, *Penmarric,* married, and had a daughter.

"*Penmarric* took me five years—along with other things—and *Cashelmara* three years," she recalled. "Now I'm working on my next book. I write about four or five drafts before a book is finished, and after each draft I like to take a break and do something different. Writing a long romantic saga set in a different period is tiring, so you get stale if you stick at it intensely for too long without a break. I also do a great deal of research for my background and period material.''

Ms. Howatch finds—like many other writers with children—that schedules change as children grow and the children's schedules change. But this kind of flexibility is also a great career plus.

"I'm a morning person, and I used to get to my studio very early," she pointed out. "But now I come here about 9 o'clock and work through to 3 or 4. I may have breakfast at home before I leave or here. Fortified by breakfast, I sit down, overlooking the river. I write the first two drafts of my books in long-hand, because I can't bear to look at a blank page in the typewriter without anything to guide me. I find that when you write in long-hand, you think about every word you put down. This makes me more economical with words.

"All people who want a career as a novelist have to find their own way to use the tools and techniques," she concluded, "and as I said earlier, that only comes by writing and keeping at it. You get better as you go along and you also find out what you do the best. But you have to be able to set your mind to it and realize how much time it will take and what a commitment you must make.

"If you really want to be a novelist and are willing to learn how, the best advice in the world is, simply: 'Never give up.' ''

MEMO 65:

> CREATE AND MAINTAIN A PICTURE OF YOURSELF AS A PERSON WHO CAN SUCCEED. THIS WILL DO YOU NO HARM—AND IT MAY DO A GREAT DEAL OF GOOD.

Elise Gould:
"If you always have your nose in a book, a job as a TRADE BOOK EDITOR *may be the right one for you.*

"When you're a book editor you can work on fiction or non-fiction, children's books, paperbacks, or technical, educational, scholarly, or reference publications," said Elise Gould, a project editor in social studies for a large publishing firm.

"You read, evaluate, and select manuscripts," she continued; "work with authors and artists; suggest revisions; rewrite and reorganize material; edit, copy edit, and proofread for spelling, punctuation, clarity, accuracy, and consistency; and help decide design, format, and typography.

"In some jobs you originate ideas and search for writers to produce the books. In others you attend writers' conferences, conventions, and workshops to look for talent. In still others, you specialize in one kind of book."

Elise Gould is project editor of 18 titles in a series called "Inquiry Into Crucial American Problems." Three of the books, which are directed to 12th-grade readers, are *Peace or War: Can Humanity Make The Choice? Values, Rights, and the New Morality: Do They Conflict?* and *Prejudice and Discrimination: Can We Eliminate Them?*

She herself is author of one book in the series, *American Woman Today: Free or Frustrated?* Her most recent project is *Inquiry Into World Cultures,* which includes books on China, India, Kenya, and Brazil.

"My love of writing and reading makes publishing a natural for me," Elise pointed out. "Because of my interest in education I enjoy working with the professors and teachers who are the authors of many of the books."

Ms. Gould, a political science major from Columbia University, got her job by scoring well in a personal interview and a test for editorial work. As a starter, she was hired as a production trainee in the educational book division. From there she worked up to her present job.

Her advice to prospective editors is to read widely. A college degree is a requirement. While the major is often English, a master's degree in any subject area can be helpful, especially in technical and educational publishing. Other prime qualifications are good concentration, ability to read rapidly, sound critical judgment, tact in offering criticism and suggestions, accuracy and dedication to details, a talent for organizing ideas, and well-developed language skills. It is helpful to enjoy the social aspects of the job since friendly relations with authors establish the rapport necessary to create a product mutually satisfactory to writer and publisher.

Beyond this, you must understand the commercial end of the book business and be able to see a manuscript from the viewpoint of its appeal to a potential audience. A knowledge of printing and illustrating techniques will be beneficial.

You usually begin as an editorial trainee or assistant in a publishing house. Another possible course is a spot as a job trainee in sales, public relations, or production. Occasionally you can start as a secretary, but Elise Gould would de-emphasize typing and secretarial skills as a means of entree.

"Women in clerical jobs have little opportunity to demonstrate editorial ability," she said, "and in my experience they are usually kept doing what their superiors recognize they do well. A woman would be better advised to get more education, or (in the case of educational publishing) to teach for a few years. Most companies use editorial tests and start people as trainees.

"One thing is very certain, though," she warned. "You won't begin in a private office with a door that says 'Senior Editor.' In your first job you may log manuscripts in and out, do the preliminary weeding out of unpromising manuscripts, and send the promising ones on to a higher editor with a written report. As you progress, you may do research and start writing copy for teachers' manuals and exercises."

MEMO 66:

REFUSE TO SPEND THE REST OF YOUR LIFE IN THE KIND OF COMPROMISE JOB IN WHICH YOU DO LESS THAN YOUR BEST AND IN WHICH YOU FAIL TO USE ALL OF YOUR TALENTS.

Glory Read:
"PUBLIC RELATIONS COUNSELING *is a good career for imaginative individuals who want to mold opinion and*

> *point out the most beneficial side of a company, product, service, or institution."*

As a gentle persuader in public relations, you promote your client through such media as news releases, publications, booklets, brochures, radio, television, speeches, films, displays, posters, and signs.

"But," explained Glory Read, president of Public Relations Counsel, Inc. in New York, "exactly what you do in your job will depend on whether you work for a large or small agency, in the public relations office of a large corporation, in government, in an educational institution, a research group, or a philanthropic or cultural campaign.

"In a large agency or corporation you may specialize in one thing, for example, writing releases, booklets, or speeches. In a small agency, like mine, you may do all the jobs connected with public relations. My account executives take charge from start to finish," Glory pointed out. "They write, work with clients, contact editors, present ideas, create programs, plan press parties, et cetera.

"Generally speaking, a job in an agency is more highly pressurized and hectic than one in the public relations department of a corporation."

Glory Read cut her teeth in communications on a newspaper in North Carolina. Later, she switched to a job with the News Bureau and Public Relations Office at Duke University, her alma mater.

"When my family and I moved to New Jersey I wanted New York experience," she continued, "so I took a copywriting job and followed that with work as a technical editor.

"Through answering an advertisement in a New Jersey paper for a copywriter, I met a man who was starting a public relations firm. I took a job working with him."

When the firm moved across the Hudson River, Glory Read went with it. As the business expanded, she became vice-president. For the new account of Johnson and Johnson, Glory originated the "Baby Yourself" campaign aimed to push adult use of baby products. Even though the birthrate was declining, sales increased. When the president of the firm died, Glory assumed the top job.

"One of the most important prerequisites of a public relations career is a liking and understanding of all types of people," she contended. "You *have* to be a friendly person."

Also necessary are writing and speaking ability, a respect for facts and details, judgment, intelligence, objectivity, curiosity, imagination, integrity, and sensitivity.

"To do a good job you *must* be sensitive," Glory Read maintained. "On the other hand, you have to develop an awfully hard hide, since the work has frustrating, discouraging moments.

"You need a creative nature. But at the same time you must have a very practical streak too. The stability of the business is not great. You must always keep that in mind.

"I think some newspaper background is important," she advised. "Some people write and report for a paper full-time before switching to the public relations field.

"There are good salaries to be earned in public relations," she concluded. "But women seeking their first job should be more interested in opportunities than in salaries. They should look for jobs with learning potential and prove how great they are.

"Whether the economy is good or bad you'll always have competition from others who want the same job. But, generally, the person who's prepared best is most likely to be hired."

MEMO 67:

> TO GET ANYWHERE IN ANY JOB YOU NEED TO BE ORGANIZED, STAY CALM, BE THOROUGH, THINK FAST, AND BE PRECISE. YOU ALSO MUST TAKE PRIDE IN YOUR WORK, BE WILLING TO DO A LITTLE EXTRA, AND GAIN SOME KNOWLEDGE FROM EVERY WORKING EXPERIENCE.

Marian Burden:
"Another aspect of public relations is DEPARTMENT STORE PROMOTION.

"I feel that no one could have a more exciting, fascinating, educational, and interesting public relations job than mine," confided Marian Burden, Director of Public Relations at one of Bloomingdale's branch stores. "And I say that because I work with people—and my love has always been for people."

Ms. Burden is responsible for planning and organizing al! of the spring and fall special events held in the store's Provence Restaurant. Some of the many celebrities she has booked for programs are Lawrence Welk, Evan Hunter, Lillian Gish, Polly Bergen, Arthur Fiedler, Pearl Bailey, and Julia Child.

"I have to work as long as one, two, or three years to land some of them," she admitted, "but in public relations you must have perseverance. I was told we'd never get Julia Child, but we did—twice! Moreover, we received a beautiful letter from her following an appearance."

Other aspects of Marian Burden's job—in addition to the daily nitty-gritty—are behind-the-scene tours of the store for students and others; seminars for eighth-grade girls on grooming, speech, social graces, poise, and wardrobe planning; the annual outdoor clothesline art shows; and the painting exhibition in the store's furniture wing.

Marian came to her job after many years of volunteer work that involved doing—philanthropically—what she now does professionally. "My training for public relations began when I married at 20 and moved from Washington, D.C. to Omaha, Nebraska," she told me. "My husband was in this field, and because I wanted to understand his work I began taking courses in it at the same time we started our family. Simultaneously, I did community work—always in programming and publicity."

When the Burdens moved East Marian continued the same sort of civic work. Such major successes as an innovative church fair eventually led to the job at Bloomingdale's.

"If your're interested in public relations a constant flow of education is extremely important," she observed. "Anything you learn will be to your advantage. Be willing to settle for something less than a great job as a starter. It takes a while to get your feet wet, so regard your first years as an apprenticeship and be willing to pay your dues.

"Working as an assistant is fine. So is starting at another job—and making your way into public relations. Get the feel of PR and learn all its intricate details. Seize every opportunity for volunteer work. Whatever you do is bound to teach you something.''

MEMO 68:

> WHEN YOU UNDERTAKE A VOLUNTEER JOB, MAKE IT A SERIOUS COMMITMENT. SOMETIMES YOU CAN SCARCELY BELIEVE HOW FAR A SMALL START CAN BRING YOU.

Amelia Lobsenz:
"To learn PUBLIC RELATIONS WRITING *I took home and analyzed 50 releases on 50 different accounts when I got my job. The next day I knew how to write a release."*

As other dialogues have stressed, good writing techniques are essential for success in public relations. "They can help you get your foot in the door," declared Amelia Lobsenz, chairman and chief executive officer of Lobsenz-Stevens, Inc., a New York agency that has handled the public relations for such diverse accounts as Western Temporary Services, the Rockefeller Brothers Fund, Travelers Insurance Companies, and Trans-Lux.

"I launched my public relations career by learning how to write releases," said Amelia, as we talked in her Manhattan office. "Previously, I'd been a free-lance magazine writer, often specializing in stories about business and successful business people.

"I began to realize that if they could do it, I could too, so I started picking up pointers and using what I call the 'sponge' technique to absorb all kinds of information. When I felt I'd mastered the challenge of magazine writing and wanted to go on to something else, a friend suggested public relations and gave me a list of agencies where I could use him as a reference. A phone call on a Friday yielded an interview and on Monday I went to work for the firm.

"It was a challenge," she admitted, "so that's when I took home the 50 releases and analyzed them, as I'd never written a release in my life. The next night I took home the same number of radio fillers—and so on, straight through what you might call a self-taught public relations course.

"I worked until midnight or 1 o'clock every night for the first six months and read every book on public relations I could lay my hands on. But after that I knew the techniques and could use them effectively. Soon I was able to help in every aspect of the agency's activity, and while I worked I gained the solid background I needed for opening a business of my own. Actually, I didn't plan to set up my own firm, but it happened, and I loved it.

"I began in the mid-Fifties and started in my own apartment. First one prospective client and then another asked me to handle an account as an individual PR practitioner. I named my business Lobsenz Public Relations Company and bridged the gap between initial income and expenses by acting as a consultant to the firm where I was formerly employed and writing magazine articles at night. I took no clients from my former employer—a practice I deplore."

As more clients began to approach her, Amelia was able to move out of her apartment to her first modest office space on Fifth Avenue. There were three other moves within the same building, always to larger quarters. In 1975 her firm merged with Stevens Public Relations Company to become Lobsenz-Stevens, Inc. Soon after the agency moved to the new Pan Ocean Building on Madison Avenue, and Amelia became chairman of the board and chief executive officer.

"Public relations," she concluded, "combines the creativity of writing with the opportunity to work in depth with varied lists of clients. Mastering good techniques for writing will always be vital to people who want to enter this field."

To this we say "Amen." Here are Ms. Lobsenz's pointers for becoming a public relations writer.

Learn your subject well. Research and even over-research; you must become an authority in order to properly "sell" your concepts. The deeper your knowledge the more varied your angles can be for shaping and re-shaping the same basic material for different newspapers, magazines, and wire services.

Slant your writing to the desired audience. Don't write "down" to any reader, but do make sure that you are targeting your messages correctly. For example, the person who is accustomed to preparing food on a strict budget won't be impressed by recipes that require expensive ingredients. The young mother is apt to be more concerned with tips on childrearing than with a new approach to chess or a story on foreign cars.

Get across your desired credits or "plugs" early in the copy. Editors often cut from the bottom of a story up. Develop ways of weaving in your public relations mentions subtly. Don't let credits look like credits—let them appear to be a natural part of your story.

Put yourself in the editor's and the reader's place. Remember always that editors want material that helps sell their publications by appealing to readers. Your material should be inspirational, informative, or amusing.

Become familiar with each publication you want to reach. Admittedly, this takes time, but back issues of most magazines are available at public libraries. Consult *Readers' Guide to Periodical Literature* for the last five years on the subject you want to promote. Then, when you contact an editor, you know exactly what he or she has used on your topic.

MEMO 69:

> EACH YEAR BREAK YOUR PREVIOUS JOB RECORD BY RAISING AND REACHING NEW GOALS.

Janet Anderson:
"Being a BOOK DESIGNER can afford a satisfying life."

For Janet Anderson the decision to go to art school was a last-minute choice. "While growing up in Pennsylvania I was interested in art," she revealed, "but I was really programmed for music, which I studied all through high school. When it was time to choose a career, however, I was suddenly convinced that I didn't want to earn my living in music. I decided to go into art and study music on the side, something I still continue."

Janet spends her working days translating the manuscripts of books into ultimate visual packages that—hopefully—will attract purchasers. "I'm involved with all the graphic steps that turn a manuscript into a book," explained Janet. "And each trade book is a different job, because the subjects are varied and the markets diversified."

In general, the designer selects type faces, lays out title pages, determines the placement of pictures or art, designs the chapter opening pages, color-coordinates the endpapers, chooses materials and colors for hard-cover books, and creates jackets. Book designers are also responsible for selecting paper, page sizes, and bindings.

"A lot of our work is pretty well defined by a budget and schedule," Janet pointed out. "Often it is frustrating to have to settle for compromises because of hard, cold business considerations. But still there is joy in the doing and a challenge in communicating graphically with readers.

"Usually you work on 40 to 50 books a season," Janet went on. "It's always fun to be in on the bestsellers. I particularly enjoyed working on the two-volume biography *Jenny* and on *Up the Down Staircase*. I also love to design cookbooks."

Pratt Institute introduced Janet to book illustration and type and graphic art. "This matched my personal inclinations," she said, "and upon graduation I got my first job as a jacket designer with a major publisher through Pratt. I've been with the same firm ever since."

If book design is work that appeals to you, you need training in a good art school or a college art degree. The major job opportunities will be with publishers and book packagers (firms that produce books and submit them as packages to publishers). You can work as a staff artist or free-lance. Some designers take staff jobs for bread-and-butter expenses and free-lance nights and weekends for extras.

"Realistically, the field is competitive," Janet Anderson conceded. "But there's something lasting about a book and being part of it. And when it means something to readers it makes you feel good, too."

MEMO 70:

EXAMINE THE WAY THE LEADERS IN YOUR FIELD SUCCEED. THEN BASE YOUR OWN BLUEPRINT ON THEIRS.

Chapter 7

Health Care and Social Services

Dr. Priscilla Bollard:
"There are many wonderful moments in an AUDIOLOGY *career.*

"At the Rockland County Center for the Physically Handicapped where I work we determine and evaluate hearing disorders and problems from babies through people in their 90's," declared Dr. Priscilla Bollard, a certified audiologist. "For those diagnosed as hard-of-hearing we develop speech and language skills by coordinating therapy and corrective measures. When sound suddenly means something to a person with a hearing difficulty, it's unbelievably exciting to witness.

"As an audiologist, I perform diagnostic and therapeutic work," she explained. "I make molds of ear impressions, teach lip reading, evaluate hearing aids, and test a variety of devices on patients so that the most effective one can be prescribed.

"Another of my responsibilities is to work with the teacher who goes into homes to help parents get started in the treatment of deaf babies. After the initial training the babies are brought into the center for daily therapy. Naturally, there are many meetings and conferences with the center's personnel and with outside consultants, besides reports to be written."

Together these activities add up to the kind of job Priscilla Bollard

153

wanted when she was ready for a second career after becoming a widow.

"I was brought up in England and France," she said. "After obtaining a B.A. in literature and drama from London University I had a first career in the London theater.

"Following my marriage I gave up the theater and came to the United States. I obtained a B.S. in general education at Columbia University and subsequently taught voice. When my husband died I wanted to prepare for a broader career, so I evaluated the potentials and eventually decided I'd like to work with people and combine several areas of interest—specifically medicine, teaching, drama, and language. It seemed that audiology would be a good way to use them all."

Dr. Bollard returned to school to obtain a M.S. in speech pathology and a doctorate in audiology from Teachers College at Columbia. She performed her internship and residency at a hospital in Queens and worked elsewhere before joining the Rockland County Center.

"For a career in audiology you need four years of undergraduate work," she stated. "And for certification by the American Speech and Hearing Association, you must have an M.A. or the equivalent plus 300 hours of supervised clinical practice and nine months of paid experience.

"My undergraduate work happened to be in liberal arts. But some people do undergraduate work in speech and then take an M.A. in audiology. Some background in speech and language is very important, because a large portion of hearing evaluation is speech testing and knowing how much or how little people understand."

Audiologists may be employed by speech and hearing clinics, hospitals, rehabilitation centers, universities, physicians' offices, industry, manufacturers of and dealers in hearing aids, schools for the deaf, and other special schools. Priscilla Bollard looks forward to the time when audiologists will be on the staffs of public schools.

"Many of the places of employment are rather far apart from each other. "Even though the need for audiologists is great," she pointed out, "this often necessitates commuting to a job or relocating, which is important for women to know. Part of the reason is that the logistics of setting up an audiology clinic are complicated. The equipment, for instance, is expensive and has to be replaced periodically because of new developments.

"At the moment jobs are generally more available in smaller towns and rural areas, because people are seeking employment in cities and in university hospitals," she continued. "However, the salaries are frequently better in less populated areas. But the field is changing rapidly—with more jobs developing in industry because of noise pollution and laws governing noise levels and in the hearing aid industry.

"So with that prognosis," she concluded, "I feel that audiology will open up in many different directions."

MEMO 71:
> EXTEND YOURSELF TO PEOPLE WITH FRIENDLINESS, WARMTH, UNDERSTANDING, PATIENCE, ENCOURAGEMENT, AND GOOD WILL.

Hazel Miller:
"It feels good to know you're helping someone. But when DRUG REHABILITATION *is on your mind you must realize that it's a complicated field.*

"There's something very appealing about working with adolescents," reported Hazel Miller, superintendent of a therapeutic residential facility for juvenile drug users, "but it's important to know that adolescents and drugs add up to a complex situation.

"At Harold House where I work we're involved with the intervention and prevention of drug use among the young and the rehabilitation of youths who need in-patient care," she explained. "We also admit socially maladjusted young people who might be predisposed to drug use. Our residents come to us voluntarily or through referrals from the courts, parents, schools, churches, and mental health centers.

"Our staff includes a physician; a psychiatrist; psychologists; counselors; a social worker; nurses; teachers; supervisors of arts and crafts, education, and activities; a chef; and paraprofessionals. The residents help with much of the work and, through a point system, earn their privileges. The program is basically of the behavior-modification type.

"I came into adolescent drug rehabilitation via a career as a nurse," revealed Hazel Miller. "I always worked with youngsters in one capacity or another—at a training school, for a pediatrician, as a public school nurse, and with a drum corps during the summer. As a school nurse I became very concerned about the growing drug problem among younsters, so when the county in which I live and work opened the Monsignor Wall Social Service Center I assumed the job of supervisor of nurses on a voluntary basis on weekends but remained a school nurse during the day. Eventually, I gave up school nursing to work on a salary at the center full time as supervisor of nurses and assistant director. This involved me in the initial planning for Harold House, which opened in 1971. The next year I became superintendent.

"In drug rehabilitation I can't stress enough that just having good intentions and wanting to help isn't enough. You're lost and ineffective unless you can bring adaptability and objectivity to your work. I might add that it is sometimes a hindrance to be in the early 20's, because it is easier to identify with the youth than to remain objective.

"Consequently, I'd advise young women considering rehabilitation to obtain your intial work experience with younger children and to give themselves time to live and grow before they start working with adolescents.

"I emphatically advise *everyone* who wants to work with adolescents to get some prior experience with this age group in a voluntary job to make absolutely sure that they'll be able to cope eight hours every day—and, maybe, be on call for 24 hours. If they can cope, the opportunities are there, because there will always be adolescents!"

MEMO 72:
> MAINTAIN A COMPASSIONATE HEART THAT IS SENSITIVE TO OTHERS' UPS AND DOWNS.

Marilyn Adair:
"As far as I am concerned there is no other area of nursing that offers greater personal rewards than PUBLIC HEALTH NURSING.

"A public health nurse is many things to many different people," said Marilyn Adair, supervisor of a hospital's community nursing service.

"To clarify terms, let me say, first, that a visiting nurse or community nurse is in public health nursing," she explained, "and public health nurses may be employed by an *official* agency, such as a state or county health department, or by a *voluntary* agency, such as a hospital or visiting nurse service.

"Generally, the *official* agency does not offer bedside care, though a qualified home-health agency may be under the same roof.

"The nurses of the voluntary home-health agency participate in bedside care. The agency may also run child-health conferences in municipalities and by contract provide school nursing, staff senior health clinics, or perform municipal nursing. A voluntary agency does not follow up on venereal disease, tuberculosis, or other communicable diseases unless by contract with a municipality.

"The nurse's role in a home-health agency is more challenging because she works with her hands as well as her mind," continued Marilyn, "but regardless of where you work a job as a public health nurse is highly diversified.

"When a community nurse service is offered directly by a hospital," Marilyn added, "a coordinator meets with the family prior to the patient's release to discuss the physical layout of the home, which members of the family can offer supplemental care, what arrangements need to be made for any special equipment, and similar matters.

"Our office divides the staff into five teams, and each day the team leader helps to arrange the case load so that each nurse consistently sees the same patients as much as possible," she said. "The supervisor assists team leaders in arranging case loads so all areas are covered.

"Usually the team leader is the first nurse to visit a home. She explains the nursing service to the patient and family and assesses them physically and emotionally. In accordance with their capacity to learn, she sets up a plan of care that her team member will follow. Adjustments are made as needed.''

According to Ms. Adair, the team member stresses proper care and comfort, for example, the importance of frequent repositioning of bed patients and of keeping skin dry and clean to help prevent bed sores. She checks the changing of dressings, supervises diet and liquid intake, and offers patients the hope and reassurance that they will be stronger in time. She checks the labeling of drugs and reviews medications with patients, so they'll know what they're taking and what results or possible untoward reactions to look for.

As the agency supervisor, Marilyn's job naturally goes above the beyond this. "I deal with special situations, as well as a lot of standard ones," she said. "For instance, I will visit a hostile, complaining family to get to the bottom of things. Or I'll travel with a staff nurse if she's not sure of a procedure or if I need to observe her function. On the other hand, I may visit instead of the staff nurse if she is facing a time problem or a question about the appropriateness of home care. Plus this, I'm involved in evaluating the staff nurses for needs in in-service training, performance, and readiness for promotion or increments. And I may represent the agency at community or other meetings. There are always the days, when after getting the work arranged, I go out and function as a staff nurse or team leader because we lack adequate staff to see everyone who needs us. In some situations I carry a few cases consistently on my own."

By many professional standards, the only nurse really trained for public health nursing is a college graduate with an R.N. and B.S. that add up to four-plus years of training—as opposed to a licensed practical nurse (L.P.N.) with as little as one year of training or as much as two, or an R.N. with an associate degree gained in a two-year course at a junior college.

Though diploma school graduates (R.N.'s with three years training in a diploma-hospital training school) may work in public health agencies, they have had, at most, observational experience. The college graduate has the edge because her program includes both classroom courses and practical experience in public health.

"I studied for my work at Skidmore College," Marilyn informed me, "and I lived and worked in New York while obtaining clinical training and experience. During that time I decided that public health nursing was the right job for me."

After graduating from college Marilyn worked as a visiting nurse in New York's Spanish Harlem. Later she moved from New York, took time out to have a family, and then returned to nursing as a team leader in a community nursing service.

"Once you have a nursing background you always have something to go on," she pointed out. "It's a profession where the door is open."

Though Marilyn is happy with her job choice she points out that the work can have its frustrating moments if, after trying several approaches, a nurse still can't master a situation.

"At these times, the nurse comes back to her team, discusses the situation, and tries other team members' suggestions," she advised. "If necessary, another nurse will go to assess the problem and, perhaps, take over if we feel there's a personality problem.

"One of the major difficulties in the visiting nurse field is the weather. In summer you may go from a very hot house to one that's air-conditioned. In winter you have snow storms and driving hazards.

"At times it's difficult to explain various matters: what medical bills are all about and why Medicare will not cover all the treatment the patient feels he needs; why a health aide can't be kept in a home indefinitely at the expense of health insurance and that she is an assistant in patient care and not a housecleaner; and why patients and families must learn to do for themselves eventually without the visiting nurse.

"But despite these drawbacks, public health nursing is terrifically rewarding work," concluded Marilyn. "You are many things to many people, and the thought that you've helped a patient and family through an often-discouraging at-home recovery can be a bright spot in your working day."

MEMO 73:

> IF YOU STOP TO CONSIDER ALL THE OBSTACLES IN THE WORK YOU WOULD LIKE TO DO, YOU WILL NEVER ACCOMPLISH ANYTHING.

Joan Schreiber:
"The primary intention in OCCUPATIONAL HEALTH NURSING *is to keep healthy people well.*

"Occupational health nursing gives you a chance to get to know people better and to see them more regularly than any other type of nursing," commented Joan Schreiber, who is employed by a large manufacturing firm. Joan treats headaches, colds, and minor ailments and injuries; provides emergency care; promotes industrial safety and accident prevention; shows educational films (on such subjects as Pap tests and breast cancer); counsels on sound health education and practices; administers pre-employment health examinations, annual eye check-ups, and special tests; prepares and maintains records; and processes all health insurance forms and claims.

"In brief, I'm responsible for the health program for 500 employees," she told me, "though, naturally, we always have a doctor on call. In the time I have left over, I conduct exercise classes two days a week after work."

Occupational health nurses were once thought of as a company's "Band-Aid pushers." But this no longer exhausts their responsibilities in pharmaceutical houses, banks, factories, oil fields, department stores, construction projects, mines, laboratories, offices, and any number of other places where employees and patrons sometimes need nurses. Even when the economy is bad their profession is alive and well.

Joan Schreiber, who lives in Pearl River, New York, received her training in Brooklyn. Following her graduation, she was a hospital nurse for a while before switching to a job as an office nurse for a private physician. Later she worked at a hospital.

"Each job gave me a different type of background," she pointed out. "This is a plus because most employers prefer occupational health nurses to have had some previous nursing experience. I switched to occupational health nursing, because, as a widow with a child, I felt the regular hours industrial nursing offers would fill my own personal needs best."

If you want to be an occupational health nurse, plan on being trained in an accredited or state-approved school of professional nursing, on acquiring the variety of experience Joan Schreiber recommends, and on taking courses to enrich your background. It is also very helpful to participate actively in professional organizations.

The personal qualifications you'll need are those of any nurse: physical capability; emotional stability; initiative; diplomacy; tact; judgment; resourcefulness; a willingness to accept responsibility and work independently; an eagerness to learn; intelligence; sensitivity; kindness; adaptability; patience; and, above all, an interest in people.

MEMO 74:

NEVER BE AFRAID TO CHANGE FROM ONE JOB TO ANOTHER WHEN YOU FEEL IT IS TIME TO MOVE ON.

Elaine Reinitz:
"To me, RECOVERY ROOM NURSING *is real nursing."*

The recovery room is a good place to be in following surgery if you're being watched over by a dedicated nurse who's as comforting as Elaine Reinitz.

"The purpose of the recovery room," said Elaine, who is the head nurse in one, "is to have people of all ages in a place where they can get the best possible care in the interim between surgery and return to their rooms.

"There are four nurses in the recovery room where I work," she explained. "After surgery the patient is brought in by his anesthesiologist, under whose care he remains. It's our job to monitor patients, watch their breathing and pulse, check the dressings and tubes, give medication as needed and directed, and be with them so they are not alone when they come out of anesthetic. Usually we take care of 23 to 25 patients a day.

"We do our best to talk to them and reassure them when they

awaken after surgery. Since we're beside people right after one of the most difficult periods of their lives, it's obvious that recovery room nursing requires a great deal of sensitivity.

"At career-choosing time I never thought of anything but nursing," Elaine Reinitz told me. "In fact, I wanted to be a nurse by the time I was nine years old."

After growing up in the Midwest, Elaine trained for a nursing career in Indiana. Following her graduation during World War II she became an Army nurse. While in service she met her husband. After the war the couple settled in Brooklyn, and Elaine worked until she had her family.

"Eventually we moved to the suburbs," she informed me, "and I kept busy with school activities while the children were growing up.

"I enjoyed that period of my life. But, looking back, I now feel that if I had been near the school where I trained and had been able to attend alumnae meetings where I would have heard, 'Why don't you come back to work?' I might have considered returning to nursing sooner."

As it was, Ms. Reintiz decided to resume her nursing career when her younger son went into the Air Force and was sent to Vietnam. "I saw a newspaper notice about a refresher course for nurses at Holy Name Hospital," she said. "I wanted to investigate. But, frankly, it took me a while to nerve myself to pick up the phone and call." Fortunately Elaine made the call and discovered recovery room nursing when she enrolled in the course.

"I'd never been in a recovery room before," she admitted, "and it appealed to me immediately. I began working in the recovery room as soon as my course was over. This is my eighth year there and my fourth as head nurse."

In addition to the basic nurse's course, you need special on-the-job training for recovery room work, for example, in electrocardiogram interpretation, cardio-resuscitation, and respiratory and intravenous therapy.

"You're committed to both mental and physical work," pointed out Elaine Reinitz. "You're on your feet practically every minute of the day, and you must be constantly alert to each person's condition. There's no sitting down and relaxing while you're on the job.

"You must also feel that each person is important to you and someone about whom you care!"

MEMO 75:

> IN EVERYONE'S LIFE DOORS OPEN WHEN LEAST EXPECTED. BUT WHEN YOU'RE AFRAID TO OPEN THEM WIDE AND LOOK ON THE OTHER SIDE, YOU DON'T GIVE YOURSELF A FIGHTING CHANCE TO MAKE SOMETHING OF YOUR LIFE. INSTEAD YOU LOCK YOURSELF IN A BOX AND THROW AWAY THE KEY.

Margaret Corcoran:
"One of the most important qualifications for a CERTIFIED MEDICAL ASSISTANT *is the ability to exercise good judgment in emergencies and appear cool on the outside, even when turning upside down inside.*

"As the delivery of health care progresses, more and more allied help is needed," pointed out Margaret Corcoran, a certified medical assistant. "The computer is never going to replace human beings."

As a certified medical assistant, Ms. Corcoran is equipped for both administrative and clinical work. "I've done each in the past," she stated, "but my present job is mainly administrative. I'm responsible for scheduling and receiving patients, obtaining patient data, maintaining medical records, and handling telephone calls, correspondence, and reports. I also purchase and maintain supplies and equipment; work on accounts, fees, and collections; take care of insurance; and assume general responsibility for the running of the office.

"A medical assistant who does clinical work has more of what we call the 'back office' jobs," she went on. "She may sterilize instruments, prepare and assist in examinations and treatments, and, if she has had the necessary education and training, be involved in laboratory procedures."

If helping a doctor with clinical and administrative (or clerical) work appeals to you, you need a high school education plus one or two years of training in a medical assistant's program. For even a starting job as a medical secretary you must have good clerical skills, plus a basic knowledge of medical terminology.

Today the American Association of Medical Assistants, a national organization approved by the American Medical Association for people employed by an M.D., encourages taking the two-year course, often offered at a community or junior college. For certification and the C.M.A. degree, you must pass the full-day examination the association gives nationally each year. It covers a broad range of subjects, including anatomy, physiology, psychology, law, and administrative and clinical procedures.

"Once you are a member of the professional society there are additional opportunities for seminars and other courses that help you grow and develop in your career," Ms. Corcoran added.

Margaret Corcoran got into the health field when she and a friend decided after high school that they didn't want to be run-of-the-mill secretaries, so both enrolled in a one-year course in a medical secretarial school.

"When the course concluded I obtained my first job through the school," Margaret told me. "It was in a dermatologist's office, and when I found I didn't like dermatology I lasted just three weeks!"

After marriage Margaret moved on to her second job, with an obstetrician-gynecologist, and she has been with doctors in that specialty ever since. For two years she worked in New Orleans, beginning as a medical secretary and progressing to a medical assistant's status as she assumed both clerical and clinical work. When she and her husband returned to the New York area she continued working in the field. From the first she has constantly upgraded herself by taking a wide range of continuing education courses and expanding her knowledge through workshops and seminars.

"As the health field grows the terms that are used to describe persons working in it can become very confusing," she stated, "and people often ask what's the fine line of difference between a medical assistant, a paramedic, et cetera. Paramedical (or allied help) includes everybody on the team who works together with physicians to deliver health care. Each of the various levels works within the limits of its training and experience. There are guidelines for paramedical training established by the professional associations and the Council of Medical Education of the American Medical Association.

"In addition to the confusion over the broad term paramedical," I reminded her, "there's an equal amount of perplexity about physician's assistant. What can you say about that?"

"The latter is a new category in the health field which started several years ago when some people felt there should be a place in civilian medicine for medics returning from Vietnam," she answered.

"Physician's assistants (PA's) are persons who have had armed forces medical corps training or gone on for special physician's assistant's training."

Once trained, a PA can perform many functions of a physician, but may not prescribe medicine or admit patients to a hospital. Usual duties include physical examinations, taking medical histories, ordering X-rays, and sewing the skin around minor cuts. A growing number of medical schools are offering a PA degree, for which five years of training is now generally required.

Another term causing confusion and controversy is "nurse practitioner"—a new discipline in which the nurse plays a more independent role in the care of patients, performing some routine duties once handled by doctors.

At this time training is available in only a few places. Besides basic nursing education and a B.S. degree, nurse practitioners need a period of intensive training and an internship. They act under a physician's guidance. While performing standard physical examinations and complementing doctors in other ways, they also look for the psychological and social factors which may underlie a disease.

"At whatever level you work in the health field there's a great joy in being of service to people," Marge Corcoran said in conclusion. "And when you're willing to go out and learn, the employment outlook is good."

MEMO 76:

ALWAYS GO FORWARD BECAUSE WHEN YOU MOVE IN THIS DIRECTION THINGS CONTINUE TO BE FRESH AND NEW.

Nancy Lewison:
"The field of SPEECH PATHOLOGY *makes for a fascinating career.*

"There's enormous gratification in helping to facilitate growth in language or modifying a problem in the ability to communicate," advised Nancy Lewison, director of a private facility for the diagnosis and treatment of speech and language disorders in both children and adults.

As director, Nancy supervises the other speech pathologists and staff members, conducts staff conferences, and provides on-going guidance for all patient care. "Our patients are seen weekly or bi-weekly, and I conduct all intake evaluations, determine the diagnosis and extent of the problem, and outline a course of therapy."

Nancy and her staff treat varied childhood problems, including delayed speech, stuttering, articulation disorders, cerebral-palsied speech, adjustment to cleft palates, and voice disorders. With adults they work on aphasia (difficulty in understanding language or speaking following stroke) and on vocalizing after having the larynx removed because of cancer.

An interest in aphasia sparked when she was in high school led Nancy into speech pathology. "My father is a clinical psychologist," she reminisced, "and while I was in high school I came across some of his books on aphasia. The problem interested me so much that after I graduated from the City College of New York with a major in psychology I went on to Teachers College at Columbia to obtain a master's degree in speech pathology."

Following this graduate study, Nancy worked two-and-a-half years in a hospital's speech and hearing program. She then returned to Teachers College as a clinical instructor of graduate students of speech therapy.

"I worked at Teachers College till I had my first child," she said. "Then I took six months off and subsequently went back to work part-time as a research speech pathologist at a treatment center for emotionally disturbed children. Later, I became director of this communications center, though I still work at the center for emotionally disturbed children part-time.

"The field of speech pathology is relatively new in its more sophisticated aspects," she pointed out. "We have had speech correction teachers for a long time, of course. But it has only been since the early and mid-sixties that we have been studying the pathology and development of language—and how words and thinking emerge—in the current way. Our knowledge is proliferating.

"There are many reasons for speech problems and a wide variation in the rate of which children acquire language skills," Nancy went on. "Usually the best success is achieved when a child with a speech problem is started on an intensive program fairly early.

"To work in this field you need enormous patience, rapport, and compassion," she continued, "because the modification of something that's as personal and close as speech and language is a very slow process. For instance, I might work with a child in correcting the 's' sound for a year. But when, after that year, I hear her speech improve it's terribly satisfying.

"The recommended training for this work is a master's degree in speech pathology and a certificate of clinical competence from the American Society of Speech and Hearing Association. In order to obtain that certificate you must have had paid professional experience in an internship.

"This job field, like many others, is tight when the economy is tight," Nancy admitted, "because hospitals, schools, and speech centers do not expand their use of speech pathologists and clinicians during such periods. But when the economic picture is bright, the job situation grows brighter, too."

MEMO 77:

> MAINTAIN A HAPPY APPROACH TO YOUR JOB INSTEAD OF A TIRED, GRIM ONE. NATURALLY, THIS WON'T ALWAYS MEAN THAT EVERYTHING WILL COME UP ROSES. BUT IT WILL EQUIP YOU TO BEAR A DAY'S WRONG WITH A POSITIVE SPIRIT.

Helen White and *Kathleen Conyers:*
"The great reward in OCCUPATIONAL THERAPY *is*

> *seeing people go home because of the improvement you have helped them make.*

"Some people still misunderstand occupational therapy as weaving, woodworking, or making potholders," declared Helen White, chief occupational therapist at a large county hospital.

"But occupational therapy, as opposed to recreation, is treatment-oriented. It's given when a doctor feels a specific type of treatment will help a patient reach a goal or attain the the highest level he or she can achieve.

"All of the activities and arts and crafts have a therapeutic purpose, whether it's to help a patient relate to other people, assume increased responsibility, strengthen a muscle, improve coordination, or achieve something else that will contribute to his mental and physical well-being," added Kathleen Conyers, a staff occupational therapist.

As a registered occupational therapist (or OTR) you work in general or military hospitals, psychiatric clinics, rehabilitation centers, community health centers, nursing homes, special schools, home care programs, and sheltered workshops.

You will help patients with such complaints as strokes, multiple sclerosis, arthritis, emotional illness, physical injuries, perceptual deficiencies, and birth defects. You'll also be involved with the problems of the aging. And after you evaluate individuals to determine their current level of functioning, you'll work as a member of a treatment team in collaboration with physicians, physical therapists, speech therapists, social workers, and other specialists.

"In occupational therapy we work both in rehabilitation service with people with physical disabilities and in general psychiatric service," Helen White continued. "In psychiatric service we use different types of modalities to get patients back into the community whenever possible.

"A revealing activity is ceramics, because a person can sometimes indicate his problem by what he makes. I worked with a patient who made a pig. But it was a pig with rabbit's ears. Later, the doctor told me the patient was a paranoiac who thought people were talking about him and the large ears indicated he was trying to hear what they were saying. Clay is fantastic as a therapeutic craft, because in throwing it a patient can work out some of his feelings—frustration, aggression, anger.

"In rehabilitation—where I work—we strive to help patients become as independent as possible after we evaluate and test them to find out where their weaknesses are," explained Kathleen Conyers. "We set up a treatment plan geared at bringing the patient from a state of disfunction to one of function.

"We teach one-handed dressing and cooking to patients paralyzed on one side. We have a kitchen which we use to show them how to solve cooking and homemaking problems and organize their work."

If you are interested in occupational therapy, both Helen White and Kathleen Conyers suggest going to a hospital (or other center where it is used) to talk to people in the field and observe them working at it. If it's for you, you will need four years of college training plus nine months of clinical affiliation. After that you'll take your registration examination and receive an OTR.

"When your training period is over you'll find that professional publications list jobs all over the world," advised Helen. "I have seen openings in Australia and Africa."

In every way you have the freedom to make your job a really worthwhile experience in occupational therapy, both women agreed, and to know the joy of seeing people leave a hospital when you know you have had a part in helping them learn to do things for themselves.

MEMO 78:

> REFUSE TO WORRY ABOUT HOW BIG THE JOB AHEAD OF YOU LOOKS. BREAK UP THE PICTURE OF ONE BIG JOB INTO SMALLER JOBS AND START ON ONE AT ONCE.

Gloria Warshaw:
"Women considering SOCIAL WORK *should know that long-time commitments are necessary.*

"Helping families and individuals discover new ways to grapple with life's problems is what social work is all about," said Gloria Warshaw, executive director of two offices operated by the Family Counseling Service, Inc. She supervises five full-time and four part-time counselors and keeps on top of what is being done to aid each client who comes for help.

"I hold weekly staff meetings to discuss cases that need further review or that would be enlightening to the other counselors," she stated. "I handle the correspondence concerning financial matters, for example, reports to organizations that give support to the agency, I run seminars, hold weekly group and family therapy sessions, and meet with the agency's consulting psychiatrist to review all cases.

"My mother was a social worker who became the executive director of her agency," Ms. Warshaw reminisced, "so my knowledge of social work goes back to my childhood. I obtained my B.S. from New York University and my master's from the University of Pennsylvania's School of Social Work.

"My first job was with the United Hebrew Immigrant Aid Service in Manhattan," she continued. "Later I worked in a number of other agencies before coming to Family Counseling Service, Inc. I started here as a psychiatric social worker and became executive director.

"The long-term commitments necessary in social work," Gloria Warshaw re-emphasized, "demand an on-going investment in both professional and personal growth. Like any other, this career field has both its frustrations and its joys. To me, the greatest frustration is a society in which people and their needs often have such a low priority. Inadequate finances to pay for services and inadequate training facilities are tremendous obstacles to giving help to all who need it."

The minimum educational qualification for a social work career is a bachelor of social work degree. In most counseling agencies, an MSW is required.

Since you will work with persons from all socio-economic backgrounds, your most essential personal qualification is empathy. You will need to like your clients and be able to understand not only what they say but also what they *mean*. You must be able to control your personal opinions and feelings—it's what the clients think and feel that's really essential.

"You need a willingness to allow people to struggle for their own solutions instead of always providing ready answers, some of which cannot be used," added Gloria Warshaw.

Opportunities for social work careers exist in public and private welfare and counseling agencies, hospitals and clinics, schools and colleges, community centers and settlement houses, senior citizen centers, and elsewhere. As you pursue your career, you can become a specialist, supervisor, administrator, teacher, or research worker—and still be involved with counseling in general.

"When money is difficult to come by the job situation is not always promising, even though many more workers are needed," concluded Gloria Warshaw. "Besides, with the growing number of professionals in the field, the standards for hiring have become more demanding. So the more professional training you can get, the more acceptable you will be in the social work field."

MEMO 79:

> REGARD EACH DAY AS SOMETHING TOO GOOD TO PASS UP. LEARN A LITTLE MORE. THINK A LITTLE MORE. DO A LITTLE MORE.

Rita Bloomfield Levin:
"Both full-time and part-time job opportunities are available in PHARMACY.*"*

When Rita Bloomfield Levin was a baby in her mother's arms, her grandfather looked at her and said, "She'll be a pharmacist." Today that prophecy has come true in every sense, because Rita Levin has had a varied career in retail and hospital pharmacy and is extremely active in professional pharmaceutical associations.

"There are many areas in this field," said Rita. "With today's emphasis on drug therapy, pharmacy is a vital part of health care."

If you choose to become a pharmacist, you must understand drugs fully—their composition, chemical and physical properties, manufacture, and uses and activity in the body of both the healthy and the ill person. You must be able to test for purity and strength.

You can work in teaching or research, community or chain drug stores, a pharmacy of your own, a government agency, notably the Food and Drug Administration, the drug or chemical industry, nursing homes, or hospitals. In the last type of employment you will concentrate on compounding and preparing prescriptions, making sterile solutions, maintaining an adequate inventory of drugs, and advising the medical staff on the selection and possible effects of drugs. "In addition, pharmaceutical law is a growing field," Rita Levin put in.

Rita grew up in a family in which the men were pharmacists. She was the first woman in the family to enter the field. "My father, who owned a pharmacy with his two brothers, was financial secretary of a county pharmaceutical society for years," recalled Rita. "I credit my going to meetings with him with my own heavy participation in professional societies today. When I was just 13 I played the accordian at one of the society's dinner dances, and I haven't missed many activities since."

As Rita attended the meetings and absorbed the atmosphere of the family's community drug store, she shared her grandfather's feeling that she would become a pharmacist. To prepare she entered Temple University College of Pharmacy. During summer vacations she worked, first in a hospital and then in a large department store pharmacy. After graduating she interned for one year in a retail pharmacy. "I continued in retail pharmacy," she informed me. "Later I worked in hospitals for a number of years. Then, when I felt ready to return to the retail or community pharmacy, I began working in my father's business."

Rita stayed there till the pharmacy was sold. Then she began doing relief work in other pharmacies and devoting a great deal of her time to serving on committees in professional associations and in legislative activities. She has traveled to England and Israel to attend pharmacy seminars and meet with heads of pharmaceutical associations.

"The percentage of women in the field has grown considerably in the past few years," Rita said. "And though statistics always fluctuate, women now account for about 50 percent of the students in pharmacy schools.

"To train for this field today, you need five years of study in a college of pharmacy," she concluded, "and in most states after you graduate you must serve a period of internship and pass a state board examination to obtain a license and be registered to practice."

MEMO 80:

> REMIND YOURSELF DAILY THAT IF YOU WILL BE AS INDUSTRI-
> OUS AS YOU POSSIBLY CAN YOU WILL ALMOST GUARANTEE
> YOURSELF A CHANCE TO GROW IN YOUR JOB.

Margaret Budd:
"In PHYSICAL THERAPY *you must always be ready for an emergency. You never know what type of order you will get from a doctor or what kind of patient will come in.*

"I have worked with individuals ranging in age from three days to 102 years," stated Margaret Budd, who serves as a hospital physical therapist. "So it's easy to see that physical therapy offers a wide scope. Treating the three-day-old baby was like handling a doll," she remembered. "The child was having trouble with her left arm, so I worked with her and taught the mother exercises she could manage at home. When we saw the baby a month or two later she was progressing well. After a year we gave the mother additional exercises. And the last time we observed, the baby was doing fine."

Physical therapy is an essential part of medicine in which you help the handicapped and injured learn to live to the limits of their capabilities. You administer treatment on prescription and under the direct supervision of a licensed physician. You too must be licensed.

As a few examples of what you'll do, you may give strengthening exercises to someone who has fractured a leg; lessons in walking and stair climbing to a patient paralyzed by a stroke; or coordination exercises to persons with neurological impairments. You can work in hospitals, nursing homes, rehabilitation centers, and patients' residences. In a hospital job, such as Margaret Budd's, you have both hospital cases and out-patients.

"I'm in charge of a department with eight physical therapists, two aides, and a secretary," said Margaret. "Our director is a physiatrist—an M.D. specializing in physical therapy. As chief physical therapist, it's my job to check new patients each morning to see if they should come to our department or receive bedside treatment from our staff," she said. "When we know what is needed, I assign other therapists or myself to patients. I discuss any problems that arise with the patients with the therapists and report progress to the doctors.

"We encourage the patients' families to visit our department and observe. For instance, when we have a stroke patient we often arrange for the family to come in every afternoon so that a therapist can show them how to get the patient in and out of bed.

"When I enrolled in Elmira College I thought I'd become a nurse," Margaret told me. "At the time, I didn't know what physical therapy was, but I had a counselor in college who advised me never to close my eyes to any career potential and who arranged for me to go to the local hospital and look at the various job opportunities there before I decided—definitely—on my career.

"When I saw the physical therapy department that was it— particularly when I remembered a very good family friend who had lived in an iron lung from the age of 13 to 33. After my four years at Elmira I took a one-year graduate course at Columbia University and obtained my certificate in physical therapy."

Following her certification, Ms. Budd was advised to work in a hospital for a while to acquire experience in all kinds of cases. "But I liked hospital work so much I've never left it," she confided. "Two years ago I received my master's degree in education with a specialty in rehabilitation counseling from Seton Hall University.

"When I started at this hospital we had an 18 × 20-foot room and the staff consisted of three—the director, a part-time therapist, and me," she said. "Now, 10 years later, we're in the hospital's old emergency room, and we have a staff of 11. That alone shows you how physical therapy has grown.

"It's a marvelous career and one you can always work in," she added. "You can leave it if you choose to be away a while—say, to raise a family. When you return you'll find your maturity is an asset.

"Physical therapy has bad aspects as well as joys," she conceded, "so anyone considering it would do well to visit a nearby hospital or other place where it's practiced and observe the day-to-day routine first-hand.

"But if you discover it's the right job for you it's really wonderful work!"

MEMO 81:

> INTEREST IS WHERE YOU FIND IT, SO NEVER CLOSE YOUR MIND TO ANY CAREER TILL YOU EXPLORE ALL ITS ASPECTS. ALL YOU NEED DO IS OPEN YOUR EYES TO THE WHOLE WIDE SPECTRUM OF POTENTIALS.

Chapter 8

Fashion and Beauty

Evelyn De Jonge:
"If you can make it as a DESIGNER *in the garment business you can make it in any business in the world, because our work involves such pressure and so many different facets.*

"The ready-to-wear fashion field doesn't offer easy careers," said Evelyn De Jonge, a youthful designer of fashions for women. Along with her husband Gerald Buxbaum, Evelyn runs Evelyn De Jonge, Inc. and EDJ Sportswear. While she designs and shops the fabric market, he manages the business and supervises manufacturing. Together they merchandise their line.

"Our business starts with the designer," Evelyn pointed out, "but after that it involves many people and an unbelievable number of details. First, you have to design your line several months in advance. Then you order the fabric and hope it will be delivered on time, because if it's late you may miss the delivery date you have given buyers.

"Once you get the fabric you must have your patterns made and marked and graded for sizing," she continued. "Next you cut the fabric and have the garments sent to a contractor to be sewn up. They're returned to you for trimming and, finally, go to the shipping department to be sent to the stores that have ordered them. From that point on you keep your fingers crossed and hope the customer is going to like the garments.''

Evelyn's hopes for her designs have come true, because in only a few years as head of her own firm she has succeeded in attracting attention to her women's dresses and sportswear.

"I got into designing almost by accident," she recalled, "though I've always loved clothes—and I'm told that all through childhood I had a real artistic flair that I wasn't conscious of. I went to an industrial arts high school, where I received a taste of drafting, sculpture, water-colors painting, draping, fashion illustration, and other aspects of art and design. Since I found all this very interesting, my father who was in the accessory area of fashion told me I belonged in the garment business."

Evelyn herself wasn't really sure what she wanted to do. But when she passed the entrance test for the Fashion Institute of Technology, she decided to study there with a major in merchandising. "That was my choice," she explained, "because I was afraid that if I trained for design I'd be cooped up in a room doing nothing else all day."

After Evelyn graduated from FIT, the school's placement office found her a job as a fabric coordinator for a large juniot clothes house. She had to shop for fabrics—excellent experience that gave her a chance to see a large segment of the market and meet many of the people in it. An interest in creating designs from the fabrics she picked was born. When Evelyn grew tired of working for a large house she took a job with a smaller children's wear firm.

"There I started out selling in the showroom and preparing publicity for the clothes in the fashion press," she said. "I also met Gerald Buxbaum, who gave me a chance to do some designing." A few months later Gerald Buxbaum left to start a business of his own and Evelyn went along—first as his right-hand person and then as his designer of children's clothes.

"We were in the children's clothes business for about nine years and were married during that time," she disclosed. "But when the era of jeans and T-shirts arrived, we closed the business and opened our women's wear and sportswear lines."

Since the fashion business had its share of doldrums in the early Seventies, Evelyn De Jonge is the first to admit that she didn't achieve her progress easily. "The tremendous pressure in this work starts with the designer,'' she said. ''But whether times are good or bad, *some* women are going to make it. You just work that much harder to give people what they want for the money that they can spend. Like so many other things in life you need both talent and training,'' she concluded. ''But luck plays a big part, too.''

MEMO 82:

> NEVER STOP TRYING TO MAKE YOURSELF BETTER. THE FASTEST WAY TO GET INTO A RUT IS TO SIT BACK AND STOP TRYING.

Bette Carrey:
''To run a fashion shop or be a BOUTIQUE OWNER *is much like playing the long shot, because it is so competitive—and you have to keep working so hard.*

''But it's also the dream of many of us who are dedicated to fashion,'' said Bette, ''since having a shop of your very own provides you, as the saying goes, with a way to do your own thing. To beat competition, however, you need several things going for you.

''As a starter, you have to be sure there's a need for the boutique you plan,'' pointed out Ms. Carrey, who runs a thriving one. ''Next you must find a location that's easily accessible and well-suited for parking. Ideally you should also possess business and selling experience and a strong artistic flair so you can create an attractive shop and select merchandise that will move. Beyond that, you need sufficient capital, dependable sources of supplies for merchandise, and sound financial advice.

''I don't consider myself particularly typical when it comes to starting and running a shop,'' Bette Carrey confided, ''because before I began selling fashions my thing was decorating homes. In fact, I was decorating 11 homes when I first saw the building which is now my shop.

''But I'm always dreaming up new things to do, and my mind just can't be idle. Consequently, when I saw a 'For Rent' sign while driving along a highway one day I glanced at the small white structure and found myself thinking, 'Wouldn't that be a great place for a shop where a total fashion look could be created?'

"Since I'm notoriously impulsive I pulled into the driveway, jotted down the phone number on the sign, and called up the owner, a man, to express my interest. At first he didn't want me as a tenant—because he wondered whether a woman could pay the rent! When I convinced him and rented the building, I decorated it in Salvation Army style while I finished the 11 houses I was engaged on. In the snatches of time I had left over I rushed into New York to buy clothes from the manufacturers and to plan the party with which I opened the store one month later. I've been in business ever since, and I love helping women create fashion looks."

If your thing is a boutique of your own, here's a blueprint based on my talks with Bette Carrey and others equally successful.

Learn all you can about fashion so your future customers will feel confidence in you. Be sensitive to trends—in fashion and people's desires.

Acquire selling experience—part-time, if necessary, and talk to people in similar but not competitive businesses and keep your eyes and ears open.

Obtain booklets on the business from the Small Business Administration (address in Chapter 10) and familiarize yourself through courses or on-the-job training with management techniques, buying and pricing, inventory control, and business promotion.

Think and dream about the image and personality you want your shop to project. Help them grow by lining up ways to develop your "own thing." While you're indulging in these dreams, prepare for the periods of drudgery you'll have to endure to achieve them.

And if you doubt there's drudgery involved ask any shop owner how she feels about handling and opening boxes!

MEMO 83:

> WHEN YOU'RE WELL PREPARED AND DOING YOUR BEST, A HAPPY OR FORTUNATE ACCIDENT CAN TAKE YOU TO A WORTHWHILE JOB YOU DIDN'T PLAN OR FORESEE.

Barbara Burditt:

"Work as a BEAUTY CONSULTANT *in the direct selling field offers opportunities to women who want a 'people' job.*

"My work is very social," said Barbara Burditt, a beauty consultant for a nationally known direct-selling firm. "I teach beauty classes in homes for groups of six women. I instruct in skin care and make-up techniques and give the women facials. There's no obligation to buy, but moderately-priced products are available for purchase.

"As a director it's also my job to train other consultants to teach people our skin care treatments and glamour make-up techniques," she stated, "and to hold weekly sales meetings.

"The history of the product to which I'm dedicated goes back to the early 1900's to a little town in Arkansas where a tanner supported his wife and nine children by taking stiff, ugly, big-pored pieces of hide and turning them into beautiful, soft leather," she told me. "As he worked with the tanning solution, he noticed that while the rest of his body aged, his hands remained smooth and young. He established that the same substance worked on his face. When he died at age 73, he looked as young as his children."

One of the children, Ova Spoonemore Standridge, shared her father's dream of perfecting the substance for the face and became a cosmetologist. In 1933 the family product was put on the market as Beauticontrol.

"I heard about it while I was working as a secretary in Wyoming," reported Barbara. "I had a serious acne condition that had troubled me since adolescence. One day a typewriter salesman told me his wife sold beauty products that might help me. I had some facials from his wife and followed the skin treatment she outlined.

"Gradually friends and acquaintances began to notice the difference in my skin, and I became so enthusiastic about what was happening that I began to encourage more and more women to follow this skin care plan."

Ultimately Barbara decided that she might as well get into the business herself. Soon she was earning more money part-time evenings as a beauty consultant than as a secretary in her daytime job. She worked her way up to a director's spot, the level above consultant.

"When I came East a neighbor lent her home for my first class," she recalled. "After that one woman told another and that provided me with my start. Now I hold between five and ten classes a week—in the morning, afternoon, or evening."

The first requirement for her type of work is believing in the product, says Barbara.

"Our requirements are that consultants be attractive and neat and use our products on their skin. We have no age or figure qualifications," she stressed. "In fact, the top saleswoman for our company one year was a Michigan woman who weighed every bit of 300 pounds. But she wants to do what she's doing—and she's also the living proof that there *is* a right job for all dedicated and hard-working women.

"It's important to discipline yourself to work on your own. Some people who start in this field can't organize themselves to do the necessary amount of work—even with our sales prizes and incentive programs.

"The money you earn depends on how much you work. If you *don't* work there are no commissions. If you *do,* they're excellent. Twenty hours a week, for example, should earn you approximately $500 a month.

"When I'm holding classes, however, I often forget about money and think I'm playing and visiting because the job is so social. And when you see women who don't feel atractive start to look really pretty the feeling is fabulous.

"Regardless of how much your earnings are, money can't buy that reward."

MEMO 84:
>WHEN LIFE OFFERS YOU SOMETHING, TAKE IT. ASSUME IT'S A
>BREAK AND TRY TO WORK IT OUT.

Kay Seiler:
"A career as a FASHION ARTIST *in which you illustrate*

finished children's and adults' wearables can be both fun and fulfilling.

"As a staff artist for a clothing manufacturer one of my jobs is to create scenes from the animal kingdom for babies' bibs," Kay Seiler informed me. "I also design appliqués for infants', children's and teenagers' garments.

"From an artistic point of view a child's bib seems to be a prosaic article with utility value only," she said, "but with a funny story printed on, it becomes imaginative. I sign most of my creations with my artist's name; this helps sell bibs to parents. Mealtime is a more pleasant experience for parents and children alike.

"It's gratifying to know that many thousands of my bibs are sold each week all over the United States and abroad, and it thrills me to travel to some far away town and find my creations in the stores there.

"Every morning, the head of our company and I discuss the assignments for the day," Kay Seiler continued. "After deciding on priorities, I dream about what I want to do, think of ideas, and make several designs. The approved designs are broken down into several colors and made ready for silk screen production. This is a stencil process that forces ink through the open meshes of several silk screens, one for each color. The printed designs are heat sealed on the garment.

"From a fashion point of view, one of the things I find most appealing is our line of silk-screen-printed T-shirts for adults and teenagers. I create decorative, whimsical or topical designs for the shirts, and, as fashion grows more individualistic, more and more people buy them to communicate their self-image."

If fashion art appeals to you, you can be employed by department stores, manufacturers, and mail-order houses, to pinpoint a few potentials. You may prefer to free-lance in your home or studio. To equip yourself for a career in the field, plan on training in art, design, and fashion at an art school, fashion institute, junior college, or college. When applying for entrance to art school you'll need samples of your work.

"For a starter, learn all you can about all the branches in the art field—including the fine arts," Kay Seiler suggested. "You can always specialize later. Moreover, when you have a broad background, your specialization can be versatile and flexible."

Kay Seiler followed her own advice by attending art school in her native Vienna before coming to the United States. She studied also at New York's Art Students League and the Fashion Institute of Technology. Before assuming her present job she was in fashion illustration.

Her checklist of qualifications for women who want to be fashion artists includes creative talent, imagination, visual orientation, a feeling for figure drawing, style, and line, adaptability, perseverance, ability to work under pressure, and plenty of stamina.

"Build up your portfolio in art school," Kay Seiler emphasized in conclusion. "You will have it as your window display when you look for a job."

MEMO 85:

> TO KEEP A CAREER GOING YOU MUST CONSTANTLY HARVEST BRIGHT IDEAS. BUT REMEMBER THAT EVEN THE BEST IDEA IN THE WORLD WILL NEVER AMOUNT TO ANYTHING IF YOU DON'T NAIL IT DOWN.

Helen Bohn:
"A BRIDAL SERVICE *is a happy business—though it has its share of tension and details and there's always a fight against time.*

"My business is weddings," stated Helen Bohn, owner of a bridal shop that specializes in the personal touch.

"I buy from the largest bridal houses in the world and carry gowns for the bride, the bridesmaids, the mother of the bride—and also dinner and prom gowns.

"If our clients wish, we take care of the whole wedding or any part by recommending florists, photographers, limousine service, and whatever else the bride needs to make the occasion the big day it is," she continued.

From an early start sewing doll clothes, Ms. Bohn has been in fashion for most of her working life.

"I started at age 17 in unit control for Sears, Roebuck and Company in Chicago," she told me, "and I still use some of the methods I learned there. Later I went into buying, so most of my training for my present work came from on the job experience plus business school and college courses."

From Chicago Helen Bohn went to Missouri to buy for a large fashion store. When she moved to the New York area she worked as a department store buyer.

"After I had two sons I retired from working for a while," she said. "When I was ready to go back to work I decided on a bridal business because I enjoy serving people."

If a service business such as this seems right for you your best training will be courses in retailing, merchandising, and fashion at fashion schools or a college. Learn everything that you possibly can about styling, fabrics, colors, and trends.

To run a consultant service as an offshoot of a bridal shop, you will need the cultural background to cope with clients on all economic, intellectual, and social levels, and a wide knowledge of the etiquette and customs involved in wedding preparations for different religious and ethnic groups. Also in your sphere will be knowledge of the proper allocation of the wedding budget, planning menus and ordering wines and liquors, seating arrangements, and flowers. Additional parts of your stock in trade will be lists of good printers and engravers, suitable halls, hotels, and restaurants, catering services, musicians, photographers, limousines, and men's formal wear rental businesses.

Good training could be working in a trousseau or bridal shop or in the linens, glassware and china, or bridal registry department of a store, or assisting a florist or banquet manager in a hotel. You might also look for work with a manufacturer of bridal gowns or a custom dressmaker.

The qualifications you need are good taste and a feeling for fashion, a liking for people and an ability to relate well to them, a creative approach, an excellent head for figures and detail, and ability to supervise. To get started it's a good idea to compile a list of brides-to-be from the engagement announcements in the newspaper, send your publicity to them, and follow up with phone calls. Later, newspaper and word-of-mouth advertising will keep your service in people's minds.

"It's a business where you often have to work when other people are free, because evenings and Saturdays are usually the times when they can come to you," Helen Bohn pointed out.

"But even with the long hours and constant fight against time, it's lots of fun to be involved with a wedding!"

MEMO 86:

> IF YOU HAVE TO PLAN EVERYTHING AND HAVE A PERFECT SITUATION BEFORE YOU BEGIN A JOB, YOU'LL NEVER GET OFF THE GROUND. THERE WILL ALWAYS BE EXCUSES WHY YOU CAN'T GET STARTED AND SITUATIONS WHEN TOO MUCH INTERFERES. WISHING WILL ALWAYS WIN OVER WORKING.

Edith Imre:
"When there is no career struggle, achievements have no real value.

"Many Europeans feel and smell the opportunity and new chances that still exist in America," declared Edith Imre, a Hungarian-born beauty specialist and importer of WIGS AND HAIRPIECES. "And we're willing to struggle to achieve this opportunity.

"When I came to America from Hungary in the late 1930's I was a graduate cosmetologist," she explained. "In Europe I had held a position working for a doctor, but in America there were no such jobs available."

Finding *some* job was imperative, however, because Edith's husband was ill and unable to work. She started out in true bottom-rung style by taking unskilled work in a factory. Every night after the factory shift, she practiced cosmetology by giving her neighbors facials.

"I made the creams from my European formulas in my own kitchen and carried the machinery from house to house," she remembered. "I charged 35¢ a facial, because, in *that* depression, 35¢ was the equivalent of three and a half loaves of bread."

When Edith lost her factory job, the demand for her facials was growing by word-of-mouth advertising. She gave up carrying her machinery and creams from house to house and worked in a New York salon.

"On a client's recommendation, I moved to a salon in a high-fashion area that was looking for a cosmetologist and opened my own facial rooms there," Edith said. "My regular clientele followed me and gradually new customers—including celebrities and name personalities—began to come in."

When the salon was unexpectedly sold, Edith opened her own in Manhattan, and from the first her special line of cosmetics and her pioneering use of hormones in beauty creams caught on. She made it her policy to keep something new going all the time, because, in her words, "Last year's ideas for business aren't new enough for this year."

Consequently, when wigs and hairpieces became best-sellers in beauty, Edith Imre began importing and designing a wide variety and today is one of the largest importers of them in the United States.

"Now in this unisex world I've been working on hair addition, or hair weaving, so I can glorify the heads of men as well as women," she told me. "In the past I've been fascinated with the idea and depressed with some of the practices, so I have perfected a method of my own that seems to be the right approach to this new idea of having more hair where nature made you sparse.

"I am always my own first model," she went on, "and thus I can determine the comforts and pitfalls of a new idea. I've now come to the almost perfect approach on the basis of individual design with the pieces attached to the existing hair with my own way of stitching."

Because Edith Imre feels so strongly that life in America has been good to her, she, in turn, has always felt a compulsion to give something back. For instance, she found herself thinking of how important psychologically a pretty hairdo—and the knowledge of how to create one—could be to troubled women. With this as a priority project, she visited New York's Women's House of Detention, hurdled all the obstacles, and donated and organized a licensed beauty school where the inmates could keep each other looking nice at the same time that they obtained job training for the outside.

And to pave the way for them to earn a living, this pint-size entrepreneur from Hungary was instrumental in having a state law prohibiting women with criminal records from working in beauty shops re-written.

MEMO 87:

> A WOMAN WITH A GOOD IDEA SHOULD NEVER BE AFRAID TO GO TO SEE ANYONE OR ASK ANYONE FOR ANYTHING THAT WILL HELP HER WORK IT OUT.

Marilyn Pignoni:
"The showroom end of the fashion business offers good opportunities to women with high school diplomas who are willing to train on the job.

"There are not enough women who work as a FASHION SHOWROOM DIRECTOR," said Marilyn Pignoni, director of sales for John Kloss, a Coty Award-winning fashion designer.

"Yet showroom work offers excellent potential to high school graduates who have a flair for clothes and selling but no talent for designing," added Marilyn, as we talked in John Kloss's showroom.

Throughout the year buyers from all over the country come to showrooms in Manhattan's West 40's and Seventh Avenue to preview the latest styles displayed by models and discussed by commentators.

The people who work in showrooms have often been called the unsung heroes of the fashion business, because, almost more than anyone else, they're responsible for the fashion "sell."

Marilyn got into showroom work when she started modelling at age 17 because that was the only job open to her. "But any woman who wants to learn the business can come right to the garment center, begin as a clerk or switchboard operator, and get her foot in the door," she explained. "If she helps out where she is needed, gets to know the people who come in and out, and learns how everything is done, her chances to progress to the point where she shows and sells clothes can be very good. This was the approach that I used, and I advanced very quickly."

After a few years, however, Marilyn tapered off and stayed at home while her son was young. But she kept her finger in the fashion pie by running a suburban modeling school and occasionally taking on other fashion jobs. When she was ready to go back to work, she prepared shows for designer Geoffrey Beene and later worked as his director of sales.

Ms. Pignoni moved onto six years as director of sales for Oscar de la Renta. She showed and sold his clothes in the boutique department of the showroom, helped prepare advertising for the buyers, wrote and coordinated fashion shows, and served as a commentator to buyers in the showroom.

Early in 1975 she left Oscar de la Renta for her present job with John Kloss. As director of sales she stays on top of everything that goes on in the showsroom and takes the pulse of all phases of the business. "This includes working with projections, designs, fabrics, colors, production, advertising, promotion, and sales," she told me. "I try to arrive by 8:15 in the morning to go over my memos and evaluate what I have to do. Then I set up a schedule for the day.

"I work by appointment with buyers and I myself take care of the major department stores all over the country and a few very fine specialty shops. In addition I sit in on all discussions concerning the salability of new designs and upcoming collections and answer at least 100 telephone calls a day. Besides, I travel to our shows in major cities, which involves bringing our entire fashion collection to the stores.

"By every standard this is a marvelous career if you love people and love being stimulated by challenges and changes," she enthused. "Every situation is different, so you're never doing the same thing twice."

If you'd like this end of the fashion business, your best first step is to seek on-the-job training in the Seventh Avenue showroom of a dress manufacturer. You'll find the names of many listed under "Apparel —Women's Dresses" in the Manhattan classified telephone directory. If you begin as a clerk you'll start out with filling orders and requisitions, keeping records, and making yourself generally useful. With experience and ambition you'll progress.

In order to do well in a showroom career you need a good appearance and personality, an ability to work at a fast pace under pressure, a natural bent for selling, and a healthy amount of drive.

"But with these attributes you never grow old," Marilyn Pignoni concluded, "because fashion is a field that is always new."

MEMO 88:

> GIVE MORE THAN IS ASKED OF YOU. IF YOU DON'T GET A CHANCE FROM 9 TO 5, SHOW YOUR *REAL* POTENTIAL—TAKE WORK HOME AND DO EXTRA PROJECTS THERE!

Allison Atwood Hunter:
"A MODEL *enjoys a lucrative and rewarding fashion career.*

"No two working days have been the same for me in the years that I've been modeling," reported Allison Atwood Hunter.

"This makes my job particularly interesting because it's exciting to work with different people and different studios," she added. "But despite the glamour, this career is not an easy one," pointed out Allison, who's represented by the Wilhelmina Model Agency in New

York. "You always have to be ready for the unexpected and you must constantly look fresh and just right, regardless of how you feel. You have to keep moving, because in one day you may have four different jobs—one uptown, one downtown, and the others across town."

Allison's day begins at 6 a.m. so she can avoid the rush hour traffic while driving from her home to New York. It ends at approximately 8 p.m., when she arrives home to fix dinner.

"I do magazine, catalogue, and TV work," she explained, "and I model all kinds of fashions from sportswear to sophisticated evening wear, nightgowns, robes, bathing suits, et cetera. Quite a few of my jobs are for Montgomery Ward, Sears, and *Good Housekeeping* magazine, and many assignments take me out of town, which is always fun.

"For example, I go down to the Caribbean islands quite a bit in the winter because the sun and beach are needed for spring and summer fashion pictures. I've been sent to New England to model ski clothes. And when I was 18 I traveled around the world—first for a Max Factor campaign in Tokyo and then for a job in London."

Allison, who grew up in a family that showed horses, got started in modeling when she was spotted by photographer Edward Pfizenmaier when she was riding in a horse show. "He asked me if I would like to be a model," she said, "and I just couldn't believe it, because it was something I'd always dreamed about and never thought would happen."

Pfizenmaier took pictures of Allison, who was 13-going-on-14, first in her home and then in his Manhattan studio. "He made an appointment for me with an agency that put me under contract. Later I switched to the Wilhelmina agency. My first job—I was just 14—was for the *Chicago Tribune*'s magazine section. When I found out I was modeling a-$300 dress I was afraid to move in it!"

Allison continued modeling while attending high school. After she graduated, she decided to stick with it so long as she was young. "You have to get into it and give it your best in those years," she pointed out. "You're in a career that won't last forever. But while you're modeling you can watch for other work in the future, because you get to see a great assortment of magazine, advertising, and television jobs and meet interesting people and make contacts."

To consider a career as a model obviously you have to be tall, slender, and good-looking. You need personality, a good face for the camera, poise, grace, intelligence, patience, and, because your days are so long and hard, fortitude.

"If you're not poised, modeling school or ballet lessons might be helpful," Allison advised, "but I'm not one who believes in a lot of expensive preparation. Agencies want you to be natural and they help you along and show you what kind of make-up is best for you. Similarly, most photographers direct you and tell you what they want. Other models are terrific in helping you too, and this is really nice.

"Pictures are important when you're breaking in, of course, and I was lucky because I had Edward Pfizenmaier's pictures. Bring your pictures to the agencies. If you photograph well, an agency may send you to another photographer, who will 'test' you as a model. This means pictures for your portfolio *and* for the photographer's portfolio, so it works doubly. You really don't have to pay a great deal of money.

"It's admittedly hard to establish yourself and get to know photographers and clients," Allison concluded. "But once you accumulate clients who really like you they can keep you very busy—and you have an exciting career."

MEMO 89:
> BE AN OPTIMIST. KNOW YOU ARE GOING TO MAKE IT. KNOW YOU ARE GOING TO SUCCEED.

Chapter 9

*A Service
or Business
of Your Own*

Janet Sterling:
*"Think in terms of filling a need in a way that hasn't been
done in your area before. Then go about it in the most
professional way possible."*

"Find a need and fill it" is the basic business advice that has started
many a woman on the road to career success—and that's Janet
Sterling's story of her HOUSE SITTING SERVICE.

Through her unique Collegiate Home Service Janet provides a long
list of clients with a choice of approximately 75 young married
couples who serve as live-in babysitters, house-watchers,
chaperones, tutors, and home-caretakers while families go away.

"Our couples are available for overnight or long-term assignments," she explained, "and our service differs from the usual type in
that we use local married couples to act as substitutes while the parents
are away. Most of the couples are college students or recent college
graduates, and they have great rapport with children. As bright,
interested, and caring people we find over and over again that they
display much resourcefulness in the face of unexpected problems and
situations.

"Our clients enjoy great peace of mind knowing there is a responsible man in the house and that they have two loving adults (for the

price of one) in their homes while they are gone. For example, a family asked us for a sports-minded man who would play games with their athletic son but would also see that he did his homework. The husband of the couple we supplied was a physical education teacher— so both homework and games worked out fine.''

Janet began her now-thriving business by answering a need of her own. ''When I moved to a new area I needed people to stay with my children when I was away,'' she told me. ''After trying several I found that what I wanted most was often hard to come by—a caring individual flexible enough to run the house in the manner to which the children were accustomed and who would put the children's needs and welfare first.

''I began to think how ideal it would be to leave the children with young substitute parents who would fit in with our life-style and do things the way we would. The idea of a couple appealed to me, because should one person become ill, there would be a back-up.''

When Janet found out her idea represented a service that was really needed, she began taking steps to establish the business that is now licensed by the state and completely insured and bonded. ''I started by contacting colleges in the area to locate couples for interviewing and screening,'' she stated. ''I lined up some of my first clients through colleges, since families sometimes call them when they need child or home care help. I also obtained clients through advertising and, later, through word-of-mouth as news of my service spread.''

In Janet's business, couples must provide references before being interviewed for the registry and are screened by both the service and the clients.

''We try to have the sitting couple visit the home a few days before the clients' departure,'' Janet said. ''This helps spare the children anxiety and gives the clients a chance to instruct the couple personally in the way they would like their home run while away.

''The usual procedure is for the substitute couple to prepare all meals (including school lunches), participate in car pools, maintain homes according to the clients' standards, and do necessary laundry.

''In an unplanned and unanticipated way my whole background seems to have led to what I am doing now,'' revealed Janet. ''For example, at college I majored in business and administration and minored in psychology, even though at the time I had no idea how I would use them. After college, I worked in personnel and interviewed and screened people for jobs.

"This training and my background in psychology are invaluable because of the extreme care I must exercise to sense the needs of clients and determine how well couples we interview can satisfy them.

"In starting a service of your own," Janet concluded, "in addition to filling a need, you should bend over backwards to find the work for which you have a background and a good intuition and use them to the hilt."

MEMO 90:

> TRY TO SENSE WHAT THE COMING THING WILL BE AND TAKE YOUR CUE FROM THAT WHEN YOU START A BUSINESS OR SERVICE.

Edna Michalzik:
"A husband, a wife, and a child—plus a business selling WEDDING FLOWERS—*add up to a great way to live and to work."*

As owners of a shop called Wedding Day, Inc., Edna and her husband Paul have a specialized service that deals exclusively in wedding flowers. And, in addition, they have kept their daughter at work with them since she was two weeks old.

"We think it's a beautiful arrangement," declared Edna, "and from the first our daughter had a great love of flowers. We let her touch each bridal bouquet and she feels the flowers very gently.

"Besides bridal bouquets, we make flower arrangements for the church, reception, attendants, and mothers," she advised. "Our stock in trade is personalizing every wedding just as much as we possibly can. For example, one of our first brides—a very beautiful,

Bohemian-type girl—wanted a wedding with a Mexican theme. She planned to arrange a combination of dried and paper flowers and wanted us to add fresh flowers. This seemed like a strange request, but we worked to create what she wanted. Ultimately, when we combined the dried and the paper flowers with just the right fresh flowers she had a most unique and beautiful bouquet.''

Edna Michalzik became a florist through the roundabout route of coming from her native Puerto Rico to New York to take a job in an office. ''The job turned out to be secretary in a bridal service,'' she informed me. ''It was all right for a starter. But my ambition from the first was to prepare myself for a business that would offer me a future and provide me with the means to live as I wanted to.

''As I thought about several potentials, I could see from my company's volume—60 weddings a week—that there was a market for wedding flowers. Consequently, I decided to learn to be a top-notch bridal florist. I knew I could use that background for either a business of my own or a job in someone else's shop.''

Edna began watching the florists at work after finishing her daily stint as a secretary. Before too long she gave up her secretarial position to devote full-time to working as a florist and learning on the job. ''It was a great place to learn, too,'' she said, ''because we had so many weddings on the weekend that we used to start working at 5 a.m. on Friday and continue almost around the clock—till about 3 a.m. on Saturday. By 7 we were on the job again.''

At the florist's Edna met her husband-to-be, who was employed as a salesman and had been a plumber and electrician.

''When we married we talked of a business of our own in which we could combine our experience and skills,'' she commented, ''so the idea of working as husband and wife in a specialized wedding flowers service seemed the perfect step.''

They began from their home. ''This was our in-transit period,'' she recalled. ''I'd improvise by emptying our refrigerator of all the food and setting it at the right temperature for the flowers I was using. Then a few years ago we moved to a new area to start a full-fledged bridal flower business. We took an inexpensive store, fixed it ourselves, and booked our first wedding while we were getting ready to open. Later, we established a tie-in with a bridal shop to get a flow of business.

Eventually we moved to a complex that—along with our wedding flowers—includes a bridal gown salon, gift shop, photographer's studio, and tuxedo rental service.

"Despite today's social changes, people still get married to the tune of thousands of weddings a year," continued Edna, "so there's a good market for this type of business—especially since very few people specialize in bridal flowers alone. However, anyone who wants such a career needs to realize that the hours are long and the work is hard. Weekends are usually the busiest times, which brings me back to my start—that working this out as a husband and wife with our daughter right beside us is a beautiful and wonderful way to live."

MEMO 91:

> WHEN A WOMAN WANTS A BUSINESS OF HER OWN SHE MUST BE WILLING TO DO ALL KINDS OF HARD WORK—INCLUDING THE DRUDGERY—WHILE STARTING AND PROGRESSING.

Syril Ivler:
"If you want to launch your own business the smartest thing you can do is learn the facts about what you hope to do.

"To prepare myself for a career in GOURMET FOODS I attended the University of Wisconsin and graduated as a bacteriologist-biochemist from Pennsylvania State College," said Syril Ivler, who now has a business in which she packages and sells frozen and canned snails. "But jobs were scarce when I finished college, so as much as I wanted to enter the food industry I started by working in hospitals. At one point I was a medical technician at a large hospital for the mentally ill."

After this detour on the job route Syril found a spot in a doughnut factory. Later she worked as a home economist for a large food concern and did sales promotion and publicity for foods. In all, she accumulated 20 years of experience before she began her own business. "When I was looking for ideas for a project of my own I tested several different foods," she said. "Ultimately I hit upon the thought of preparing and freezing snails for sale.

"For a catchy name—a *must* in every business—I chose 'S-Car-Go,' phonetic for 'escargots.' Eventually, I added 'Mussels Mar 'N Year,' then canned snails.

"I began by testing and perfecting the product in my kitchen. My son was chief tester for the snails, my daughter for the mussels.

"When I felt ready to begin, I stuffed imported snails with seasoned parsley-butter sauce, packaged them in disposable oven-ready pans, labeled them, and sold them to department stores, supermarkets, and food shops. I made my first sales by going to stores and showing S-Car-Go to buyers. I also displayed the product at food shows and used my previous promotion experience for the publicity and photography. For a gimmick I wore—and still wear—a snail pin."

As business developed Syril moved from her kitchen to larger quarters and trained a staff of helpers. When people from all over the country who had eaten her snails began writing or telephoning to ask where they could purchase them, she engaged brokers to handle the selling and distribution. Her business expanded nationally to restaurants, hotels, motels, country clubs, caterers, and college and hospital administrative dining rooms.

"Despite expansion, however, I'm still chief cook and bottle washer on occasion," admitted Syril, "because we remain a small concern. But as head I'm responsible for planning the work with the women in the plant, taking care of the mail, contacting brokers and distributors throughout the United States, and making arrangements with truckers.

"Regardless of how much you love your career, running your own business can be full of tension," she conceded, "because nothing always goes exactly as you want. But one of the greatest satisfactions is seeing a business grow from nothing to something really substantial.

"The key to success, as I pointed out in the beginning, is learning the hard cold facts about the business you hope to enter *before* you start. If it's in the food industry, for instance, a college degree plus several years of job training in all phases of the business will help you.

"Beyond that, begin in a small way and expect to work hard. I often work seven days a week and, usually, many hours each day."

MEMO 92:
> THINK OF YOUR LIFE AS A TREE WITH ONE BIG STRONG TRUNK
> AND LOTS AND LOTS OF BRANCHES THAT LEAD TO A VARIETY
> OF RIGHT THINGS TO DO.

Gertrude Gardner:
"When you want to open a shop to sell GIFTS AND ANTIQUES *you need a flavor and theme.*

"Today it is no longer possible to sell merchandise per se," explained Gertrude Gardner, originator of three shops—The Store Next Door, The Party Shop, and Gardner's II—featuring unusual and provocative antiques. You must have a theme, flavor, décor that catches people's eyes and merchandise that's outstanding and not run-of-the-mill. In addition you need to be financially independent of your business for at least a year, because it takes time before a shop starts to pay.

"From the experience I gained selling and buying gift items while helping my husband, I'd tell anyone who wants to open a business to take a job in another shop first," added Ms. Gardner. "Try to work very closely with the buyer.

"A good look at an empty store that was literally next door to my husband's shop gave me my idea. That store at the turn-of-the-century had handled dry goods and general merchandise. So when I made it into a gift shop, I picked the turn-of-the-century flavor for my theme and settled on The Store Next Door as an obvious name.

"When it was on solid footing, I opened The Party Shop in response to customers' requests for party items. Later I began my antiques business. To convey the nostalgia and flavor I wanted, I left the design of the stores and the original shelves intact, installed Tiffany lamps, and painted the interiors chartreuse. Anyone who knows me knows chartreuse is my 'thing.'

"I built the décor around items that were part of an earlier era. For opening day at The Store Next Door I used an old icebox painted gold as the display case for Christmas arrangements. An old-fashioned sewing machine served as a show case for table mats and a turn-of-the-century Victrola figured in the décor."

When you want to open a gift shop, it's obviously essential to follow all this book's tips in connection with other businesses. In addition, before hanging out your "Open" sign, you should observe the tastes and shopping habits of the people to whom you'll cater, survey the competition, and visit many gift shops.

To get a broad view, read trade magazines. *The Gift and Art Buyer* and *Giftwards,* for example, will provide you with valuable information on display ideas, trends in tastes, and practical suggestions for building sales through public relations and customer service. They'll keep you current on the dates and locations of gift shows. Listings under "Giftwares—Wholesalers and Manufacturers" in the New York classified telephone directory will give you leads to sources of supply. You can order at showrooms, by phone or mail, or from representatives who call on you. Many people in the business opt for personal visits to the showrooms.

"When I started I found it was advantageous to buy a minimum number of each item I stocked," emphasized Gertrude Gardner. "As you see what your customers like, it's easy to reorder."

Once you have put together a distinctive shop and window display, launch your business with an open house with punch and cookies, coffee and pastries, or wine and cheese. At the same time, advertise in local newspapers and mail announcements to your potential clientele.

"Then, above all, prepare yourself for a total commitment to your gift shop," Gertrude Gardner concluded. "You have to work at this business and enjoy what you do.

"As for me, I love the work so much I can't wait to get down to the store each day!"

MEMO 93:

> THINK BIG AND ASK, "HOW MUCH DO I NEED?" WHEN YOU
> DECIDE ON YOUR ANSWER, ACCOMPLISH AND ACHIEVE YOUR
> END BY DOING A SUPERLATIVE JOB.

Cathy Norman:
"There's tremendous satisfaction in offering EMPLOY-
MENT COUNSELING *to job seekers and helping them
find what they want.*

"In a career in personnel counseling your main function is to screen
job seekers for employment in businesses which request their services," declared Cathy Norman, a certified employment counselor.
"You interview job applicants, test their work skills, refer them to
prospective supervisors, and—often—provide counseling."

Cathy came into this work after many years in which she combined a job during the day with courses in business school and at
Queens College at night. "In my first job in downtown New York I
worked as a biller for a perfume company," she revealed.
"Next I was a statistical typist. From that job—with experience and
business school behind me—I moved into a post as secretary to an
executive."

Marriage and children followed, and Cathy stayed home for nine
years. When she was widowed while very young, she returned to a
former employer. "I know the feeling of insecurity many women
experience when they go back to work," she went on, "but all you
have to do is try and be willing to make a new start."

With that philosophy, Cathy put her shoulder to the wheel of her
secretarial job. When commuting to New York became too hard
because of her small children, she switched to secretarial jobs on Long
Island. As secretary to the president of an electronics firm, she was
introduced to personnel work.

"I had the responsibility of recruiting people both for the office force and for executive positions. I enjoyed the opportunity to sit in on many meetings, learn what goes on in a company, and become familiar with different departments."

When re-marriage and a move to New Jersey terminated this job, Cathy Norman decided, after getting settled, to enter the job market for the third time. "I remembered that when I was a secretary a person who had run an employment agency had asked me to join her," she told me. "Thmugh I hadn't followed through then, suddenly employment work seemed like a good idea."

With personnel counseling and management as her goal, Cathy answered an ad for a secretary in an employment agency. Starting as a junior secretary, she received on-the-job training and advanced to administrative work in three-and-a-half years.

"From the first I enjoyed this work so much I realized I'd missed my calling," she confided. "I was so sure of it that my husband and I began our own agency. I started alone, with my husband, who held another job, helping me out in his spare time. Eventually he gave up his job, because he was needed so much in the business." In time Cathy put on employees. Now she has two offices and plans a third.

"This business has been the right one for me because it just grew and grew," she said. "It's true the economy affects it, but we've never had a bad year. The important thing is to build a reputation for filling orders properly. If a client wants a clerk-typist to work on a billing machine you'd better send someone who can recognize the machine."

A college education is usually required for a career in employment counseling, and a knowledge or feeling for psychology is an important prerequisite.

"In addition, you need actual working experience," Cathy Norman concluded. "In some states you cannot even become a trainee unless you have worked in industry or some other area for at least a year. And the more people I meet in agency management, the more I find they have varied backgrounds in chemicals, sales, education, or whatever. Finally, you must be licensed by your state to be a counselor. You must be in business for two years before you can qualify for

the tough, three-part examination for the Certified Employment Counselor title awarded by the National Employment Association.''

MEMO 94:
> WHEN IT'S TIME TO TAKE NEW STEPS AND MAKE CHANGES IN
> YOUR LIFE SAY "WHY NOT?" THEN GO AHEAD AND SEE WHAT
> HAPPENS.

Cynthia Krasny and Bernice Ruderman:
*"Sometimes we think of ourselves as party psychiatrists
because clients call us morning, noon, and night when they
want us for* PARTY COORDINATING.

"Actually, we're party decorators and coordinators," advised Bernice Ruderman when I interviewed the partners at their "Party Plus"
headquarters in the colorful and charming "Boutique Row" in a New
York suburb. "We arrange all types of parties, both at homes and
clubs, and we sell personalized party supplies—napkins, center-
pieces, decorations, invitations, stationery, or whatever a hostess
wants. And all our parties are highly individualized, according to the
client's taste.

"We charge a flat fee for our work and we're able to supply every
service people want, be it a tent, catering, flowers, or entertainment,"
put in Cynthia Krasny. "We book parties several weeks to several
months in advance. When clients come on their initial visit to plan a
party they pay us a retainer. From there on in we do as little or as much
as the hostess wants."

Cynthia and Bernice started their business several years ago when
they put their creative heads together and decided to turn their party
prowess into professional work. "From a business point of view we

had a good combined background," Cynthia pointed out. "I was a merchandising major with training and experience in selling. Bernice was an art major with a thorough artistic bent. Both of us had a penchant for making our own parties outstanding and interesting, so when we sensed a need for a party coordinating business in our area (where we were well known for our community activities) we said, 'This is it.' "

"From the first we have made it our practice to do everything in a very personal way," stressed Bernice, "and, as one person has told another about our parties, we have grown. We work hard to do things in a new vein and come up with interesting themes. For example, for one home party, we developed a medieval theme, including a tent with banners, troubadours, and a jousting contest on the lawn."

"Despite our success, I do want to say that party coordinating involves lots of pressures and responsibilities," warned Cynthia, "and certainly a major problem is that you must depend on so many other people to carry out your work. You run into shipping difficulties and other situations completely beyond your control.

"On one occasion we ordered 500 invitations for a corporation Christmas party from one of our suppliers. And you'll never believe what happened. First, the invitations were made up incorrectly at the plant. Next they were lost in delivery. When they were redone, arrangements were made to ship them to us by bus. But the bus was delayed by an ice storm and on top of that, the person responsible for delivering them to the bus came down with the flu. Finally we received the order. But we lived through some anxious moments."

When you're interested in being a party decorator or coordinator, the two women emphasized, you need creativity, an artistic flair, a constant flow of new ideas, a contemporary approach, business sense, leadership, an ability to relate to others, a talent for putting people's money where it counts the most, and all the working experience you can obtain selling and working in the display department of a store.

But when you have all this going for you, this business is a good one, both partners observed in conclusion, and one of the greatest rewards you'll receive will be letters from satisifed clients.

MEMO 95:

IT MAKES BOTH SENSE—AND CENTS—TO CAST YOUR LOT WITH
THE WORKERS INSTEAD OF THE DABBLERS.

Josephine Lo Re:
"DRIVING INSTRUCTION *is a satisfying business.*

"It's definitely true that there's always a right job for a woman *if* she really looks for it," agreed Josephine Lo Re, who used this philosophy to start out and later progress to the ownership of her own driving school. "I think that no person should retire, because then you start to die slowly," declared the energetic Ms. Lo Re, who began her school at a time of life when some people think of abandoning instead of starting a business.

Ms. Lo Re is very deeply involved in teaching all types of people to drive. One of her special moments of pride was seeing a great-grandmother get her first driver's license.

"I teach people from 17 to 70," Josephine informed me, "but I give special rates to senior citizens and high school students because I often find that both need an extra measure of encouragement and tender loving care. The special rate to teenagers sometimes motivates them to take the extra lessons they often need in view of the dose of overconfidence that sometimes plagues this age and may lead to fatal accidents. On the other hand, senior citizens on a fixed income—very often widows—discover the difference between independence and dependence if they can learn to drive a car.

"This is a very challenging business," she continued, "and I derive a great deal of pleasure from it. I like it so much that I also run a school with a Spanish-speaking secretary and instructor to make learning to drive more comfortable for speakers of Spanish in our area."

If anyone had told Josephine Lo Re—25 years ago—that she'd be a successful working woman performing a service for others she, by her own admission, would have been the first to doubt it.

"Originally, I was a housewife and mother," she reminisced, "and I chose to stay at home with my children. When they were 5 and 11, however, I contracted tuberculosis and had to be confined to a sanitarium for two years. After I came home, I had a relapse and had to be confined again. Although I was finally well physically, the illness and separation from my family had taken its toll psychologically. I couldn't seem to find my place, so my doctor recommended that I get a small job to give me some purpose and framework for my days without demanding too much from me."

Josephine Lo Re wondered what kind of job could help her adjust to the world again and still not be a strain. But true to her feeling that there's always a job when you really look for it, she found a part-time spot as cashier in a theater.

"I was right that this job would provide me with a chance to meet and talk with people and help me find myself," she explained. "But after it yielded those goals, it wasn't satisfying enough. My son was a driving instructor by then." He was so interested in his work that I decided to study and take the necessary written, psychological, reflex, and road tests so I could get my license and become an instructor."

For a while Josephine worked part-time in the driving school. Later she was made office and school manager. Her job involved recruiting students, arranging classes, engaging instructors, and handling the payroll and bookkeeping.

"Over a period of years I began to think of opening a school of my own where I could apply my own ideas," she said. "The schools I now have are the results."

"A driving school must meet state requirements for licensing," she concluded. "The operator must be a driving instructor in order to apply for the license.

"I find the work is highly enjoyable, and one of the constant highlights is seeing the smile on people's faces once they have their license."

MEMO 96:

> SAVE HOURS EVERY YEAR BY ASKING YOURSELF BEFORE YOU
> DO SOMETHING WHETHER IT IS REALLY NECESSARY OR

WHETHER YOU COULD DEVOTE YOUR TIME TO SOMETHING
MORE PRODUCTIVE.

Pat Palmer:
"I don't think there are many opportunities that a woman can't have if she really works and tries.

"Just doing one thing after another is what keeps a woman going and gives her good opportunities," declared Pat Palmer, owner of a Manhattan REAL ESTATE corporation.

With this as the premise that keeps her moving, Pat finds apartments for celebrities and sells townhouses and finds and rents commercial space in them for business people with special needs and tastes. She has served such clients as Elizabeth Taylor, Marlene Dietrich, Sophia Loren, Rock Hudson, Frank Sinatra, Hermione Gingold, Paul Newman, Joanne Woodward, and Johnny Carson.

In between business commitments she studies singing seriously and performs fairly regularly with Manhattan's Amato Opera Company. In the time left over she swims, rides a bike, paints in oils, keeps up with her reading, and runs an apartment in the city and a house in the country. Her latest venture is a cosmetics business with her brother.

"I originally wanted to be a lyric soprano," Pat informed me, "so I came to New York to study voice. I took a job in a real estate office to pay for my lessons. But my employer died and his family closed the office. I decided to give up working to devote full time to my music," she went on, "but my mother became very ill and I was forced to return to work."

As Pat analyzed her job potential, she realized the only thing she knew was a little bit about real estate. "So, with the confidence of youth, I cast my lot in that direction and began my own business," she smiled.

To get started, Pat went out and searched for apartment listings for the clients she was sure she would get. When she saw some spacious empty rooms in an attractive old brownstone, she knocked on the door of the building and suggested to the owner that she rent them for an office.

The owner turned out to be Countess Cassini, mother of designer Oleg Cassini. After exclaiming, "You're only a child," the countess took a liking to Pat, agreed to rent her the rooms, and even gave her a helping hand by listing with her an empty apartment that had once been occupied by actress Gene Tierney. "Food store heir Huntington Hartford came to see the apartment," she revealed, "and that gave me my start with celebrities.

"In order to launch the business, I advertised, stayed in the office till midnight whenever necessary, and obtained a do-it-yourself education in real estate by reading and studying in the public library.

"That was in the past, however; today women interested in real estate careers must begin by taking courses and working as apprentices in offices. The best way to start off on the right foot," Pat continued, "Is to go to your local real estate board and find out the exact requirements in the area where you live. Usually, a local broker can get you a temporary saleswomen's license when you're ready. Later you can take an exam for the permanent license. After you accumulate enough experience and background, you can apply for a broker's license.

"From there progress is up to you," Pat Palmer said, as we parted, "but as I stressed when we started to talk, there's no limit to where you can go.

"And I say this because of my own experience and my very strong conviction that there aren't many job opportunities a woman can't strive for and have—if she analyzes her potential and, then, gets out there and tries!"

MEMO 97:

STAND UP FOR YOUR IDEAS, PROMOTE WHAT YOU KNOW IS GOOD, AND FACE AND SOLVE YOUR PROBLEMS AS THEY ARISE.

Helen Areinoff and Norma Cybul:
"There's always a right time for someone to start a new career."

Two women who said, "This is where we're *at*—we'll begin and push right through," are Helen Areinoff and Norma Cybul, who run a service as HOME LIQUIDATORS. Their firm, Lady Liquidators, disposes of property in apartments and homes when people move to smaller quarters or elsewhere in the country.

"We sell the contents of a large house, small house, or even just one room and take a commission," explained Helen. "We differ from estate sellers in that we handle the possessions of living people rather than the contents of a house that has passed on to heirs."

"Everything is sold, including toothpicks, old shoes, and door-knobs," added Norma, "but the real advantage of our service is that most people have things that are worth more than they think, and because we know the value we are able to get more money for them."

"When someone wants us for a house sale," Helen said, "we make an appointment to look over the contents and find out what the people living there want to take with them and what they want to sell. The sellers usually sleep on their determination and then decide to make changes. When everything is finally decided, we list the items, and set a date for the sale and advertise it in the local papers. A week before the date we tag everything in the house that's being sold. Besides our mailing list that goes to antique dealers and house sale followers, we have a list of people who ask us to keep our eyes open for certain things—say, a 9 × 12 green rug."

On the day of the sale Helen and Norma arrive at dawn with a staff, if needed, and take over the whole hosue. The seller need not be present, though the partners prefer some member of the family to be at the cash box. Purchasers are responsible for removals. Helen and Norma can provide names of persons with available trucks.

"The idea for this business began after I had a tag sale in my own home," revealed Helen. "I was suddenly confronted with the problem of what to do with all my things. There's a tremendous trauma in parting with items that you've accumulated. I found it much easier to hire someone to clear out my house."

After moving to another state, Helen met Norma. The two decided a house liquidation service would be a good idea for them.

"We add up to another case of two women with backgrounds that go well together," said Norma. "I know antiques and appraising, and Helen has a background of teaching, real estate, and managing a shop."

Once the women were ready to start they obtained their first job through someone who heard about them from a friend. Today they get much of their business from referrals.

Regardless of whether times are good or bad, the partners feel you can't hold back and not start something new. You must realize that if you sit around and wait for the right time, it will never come. You must put your fear behind you and try to make things happen.

The important thing is to meet other people who are doing what they like, and then adapt yourself to something *you* would like!

MEMO 98:

    SPARKLE WITH LIFE AND BEGIN PRODUCING AS YOU'VE NEVER PRODUCED BEFORE.

Lois Lindauer:

"I founded my DIET WORKSHOP *business on a personal loss—one third of the weight I had carried throughout my adult life.*

"I always wanted to achieve," confided weight control specialist Lois Lindauer, national director of The Diet Workshop, the second largest franchised weight control organization in the country. "So after my graduation from college I set out to become chairman of the board of some company. But it took me only a month to discover that anyone who was 21, fat, and female need not apply for the top spot."

A crash course in Speedwriting led Lois to a position as a secretary-copywriter for a Boston advertising agency, until she switched to homebound ventures after marrying and having two daughters.

"At home I poured my energy into manufacturing wall plaques and wall arrangements," she told me. "I never admitted, even to myself, that my success was based on the fact that my business did not require me to be personally attractive. I could hide my fat in unattractive working clothes because I thought it made sense to wear a pair of slacks held together at the waist by a large safety pin and topped by one of my husband's old shirts. After all, I needed to be free of worrying about my clothes, didn't I?"

Finally, Lois was forced into the decision to lose weight when some of her friends steered her to one of the first weight control groups. Despite her doubts, she agreed to give the program a one-week try. It succeeded, and she continued until she reached her goal of trimming off 42 pounds.

Once she mastered the intricacies of the nutrition involved, Lois became fascinated with the mechanics of the group technique. She grew interested in starting a weight control group of her own that would take into consideration ways to assist members—emotionally and mentally—as they set about reducing.

With that as her goal, she began The Diet Workshop in Boston in the living room of a friend—Edith Berman—who had 75 pounds to lose. Today Edith is the organization's national director of research and development.

With the business successfully launched, the search for better group weight control led Lois to the office of Morton B. Glenn, M.D., one of the country's leading obesity and nutrition experts—a move designed to ensure continued growth through scientific backing for the advice dispensed to members. Dr. Glenn became the workshop's advisor and overseer of the diet and group program.

The second city to offer classes was Springfield, Massachusetts. Within a year the combined Boston-Springfield operation had burst its seams and war far too large for one woman to handle. "I decided that franchising would solve many of my problems," Lois informed me. "It would reach more people, allow me to expand without straining my personal life, and—last but not least—permit me to become the executive I'd always dreamed of being. Under the franchise arrangement we train new area directors in intensive one-week sessions in the Boston headquarters."

As an executive, Lois believes that when you start a business you need to inject yourself heavily with care and concern for all the details and all the people involved in it. "Personal interest is terribly important," she emphasized, "so I am concerned about each and every workshop member—and about each and every franchisee. I keep in touch with all the area directors in the field and visit and observe in each area at least once a year."

One of the innovations Lois has brought to The Diet Workshop is the addition of behavior modification to the existing diet and nutrition programs.

"It breaks down eating habits into six simple steps and gives dieters specific instructions that lead to changing poor eating routines to patterns that will make lifelong maintenance easier," she stressed. "I've also pioneered day-long consciousness-raising sessions on the subject of weight control. This helps large audiences focus on the many factors interwoven in the problem of obesity.

"I'm a perfectionist and hard worker by nature," Lois admitted, "and I believe I've found my natural niche with a thriving business that's helping people."

MEMO 99:

> IT'S GOOD FOR ANY WOMAN'S EGO TO PICTURE HERSELF AS THE SUPERVISOR OF A SUCCESSFUL BUSINESS. BUT BEFORE YOU CAN EVEN THINK OF BEING HEAD OF YOUR OWN ENTERPRISE YOU SHOULD KNOW HOW TO DO EVERYTHING IN IT SHOULD THE NEED ARISE.

Helga Volpe and Wini Atkinson:
"We started by dressing up hot dogs to make them more than just hot dogs."

In a stroke of inspired originality, Helga Volpe and Wini Atkinson began what they call WILD WIENERS CATERING—a service in which they take glamorized hot dog carts with different types of plain and fancy hot dogs and sauces to private and commercial parties and functions.

"Our glamorization is in the sauces," stated Helga. "In addition to the usual ones, we have Italian, Indian curry, Hawaiian, chili, creole, Armenian, and other special sauces. We also make a variety of mustards and various interesting types of bread."

"The carts which we transport to parties in our van are basically the same design as those used by hot dog vendors," put in Wini, "but we've customized and glamorized them. One has an orange and white striped side and a matching umbrella. The 'vendor' who staffs the cart also wears orange and white when not dressed in a special costume."

Typical affairs Ms. Volpe and Ms. Atkinson handle are after-football get-togethers, summer pool parties, home movie showings, sweet sixteen parties, and—naturally—cocktail parties.

"From the start we provided whatever a hostess wanted, such as a cheese board and exotic hors d'oeuvre, beer and pretzels, to champagne and caviar," Wini said. "But now we have expanded our service, so, besides hot dogs, we offer knockwurst, bauernwurst, weisswurst, and a six-foot crowd-pleaser hero. We have carts for serving kabobs, hot hero sandwiches, and Chinese food. When dessert is desired, we supply a Continental pastry and specialty coffee cart or an ice cream sundae cart with fixings for people to make their own."

"For further expansion we started an open-air restaurant in an alley in New York's Greenwich Village in 1975," added Helga.

These two outstandingly successful enterprising women met through a car pool for their children. They wanted to do something outside the home. Helga had been in advertising and Wini in nursing.

Helga was once a guest at a party at a very expensive home in which sophisticated people were entranced by a hot dog cart the hostess had obtained from New York; she told Wini about it. "We felt," explained Wini, "that in these high-cost times a hot dog service would enable a hostess to give different parties that people would talk about without going broke in the process. We thought it was time for a change from the usual turkey, ham, and Swedish meat balls.''

To get started the women talked to hot dog vendors, lined up suppliers, and took courses in New York and Long Island from culinary experts. ''We actually worked with a vendor in New York for a day,'' Helga recalled. ''We went with him to pick up his cart, and he showed us how to place the orders and prepare the boiling water. At his location, we observed him serve people and took lessons from him the rest of the day.''

''When we got our first cart we had hot dog parties in Helga's yard to experiment with it,'' Wini added. ''We spent time with the cart at the beach and experimented some more by sending all the kids in the neighborhood hot dogs with different kinds of sauces. At a hot-dog-sauce tasting party we presented our guests with cards on which we asked them to write their critiques. If changes were in order we made them.''

''When we felt ready to start we worked out of our homes for a while to test the market before we invested in our present commercial location,'' Helga commented.

''Before you bite off more than you can chew,'' she continued, ''it's essential to spend sufficient time thinking about what you're best suited for and feel sure you'll enjoy.''

''If you're married, it's also important to get genuine encouragement from your husband,'' Wini added. ''And a partnership is good for women who want to start a business, because they can divide the work according to each one's competence and interest. Partners, however, need the same business philosophy and a similar sense of priorities. There have been disasters in partnerships, but ours works because we're both very much into it, and our friendship also means a great deal to us.''

''A lot of women have ideas about going into a business as long as it's glamorous,'' pointed out Helga. ''But when they think in these terms they're not realistic and fully aware of how much hard work is involved. Wini and I are workhorses—and our work *is* hard!''

If you're willing to work very hard in the job that is right for you, both Wini and Helga are quick to agree on the wisest advice in the world. When you have an idea, they urge, *try*—and resolve to keep plugging. It's sad to sit back and say someday, "I should have," instead of "I *did*!"

MEMO 100:

FOR THE REST OF YOUR LIFE—AND AT ANY AGE—HAVE ENOUGH HOPE IN THE FUTURE TO KNOW THE INTEREST-FILLED YEARS AHEAD CAN BE YOUR *BEST* YEARS YET!

Chapter 10

Go-And-Do!
100+
Career Resources
and Referrals

This chapter is for reference—rather than rapid consumption—so if you're in a hurry, go on to the "Afterthoughts." Then return here as a directory to the further help you'll need once you decide what you'd like to do in your first or second career.

You'll find that letters and queries to the resources and referrals listed here (along with visits to your library to study suggested publications) will bring you specific and detailed information and assist you in getting started or progressing in the right job. Some names and addresses will appear more than once, because some resources serve multiple functions.

For easy reference, this directory has been divided into the following nine categories:

1. *Organizations and Institutions That Provide Career Information*
2. *Counseling and Testing Facilities*
3. *Education and Training*
4. *College Credit Examinations and High School Equivalency Tests*
5. *Scholarships and Financial Aid*
6. *Employment Services and Job-Finding Guidance*

7. Women's Groups and Organizations.
8. Women's Rights and Legal Assistance
9. Publications, Pamphlets, Newsletters, and Bulletins

I. ORGANIZATIONS AND INSTITUTIONS THAT PROVIDE CAREER INFORMATION

Accounting
Accounting Careers Council
P.O. Box 650
Radio City Station
New York, N.Y. 10019

American Institute of Certified Public Accountants
666 Fifth Ave.
New York, N.Y. 10019

American Society of Women Accountants
327 S. La Salle St.
Chicago, Ill. 60604

Actuary
Casualty Actuarial Society
200 E. 42nd St.
New York, N.Y. 10017

Society of Actuaries
208 S. LaSalle St.
Chicago, Ill. 60604

Advertising
Advertising Education Publications
3429 55th St.
Lubbock, Tex. 79413

American Advertising Federation
1225 Connecticut Ave., NW
Washington, D.C. 20036

American Association of Advertising Agencies
200 Park Ave.
New York, N.Y. 10017

Aeronautics
American Institute of Aeronautics and Astronautics, Inc.
1290 Ave. of the Americas
New York, N.Y. 10019

National Aeronautics and Space Administration
Washington, D.C. 20546

Agriculture
American Society of Agronomy
677 S. Segoe Rd.
Madison, Wisc. 53711

U.S. Dept. of Agriculture
Office of Personnel
Washington, D.C. 20250

Anthropology
American Anthropological Association
1703 New Hampshire Ave., NW
Washington, D.C. 20009

Architecture
Alliance of Women in Architecture
18 E. 13th St.
New York, N.Y. 10003

American Institute of Architects
1735 New York Ave., NW
Washington, D.C. 20006

Association of Women in Architecture
P.O. Box 1
Dayton, Mo. 63105

Boston Architecture Center
320 Newbury St.
Boston, Mass. 02115

Art
College Art Association of America
Status of Women Committee
16 E. 52nd St.
New York, N.Y. 10022

National Art Education Association
1201 16th St., NW
Washington, D.C. 20034

National Association of Schools of Art
1 Dupont Circle, NW
Washington, D.C. 20036

Women's Caucus For Art
c/o Dr. Mary Garrard
7010 Aronow Drive
Falls Church, Va. 22042

Astronomy
American Astronomical Society
211 Fitz Randolph Rd.
Princeton, N.J. 08540

Audiology
American Speech and Hearing Association
9030 Old Georgetown Rd.
Washington, D.C. 20014

Banking
American Bankers Association
Personnel Administration and Management Development Committee
1120 Connecticut Ave., NW
Washington, D.C. 20036

National Association of Bank Women
1730 Pennsylvania Ave., NW
Washington, D.C. 20006

Beauty Culture
National Beauty Career Center
3839 White Plains Rd.
Bronx, N.Y. 10467

Civil Service
U.S. Civil Service Commission
Room 1416 A
1900 E St., NW
Washington, D.C. 20415

Community Action
Community Action Program
Office of Economic Opportunity
1200 19th St., NW
Washington, D.C. 20506

National Association for Community Development
Room 106
1424 16th St., NW
Washington, D.C. 20036

Computer Programming
American Federation of Information Processing Societies
210 Summit Ave.
Montvale, N.J. 07645

Association for Computing Machinery
1133 Ave. of the Americas
New York, N.Y. 10036

Association of Data Processing Service Organizations, Inc.
551 Fifth Ave.
New York, N.Y. 10017

Data Processing Management Association
505 Busse Highway
Park Ridge, Ill. 60068

Conservation
American Public Works Association
1313 E. 60th St.
Chicago, Ill. 60637

Conservation Foundation
1717 Massachusetts Ave., NW
Washington, D.C. 20036

Ecological Society of America
c/o Dr. W. C. Ashby
Dept. of Botany
Southern Illinois University
Carbondale, Ill. 62901

Environmental Protection Agency
401 M St., SW
Washington, D.C. 20460

National Audubon Society
950 Third Ave.
New York, N.Y. 10022

National Parks & Conservation Association
1701 18th St., NW
Washington, D.C. 20009

National Resources Council
1025 Connecticut Ave., NW
Washington, D.C. 20036

National Wildlife Federation
8925 Leesburg Pike
Vienna, Va. 22180

Nature Conservancy
1800 North Kent St.
Arlington, Va. 22209

Scientists' Institute for Public Information
30 E. 68th St.
New York, N.Y. 10021

Soil Conservation Society of America
7517 Northeast Ankeny Rd.
Ankeny, Iowa 50021

Wilderness Society
1901 Pennsylvania Ave., NW
Washington, D.C. 20006

Wildlife Society
2900 Wisconsin Ave., NW
Washington, D.C. 20016

Construction
National Association of Women in Construction
2800 W. Lancaster Ave.
Fort Worth, Tex. 76107

Counseling and Guidance
American Association for Mental Health Counselors
P.O. Box 5327
Baltimore, Md. 21209

American Association of Marriage and Family Counselors
6211 W. Northwest Highway
Dallas, Tex. 75225

American Rehabilitation Counseling Association
1607 New Hampshire Ave., NW
Washington, D.C. 20009

American School Counselors Association
1607 New Hampshire Ave., NW
Washington, D.C. 20009

National Association for Mental Health
1800 N. Kent St.—Rosslyn Station
Arlington, Va. 22209

National Rehabilitation Counseling Association
1522 K St., NW
Washington, D.C. 20005

National Vocational Guidance Association
1607 New Hampshire Ave., NW
Washington, D.C. 20009

Crafts
American Crafts Council
44 W. 53rd St.
New York, N.Y. 10019

Day Care
Day Care and Child Development Council of America, Inc.
1401 K St., NW
Washington, D.C. 20005

Dentistry
American Dental Assistants Association
211 E. Chicago Ave.
Chicago, Ill. 60611

American Dental Association
211 East Chicago Ave.
Chicago, Ill. 60611

American Dental Hygienists Association
211 East Chicago Ave.
Chicago, Ill. 60611

Association of American Women Dentists
435 N. Michigan Ave.
Chicago, Ill. 60611

National Dental Association
P.O. Box 197
Charlottesville, Va. 22902

Dietetics
American Dietetic Association
620 North Michigan Ave.
Chicago, Ill. 60611

Direct Selling
Direct Selling Association
1730 M St., NW
Suite 610
Washington, D.C. 20036

Economics
American Economic Association
Status of Women Committee
Southern Methodist University
Dept. of Economics
Dallas, Tex. 75275

Education
American Association of School Administrators
1801 N. Moore St.
Arlington, Va. 22201

American Association of University Professors
1 Dupont Circle, NW
Washington, D.C. 20036

American Education Research Association
1126 16th St., NW
Washington, D.C. 20036

American Federation of Teachers
11 Dupont Circle, NW
Washington, D.C. 20036

American Studies Association
4025 Chesnut St.
University of Pennsylvania
Philadelphia, Pa. 19174

Association for Asian Studies
1 Lane Hall
University of Michigan
Ann Arbor, Mich. 48104

Latin American Studies Association
c/o Dr. Evelyn P. Stevens
14609 S. Woodland Rd.
Shaker Heights, Ohio 44120

National Association for Women Deans, Administrators, and Counselors
1028 Connecticut Ave., NW
Washington, D.C. 20036

National Center for Information on Careers in Education
1607 New Hampshire Ave., NW
Washington, D.C. 20009

National Council of Administrative Women in Education
1815 Fort Meyer Drive
N. Arlington, Va. 22209

National Education Association
1201 16th St., NW
Washington, D.C. 20036

Women Educators
c/o Ms. Carston McKay
Madison Area Technical College
211 N. Carroll St.
Madison, Wisc. 53703

Electronics
Electronic Industry Association
2110 Eye St., NW
Washington, D.C. 20006

National Electronic, Inc.
1309 W. Market St.
Indianpolis, Ind. 46222

Embroidery and Stitchery
Embroiderers' Guild of America, Inc.
120 E. 56th St.
New York, N.Y. 10022

Engineering
American Institute of Chemical Engineers
345 E. 47th St.
New York, N.Y. 10017

American Institute of Industrial Engineers, Inc.
345 E. 47th St.
New York, N.Y. 10017

Engineers' Council for Professional Development
345 East 47th St.
New York, N.Y. 10017

National Society of Professional Engineers
2029 K St., NW
Washington, D.C. 20006

Society of Women Engineers
345 E. 47th St.
New York, N.Y. 10017

Executive Housekeeping
National Executive Housekeeping Association
Business and Professional Building
Second Ave.
Gallipolis, Ohio 45631

Fashion Design
Fashion Institute of Technology
227 W. 27th St.
New York, N.Y. 10001

Food Service
Council on Hotel, Restaurant, and Institutional Education
Suite 534
1522 K St., NW
Washington, D.C. 20005

Culinary Institute of America
Hyde Park, N.Y. 12538

National Association of Food Chains Educational Council
1725 Eye St., NW
Washington, D.C. 20006

National Restaurant Association
1 IBM Plaza
Suite 2600
Chicago, Ill. 60611

Food Technology
Institute of Food Technologists
Suite 2120
221 N. LaSalle St.
Chicago, Ill. 60601

Foreign Service
Foreign Service Recruitment
Board of Examiners
State Department
Washington, D.C. 20520

Forestry
American Forestry Association
1319 18th St., NW
Washington, D.C. 20036

Society of American Foresters
1010 16th St., NW
Washington, D.C. 20036

U.S. Forest Service
U.S. Department of Agriculture
Washington, D.C. 20250

Fund Raising
American Association of Fund-Raising Counsel, Inc.
500 Fifth Ave.
New York, N.Y. 10036

Geography
Association of American Geographers
1710 16th St., NW
Washington, D.C. 20009

Geology and Geophysics
American Geological Institute
5205 Leesburg Pike
Falls Church, Va. 22041

American Geophysical Union
1707 L St., NW
Washington, D.C. 20036

Society of Exploration Geophysicists
P.O. Box 3098
Tulsa, Okla. 74101

Gift Shop
National Gift and Art Association
220 Fifth Ave.
New York, N.Y. 10010

History
American Historical Association
400 A St., SE
Washington, D.C. 20003

Society of American Archivists
Status of Women Committee
University Libraries
University of Minnesota
Minneapolis, Minn. 55455

Home Economics
American Home Economics Association
2010 Massachusetts Ave., NW
Washington, D.C. 20036

Homemaking
National Council for Homemaker-Home Health Aide Services
1740 Broadway
New York, N.Y. 10019

Horticulture
American Orchid Society
Botanical Museum of Harvard University
Cambridge, Mass. 02138

Botanical Society of America
Department of Botany
Indiana University
Bloomingdale, Ind. 47401

Horticultural Society of New York
128 W. 58th St.
New York, N.Y. 10019

Hospitality
American Hotel and Motel Association
888 Seventh Ave.
New York, N.Y. 10019

Industrial Design
Industrial Designers Society of America
60 W. 55th St.
New York, N.Y. 10019

Interior Design
American Institute of Interior Designers
730 Fifth Ave.
New York, N.Y. 10019

National Society of Interior Designers
315 E. 62nd St.
New York, N.Y. 10021

Landscape Architecture
American Society of Landscape Architects
1750 Old Meadow Road
McLean, Va. 22101

Boston Architecture Center
320 Newbury St.
Boston, Mass. 02115

Languages
Linguistic Society of America
1611 N. Kent St.
Arlington, Va. 22209

Modern Language Association
Status of Women Commission
62 Fifth Ave.
New York, N.Y. 10011

Law
American Bar Association
1155 E. 60th St.
Chicago, Ill. 60637

American Civil Liberties Union
22 E. 40th St.
New York, N.Y. 10016

Association of American Law Schools
Suite 370
1 Dupont Circle, NW
Washington, D.C. 20036

Institute of Paralegal Training
401 Walnut St.
Philadelphia, Pa. 19106

National Association of Women Lawyers
American Bar Center
1155 E. 60th St.
Chicago, Ill. 60637

National Lawyers Guild
23 Cornelia St.
New York, N.Y. 10014

Librarianship
American Library Association
50 E. Huron St.
Chicago, Ill. 60611

Special Libraries Association
235 Park Ave. South
New York, N.Y. 10003

Life Insurance
American College
270 Bryn Mawr Ave.
Bryn Mawr, Pa. 19010

Association for Advanced Life Underwriting
1922 F St., NW
Washington, D.C. 20006

Institute of Life Insurance
277 Park Ave.
New York, N.Y. 10017

Life Insurance Marketing and Research Association
170 Sigourney St.
Hartford, Conn. 06105

Life Office Management Association
100 Park Ave.
New York, N.Y. 10017

Life Underwriter Training Council
1922 F St., NW
Washington, D.C. 20006

Million Dollar Round Table
36 S. Wabash Ave.
Chicago, Ill. 60603

National Association of Insurance Women
1847 E. 15th St.
Tulsa, Okla. 74104

Management
Academy of Management
Status of Women Committee
2700 Bay Area Blvd.
Houston, Tex. 77058

American Management Association
135 W. 50th St.
New York, N.Y. 10015

National Association for Female Executives
176 Madison Ave.
New York, N.Y. 10017

Market Research
American Marketing Association New York Chapter, Inc.
420 Lexington Ave.
Suite 1735
New York, N.Y. 10017

Mathematics
American Mathematical Society
P.O. Box 6248
Providence, R.I. 02904

Association for Women in Mathematics
c/o Dr. Lenore Blum
Dept. of Mathematics
Mills College
Oakland, Cal. 94613

Medicine and Health

(Hospital Administration)
American College of Hospital Administrators
American Hospital Association
840 N. Lake Shore Drive
Chicago, Ill. 60611

(Immunology)
American Association of Immunologists
9650 Rockville Pike
Bethesda, Md. 20014

(Medical Assistants)
American Association of Medical Assistants
1 E. Wacker Drive
Chicago, Ill. 60601

(Medical Record Librarian)
American Medical Record Association
875 North Michigan Ave.
Suite 1850
Chicago, Ill. 60611

(Medical Technologist and Laboratory Technician)
American Society for Medical Technology
Suite 200
5555 West Loop South
Bellaire, Tex. 77401

American Society of Radiologic Technologists
Suite 620
645 North Michigan Ave.
Chicago, Ill. 60611

Health Resources Administration
Bureau of Health Resources Development
9000 Rockville Pike
Bethesda, Md. 20014

National Committee for Careers in the Medical Laboratory
9650 Rockville Pike
Bethesda, Md. 20014

National Health Council
1740 Broadway
New York, N.Y. 10019

Registry of Medical Technologists
American Society of Clinical Pathologists
P.O. Box 4827
Chicago, Ill. 60680

(Nursing)
American Nurses Association
2420 Pershing Road
Kansas City, Mo. 64108

National Federation of Licensed Practical Nurses, Inc.
250 W. 57th St.
New York, N.Y. 10019

National League for Nursing, Inc.
10 Columbus Circle
New York, N.Y. 10019

(Nurse Practitioner)
Health Resources Administration
Bureau of Health Resources Development
9000 Rockville Pike
Bethseda, Md. 20014

(Physician)
American Medical Association
Council on Medical Education
535 N. Dearborn St.
Chicago, Ill. 60610

American Medical Women's Association
1740 Broadway
New York, N.Y. 10013

Association of American Medical Colleges
Suite 200
1 Dupont Circle, NW
Washington, D.C. 20036

(Physician's Assistant)
Association of American Medical Colleges
Suite 200
1 Dupont Circle, NW
Washington, D.C. 20036

Health Resources Administration
Bureau of Health Resources Development
9000 Rockville Pike
Bethseda, Md. 20014

(Physiology)
American Physiological Society
9650 Rockville Pike
Bethesda, Md. 20014

(Public Health)
American Public Health Association, Inc.
1015 18th St., NW
Washington, D.C. 20036

Mental Health
American Psychiatric Association
1700 18th St., NW
Washington, D.C. 20009

American Psychological Association
1200 17th St., NW
Washington, D.C. 20036

Association for Women in Psychology
c/o Dr. Leigh Marlowe
Manhattan Community College
180 West End Ave.
New York, N.Y. 10023

National Association for Mental Health
1800 N. Kent St.
Rosslyn Station
Arlington, Va. 22209

National Institute of Mental Health
5600 Fishers Lane
Rockville, Md. 20852

Meteorology
American Meteorological Society
45 Beacon St.
Boston, Mass. 02108

Museum Work
American Association of Museums
2233 Wisconsin Ave., NW
Washington, D.C. 20007

Music
American Guild of Musical Artists
1841 Broadway
New York, N.Y. 10023

College Music Society
Status of Women Committee
Dept. of Music
State University of New York
Binghamton, N.Y. 13901

Music Educators National Conference
1201 16th St., NW
Washington, D.C. 20036

Occupational Therapy
American Occupational Therapy Association, Inc.
Suite 200
6000 Executive Boulevard
Rockville, Md. 20852

Oceanography
American Society for Oceanography
Marine Technology Society
1730 M St., NW
Washington, D.C. 20036

International Oceanographic Foundation
1 Rickenbacker Causeway
Virginia Key
Miami, Fla. 33149

National Oceanic and Atmospheric Administration
Office of Public Affairs
6001 Executive Blvd.
Rockville, Md. 20852

Optometry
American Optometric Association
7000 Chippewa St.
St. Louis, Mo. 63119

Personnel Work
American Personnel and Guidance Association
1600 New Hampshire Ave., NW
Washington, D.C. 20009

American Society for Personnel Administration
19 Church St.
Berea, Ohio 44017

International Association of Personnel Women
358 Fifth Ave.
New York, N.Y. 10001

National Association of Student Personnel Administrators
c/o Ms. E. Susan Petering
Wheaton College
Norton, Mass. 02766

Pharmacy
American Association of Colleges of Pharmacy
850 Sligo Ave.
Silver Spring, Md. 20910

American Pharmaceutical Association
2215 Constitution Ave., NW
Washington, D.C. 20037

Philosophy
American Philosophical Association
c/o Ms. Susan Ekstrom
Dept. of Philosophy
Morrill Hall
Michigan State University
East Lansing, Mich. 48824

Photography
Eastman Kodak Co.
Rochester, N.Y. 14650

Professional Photographers of America, Inc.
1090 Executive Way
Oak Leaf Commons
Des Plaines, Ill. 60018

Physical Therapy
American Physical Therapy Association
1156 16th St., NW
Washington, D.C. 20005

Piano Tuning
Piano Technicians Guild
1417 Belmont
Seattle, Wash. 98122

Political Science
American Political Science Association
Status of Women Committee
1527 New Hampshire Ave., NW
Washington, D.C. 20036

Women's Caucus for Political Science
Mt. Vernon College
2100 Foxhall Rd., NW
Washington, D.C. 20007

Public Administration
American Society for Public Administration
Suite 300
1225 Connecticut Ave., NW
Washington, D.C. 20036

Public Relations
Public Relations Society of America
845 Third Ave.
New York, N.Y. 10022

Publishing
American Newspaper Publishers Association Foundation
Box 17407
Dulles International Airport
Washington, D.C. 20041

American Society of Journalists and Authors, Inc.
123 W. 43rd St.
New York, N.Y. 10036

Association of American Publishers, Inc.
1 Park Ave.
New York, N.Y. 10016

Bowker Co.
1180 Ave. of the Americas
New York, N.Y. 10036

International Newspaper Advertising Executives
P.O. Box 147
Danville, Ill. 61832

Magazine Publishers Association
575 Lexington Ave.
New York, N.Y. 10022

National Association of Media Women
c/o Ms. Lois K. Alexander
157 W. 126th St.
New York, N.Y. 10027

National Federation of Press Women
c/o Ms. Jean Wiley Huyler
25246 106th Ave. SE
Kent, Wash. 98388

National Press Club
National Press Building
529 14th St., NW
Room 138D
Washington, D.C. 20004

Society of Technical Writers and Publishers
Suite 421
1010 Vermont Ave., NW
Washington, D.C. 20005

Women in Communications
c/o Ms. Mary Utting
8305A Shoal Creek Blvd.
Austin, Tex. 78558

Radio and Television
American Federation of Television and Radio Artists
1350 Ave. of the Americas
New York, N.Y. 10019

American Women in Radio and Television, Inc.
1321 Connecticut Ave., NW
Washington, D.C. 20036

National Association of Broadcasters
1771 N St., NW
Washington, D.C. 20036

Real Estate
National Association of Real Estate Boards Offices
Department of Education
155 E. Superior St.
Chicago, Ill. 60611

Recreation
American Alliance for Health, Physical Education, and Recreation
1201 16th St., NW
Washington, D.C. 20036

National Therapeutic Recreation Society
National Recreation and Park Association
1601 N. Kent St.
Arlington, Va. 22209

Religion
American Academy of Religion
Women's Caucus
Dept. of Religion
Smith College
Northampton, Mass. 01060

Church Employed Women
Room 1260
475 Riverside Drive
New York, N.Y. 10027

International Association of Women Ministers
1464 W. 101 St.
Cleveland, Ohio 44102

United Presbyterian Church in the USA
Council on Women and the Church
475 Riverside Drive
New York, N.Y. 10027

Science
American Association for the Advancement of Science
Office of Opportunities in Science
1776 Massachusetts Ave., NW
Washington, D.C. 20036

American Chemical Society
1155 16th St., NW
Washington, D.C. 20036

American Institute of Biological Sciences
3900 Wisconsin Ave., NW
Washington, D.C. 20017

American Institute of Chemists
7315 Wisconsin Ave.
Bethesda, Md. 20014

American Institute of Physics
335 E. 45th St.
New York, N.Y. 10017

American Physical Society
c/o Dr. Margaret E. Law
Laboratory of Physics
Harvard University
Cambridge, Mass. 02138

American Society of Biological Chemists
Status of Women Committee
9650 Rockville Pike
Bethesda, Md. 20014

American Society for Cell Biology
c/o Dr. Mary E. Clutter
Dept. of Biology—OML
Yale University
New Haven, Conn. 06520

American Society for Microbiology
Status of Women Committee
1913 Eye St., NW
Washington, D.C. 20006

Association for Women in Science, Inc.
1346 Connecticut Ave., NW
Suite 1122
Washington, D.C. 20036

Biophysical Society
Women's Caucus
c/o Dr. Mary Jacobs McCrea
George Washington University Medical School
Washington, D.C. 20037

Botanical Society of America
Department of Botany
Indiana University
Bloomingdale, Ind. 47401

Social Service and Rehabilitation
Community Service Administration
Social and Rehabilitation Service
U.S. Department of Health, Education, and Welfare
330 C St., SW
Washington, D.C. 20201

National Association of Social Workers, Inc.
Suite 600
1425 H St., NW
Washington, D.C. 20005

Social Studies
National Council for the Social Studies
1515 Wilson Blvd.
Arlington, Va. 22209

Sociology
American Sociological Association
1722 N St., NW
Washington, D.C. 20002

Sociologists for Women in Society
c/o Prof. Arlene Kaplan Daniels
Department of Sociology
Northwestern University
Evanston, Ill. 60201

Speech Pathology
American Speech and Hearing Association
9030 Old Georgetown Road
Washington, D.C. 20014

Statistics
American Statistical Association
806 15th St. NW
Washington, D.C. 20005

Translating
American Translators Association
Box 401
Camden, N.J. 08101

Travel
American Society of Travel Agents
360 Lexington Ave.
New York, N.Y. 10017

Urban Planning
American Institute of Planners
1776 Massachusetts Ave., NW
Washington, D.C. 20036

American Society of Planning Officials
1313 E. 60th St.
Chicago, ill. 60657

Veterinary Medicine
American Veterinary Medical Association
600 S. Michigan Ave.
Chicago, Ill. 60605

Weather Service
National Weather Service
c/o National Oceanic and Atmosphere Administration
U.S. Dept. of Commerce
Silver Spring, Md. 20910

II. COUNSELING AND TESTING FACILITIES

The following organizations or groups offer help in defining goals, analyzing personal priorities, and exploring job opportunities. Some are non-profit, and some charge fees. Some counsel privately; others work with groups.

The benefits from counseling and testing vary with each individual. A great deal depends upon the caliber of the counseling and the rapport established between you and the counselor. But many people have been helped, so if you are floundering you may want to think about it. Letters to any of the following addresses will supply you with a broader view of what's available.

(In addition to the places listed below, many state employment agencies and service organizations such as the YWCA and YWHA provide counseling. Check your area to find out what is available.)

American Personnel and Guidance Association
1605 New Hampshire Ave., NW
Washington, D.C. 20009

Association of Feminist Consultants
4 Canoe Brook Drive
Princeton Junction, N.J. 08550

Business and Professional Women's Foundation
2012 Massachusetts Ave., NW
Washington, D.C. 20036

Career Clinic for Mature Women
628 Nicollet Mall
Room 331
Minneapolis, Minn. 55402

Career Workshops for Women
333 Central Park West
New York, N.Y. 10025

Catalyst
6 E. 82nd St.
New York, N.Y. 10028

Center for New Directions
6950 Hayvenhurst Ave.
Van Nuys, Calif. 91406

Distaffers Research and Counseling Center
4625a 41st St., NW
Washington, D.C. 20016

Effective Feedback, Inc.
840 Brookwood Place
Ann Arbor, Mich. 48104

Individual Development Center
310 15th St. East
Seattle, Wash. 98122

Individual Resources
60 E. 12th St.
New York, N.Y. 10003

Johnson O'Connor Research Foundation and Human Engineering
  Laboratories
11 E. 62nd St.
New York, N.Y. 10021

More for Women
2 Lexington Ave.
New York, N.Y. 10010

New Environments for Women
44 Bertwell Rd.
Lexington, Mass. 02173

Options for Women
8419 Germantown Ave.
Philadelphia, Pa. 19118

Pennsylvania State University
McKeesport Campus
Pittsburgh, Pa. 15132
(Ask about "Life Work Planning")

Wells-Christie Associates
P.O. Box 3392
Beverly Hills, Calif. 90212

Wider Opportunities for Women, Inc. (WOW)
1649 K St., NW
Washington, D.C. 20006

Women and Girls Employment Enabling Services
3485 Poplar Ave.
Suite 1
Memphis, Tenn. 38111

Women's Opportunities Center
c/o Edythe R. Peters
University of California Extension
Irvine, Calif. 92664

III. EDUCATION AND TRAINING

The following resources provide help, encouragement, and information for women who want to improve their education and training through short- or long-term courses, workshops, and seminars.

Adult Education Association
810 18th St., NW
Washington, D.C. 20006

American Association of Community and Junior Colleges
1 Du Pont Circle, NW
Washington, D.C. 20036

American Association for Higher Education
1 Du Pont Circle, NW
Washington, D.C. 20036

American Society for Training and Development
815 15th St., NW
Room 800
Washington, D.C. 20005

AWARE
Association for Women's Active Return to Education
5820 Wilshire Blvd.
Suite 605
Los Angeles, Calif. 90036

Career Horizons for Women
Hofstra University
Hempstead, N.Y. 11050

Michigan State University Evening College
18 Kellogg Center
East Lansing, Mich. 48822

National Home Study Council
1601 18th St., NW
Washington, D.C. 20009

National University Extension Association
Suite 360
1 Du Pont Circle, NW
Washington, D.C. 20036

For an additional view of what's available in the field of adult education and continuing education, send for the following publications or consult them at a library:

Continuing Education Programs and Services for Women
Government Printing Office
Washington, D.C. 20402
Cost: 70¢

The New York Times Guide to Continuing Education in America
Edited by Frances Coombs Thompson
Quadrangle Books
10 E. 53rd St.
New York, N.Y. 10022

Special Degree Programs For Adults Exploring
        Non-Traditional Degree Programs in Higher Education
American College Testing Program
Publications Division
P.O. Box 168
Iowa City, Iowa 52240
Cost: $2

University Without Walls: A First Report
Union For Experimental Colleges and Universities
Antioch College
Yellow Springs, Ohio 45307
Cost: $1.75

Apprenticeship Occupations and Skilled Trades
Better Jobs for Women
1545 Tremont Place
Denver, Colo. 80202
(Provides information on formal apprenticeships in non-traditional jobs)

Human Resource Development Institute of AFL-CIO
815 16th St., NW
Washington, D.C. 20036
(Ask about Apprenticeship Outreach Programs)

U.S. Dept. of Labor
Manpower Administration
Bureau of Apprenticeship and Training
200 Constitution Ave., NW
Washington, D.C. 20210
(Send for *The National Apprenticeship Program, Directory of Apprenticeship Information Centers,* and *Steps to Opening the Skilled Trades to Women*)

Women in Wisconsin Apprenticeships
Dept. of Industry, Labor, and Human Relations
Box 2209
Madison, Wisc. 53702
(Prepares women for jobs in printings, manufacturing, construction, and other trades)

Law School
The Women's Committee
New England School of Law
126 Newbury St.
Boston, Mass. 02115

Leadership and Management Training

A master's degree in business administration (M.B.A.) from Harvard, Columbia, or the Wharton School of Finance at the University of Pennsylvania provides a five-star rating for starting a career in management. Lacking that, there are training courses and seminars offered at different locations that will teach you the principles and basics that can get you started. Here is a sampling:

American Management Association
Personnel Division
135 W. 50th St.
New York, N.Y. 10020

Distaff Group
Executive Enterprises
10 Columbus Circle
New York, N.Y. 10019

Emerging Woman in Management
P.O. Box 333
Chicago, Ill. 60411

Foundation Management Seminars
Business and Professional Women's Foundation
2012 Massachusetts Ave., NW
Washington, D.C. 20036

Graduate Management Program for Women
Pace University
Pace Plaza
New York, N.Y. 10038

Leadership and Training Task Force
c/o Judith Geschwind
2306 Greenery Lane
Silver Spring, Md. 20906

Management for Today's Woman Program
Katherine Gibbs School
200 Park Ave.
New York, N.Y. 10017

Women in Management
Elizabeth T. Lyons
1050 George St.
New Brunswick, N.J. 08701

Women's Training and Resources Corp.
Congress Bldg.
142 High St.
Suite 512
Portland, Maine 04101

IV. COLLEGE CREDIT EXAMINATIONS AND HIGH SCHOOL EQUIVALENCY TESTS

American Council on Education
1 Du Pont Circle, nw
Washington, D.C. 20036
(Send for a listing of centers where you can be tested on life experience that may qualify you to pass a high school equivalency test. Sometimes a small amount of additional study is required to earn a diploma.)

CLEP (College Level Examination Program)
College Entrance Examination Board
Box 592
Princeton, N.J. 08540
(This program allows you to get credit by examination for what you have learned outside of the classroom. Exams are given at various intervals at over 300 colleges in five general and 29 specific subjects.)

CPEP (College Proficiency Examinations)
New York State Education Department
99 Washington Ave.
Albany, N.Y. 12210
(This program permits women to obtain credit for what they have learned outside the classroom. Examinations may be applied toward degrees awarded under the New York State Regents External Degree Program. This program is not limited to residents of New York.)

V. SCHOLARSHIPS AND FINANCIAL AID

A smattering of scholarships to whet your interest follows. For further information on what's available consult reference books and pamphlets on scholarship listings in your library.

American Association of University Women
Educational Foundation Programs Office
2401 Virginia Ave., NW
Washington, D.C. 20037
(Since 1888 AAUW has granted fellowships for advanced study without restrictions of age, field, or place of study.)

Business and Professional Women's Foundation
2012 Massachusetts Ave., NW
Washington, D.C. 20036
(Until 1980 this foundation and the Sears, Roebuck Foundation will lend women up to $2,000 a year to attend one of 110 participating graduate schools in business administration.)
Clairol Loving Care Scholarship Program
345 Park Ave.
New York, N.Y. 10022
($50,000 worth of scholarships for college educations are available to women over 35 who wish to enroll in a full- or part-time degree program. The money is split 50 ways among four-year colleges.)

Founders Fund Vocational Aid
Altrusa International
332 S. Michigan Ave.
Chicago, Ill. 60604
(Women who are widowed, disadvantaged, physically handicapped, or the sole support of a family may qualify for financial aid—$50 to $350 per year—for training courses or equipment needed for self-employment or rehabilitation.)

National League for Nursing
10 Columbus Circle
New York, N.Y. 10019
(For a listing of local, state, and national financial aid programs for women desiring training as licensed practical nurses or registered nurses send 50¢ to the above address.)

Women's Resource Center
Scholarship Committee
226 Boswick, NE
Grand Rapids, Mich. 49502
(This center provides scholarships to mature women interested in academic careers on a part-time basis.)

VI. EMPLOYMENT SERVICES AND JOB-FINDING GUIDANCE

The majority of the following places maintain job listings. Those in your area will attempt to match you to the best possible job or help you change careers. Some will place you in full- or part-time jobs at any level (from beginning spots right on up the ladder); others specialize in finding jobs for highly qualified professional and management personnel.

Alumni Advisory Center
541 Madison Ave.
New York, N.Y. 10022
(A career planning organization that provides individual counseling, maintains a job reference library and issues *Job Fact Sheets* at 75¢ each.)

Boston Project for Careers
83 Prospect St.
W. Newton, Mass. 02165
(Assists both management and women in matching people to jobs.)

Distaffers, Inc.
1130 Western Savings Building
Philadelphia, Pa. 19107
(Places professional women in full- or part-time jobs on a short-term
or permanent basis.)

Flexible Careers
Young Women's Christian Association
37 S. Wabash Ave.
Chicago, Ill. 60603
(A registry of part-time or flexi-time jobs.)

Fordyce, Andrews, & Haskett, Inc.
230 Park Ave.
New York, N.Y. 10017
(An executive search firm for women in manufacturing, engineering,
industrial relations, and data processing.)

Individual Resources
Box 5346
Grand Central Station
New York, N.Y. 10017
(When you fill out the information sheet obtainable from this firm
your qualifications are put into a computer. When a job matches your
background, the computerized data bank produces your card.)

Job Search
Women's Resource Center
Young Women's Christian Association
1111 SW 10th St.
Portland, Ore. 97205
(Places women in non-traditional jobs.)

Mainstream Associates
343 Madison Ave.
New York, N.Y. 10017
(Specializing in career changing.)

Management Services
2 W. 45th St.
New York, N.Y. 10022
(Full-time and short-work-week jobs for qualified executive and professional personnel.)

Management Woman, Inc.
Plaza Hotel
Fifth Ave., at 59th St.
New York, N.Y. 10019
(For women prepared to fill high-level, well-paying spots.)

McKay and Associates
406 Westwood Drive
Chapel Hill, N.C. 27514
(Locates top women for top jobs.)

Newtime Agency
2 W. 45th St.
New York, N.Y. 10020
(Shortened-work-schedule jobs.)

Options for Women, Inc.
8419 Germantown Ave.
Philadelphia, Pa. 19188
(Full- or part-time employment.)

RLS Associates
41 Broad St.
Charleston, S.C. 29407
(Runs career weekends for women seeking jobs in management, personnel, sales, marketing, research, computer operations, accounting, and engineering.)

Today's Woman Placement Service
21 Charles St.
Westport, Conn. 06880
(Places professional and executive women in high level jobs.)

U.S. Dept. of Labor
U.S. Employment Service
Office of Technical Support
Washington, D.C. 20210
(Ask the public employment office in your area for information on the computerized Job Bank the U.S. Employment Service operates in many metropolitan locations around the country.)

Two additional places to contact for job guidance and employment information are:

Women's Bureau
Massachusetts Department of Commerce and Development
100 Cambridge St.
Boston, Mass. 02202

Women's Bureau
U.S. Department of Labor
Washington, D.C. 20210

VII. WOMEN'S GROUPS AND ORGANIZATIONS

The following groups have varying degrees of involvement with the women's movement. All provide information and support on working women's problems, status, image, and opportunities.

American Association of University Women
4501 Virginia Ave. NW
Washington, D.C. 20037

Barnard Women's Center
Barnard College
Broadway at 117th St.
New York, N.Y. 10027

B'nai B'rith Women
1640 Rhode Island Ave., NW
Washington, D.C. 20036

Coalition of 100 Black Women
c/o CTW
1 Lincoln plaza
New York, N.Y. 10023

Federally Employed Women
621 National Press Bldg.
Washington, D.C. 20004

Federation of Organizations for Professional Women
1346 Connecticut Ave., NW
Room 1122
Washington, D.C. 20036

Gray Panthers
c/o Maggie Kuhn
Tabernacle Church
3700 Chesnut St.
Philadelphia, Pa. 19104

Media Women
320 Central Park West
New York, N.Y. 10025

National Association for Female Executives
10 E. 40th St.
New York, N.Y. 10016

National Organization for Women
5 South Wabash St.
Suite 1615
Chicago, Ill. 60603

OWL (Older Women's Liberation)
c/o Peggy Fenley
3711 Oakland Gravel Road
Columbia, Mo. 65211

Professional Women's Caucus
Box 1057
Radio City Station
New York, N.Y. 10019

Stewardesses for Women's Rights
515 N. Washington
Alexandria, Va. 22314

Union Women's Alliance to Gain Equality
2137 Oregon St.
Berkeley, Calif. 94705

Women in Communications
8305-A Shoal Creek Blvd.
Austin, Tex. 78758

Women Office Workers
P.O. Box 439
Planetarium Station
New York, N.Y. 10024

VIII. WOMEN'S RIGHTS AND LEGAL ASSISTANCE

The following commissions and organizations are dedicated to advancing women's employment and educational rights and to investigating discrimatory and sexist practices.

Advocates for Women
564 Market St.
San Francisco, Calif. 94104

American Civil Liberties Union
Women's Rights Projects
22 E. 40th St.
New York, N.Y. 10016

American Federation of Teachers
Women's Rights Committee
11 Du Pont Circle, NW
Washington, D.C. 20036

American Jewish Congress
Women's Division
15 E. 84th St.
New York, N.Y. 10028

Center for Constitutional Rights
588 Ninth Ave.
New York, N.Y. 10036

Employment Discrimination Counseling Project
1736 R St. NW
Washington, D.C. 20009

Federally Employed Women
621 National Press Bldg.
Washington, D.C. 20004

Human Rights for Women
1128 National Press Bldg.
Washington, D.C. 20004

National Education Association
Women's Caucus
1201 16th St., NW
Washington, D.C. 20036

Project on the Status and Education of Women
Association of American Colleges
1818 R St., NW
Washington, D.C. 20009

Union Women's Alliance to Gain Equality
c/o Ms. Anne Lipow
2137 Oregon St.
Berkeley, Calif. 94707

U.S. Civil Rights Commission
1121 Vermont Ave., NW
Washington, D.C. 20425

U.S. Department of Labor
Citizens' Advisory Council on the Status of Women
Room 4211, 14th St. and Constitution Ave., NW
Washington, D.C. 20210

U.S. Dept. of Labor
Office of Federal Contract Compliance
14th St. and Constitution Ave., NW
Washington, D.C. 20210

U.S. Dept. of Labor
Wages and Hours Division
Employment Standards Administration
14th St. and Constitution Ave., NW
Washington, D.C. 20210
(Take complaints about violations of the Equal Pay Act to the area
office nearest you. You'll find it in the listing under "U.S. Government" in your telephone directory.)

U.S. Department of Labor
Women's Bureau
14th St. and Constitution Ave., NW
Washington, D.C. 20210

U.S. Equal Employment Opportunity Commission
1800 G St., NW
Washington, D.C. 20506

Women's Action Alliance
370 Lexington Ave.
New York, N.Y. 10017

Women's Center Legal Program
1027 S. Crenshaw Blvd.
Los Angeles, (Calif.

Women's Equity Action League (WEAL)
538 National Press Bldg.
Washington, D.C. 20004

Women's History Library
2325 Oak St.
Berkeley, Calif. 94708
(Feminist books and pamphlets)

Women Involved
1572 Massachusetts Ave.
Cambridge, Mass. 02138

Women's Lobby, Inc.
1345 G St., SE
Washington, D.C. 20003

Women's Rights Project
American Civil Liberties Union
22 E. 40th St.
New York, N.Y. 10017

IX. PUBLICATIONS, PAMPHLETS, NEWSLETTERS, AND BULLETINS

Depending upon your individual interests and problems you'll find a great deal of information and provocative reading in the following recommended references. Some of the publications will be in your library. Others are available at nominal prices (see Women's History Library under Section VIII)

Angry Woman's Arsenal Against Sex Discrimination in Employment, The
New York National Organization for Women
47 E. 19th St.
New York, N.Y. 10003

Business and Industry Discrimination Kit, The
National Organization for Women
5 S. Wabash Ave.
Suite 1615
Chicago, Ill. 60603

Encyclopedia of Careers and Vocational Guidance
J. G. Ferguson
Doubleday & Co., Inc.
245 Park Ave.
New York, N.Y. 10017

Equal Pay Facts
Women's Bureau Leaflet 2
Government Printing Office
Washington, D.C. 20402

Equal Rights Amendment—What It Will and Won't Do, The
Citizens' Advisory Council on the Status of Women
U.S. Department of Labor
Room 4211
Washington, D.C. 20210

Executive Woman, The
Executive Woman
747 Third Ave.
New York, N.Y. 10017
(This monthly newsletter for women who buy and sell products and services costs $20 annually.)

Guide to Federal Laws Prohibiting Sex Discrimination, A
Clearinghouse Publication 46
Government Printing Office
Washington, D.C. 20402

Job Finding Techniques for Mature Women
Pamphlet 11
Government Printing Office
Washington, D.C. 20402

Media Report to Women
Media Report
3306 Ross Place, NW
Washington, D.C. 20008
(A subscription to this monthly newsletter costs $10 a year.)

New Directions for Women
P.O. Box 27
Dover, N.J. 07801
(A yearly subscription to this news quarterly is $3.)

Occupational Outlook Handbook
Bulletin 1700
U.S. Department of Labor
Government Printing Office
Washington, D.C. 20402
(This 900-page bible with quarterly supplements is in most public libraries.)

Prime Time
264 Piermont Ave.
Piermont, N.Y. 10968
(A one-year subscription to this monthly newsletter if $5.)

Small Business Reporter
Bank of America
Dept. 3120
P.O. Box 37000
San Francisco, Calif. 94137

Spokeswoman, The
Spokeswoman
5464 S. Shore Drive
Chicago, Ill. 60615
(A subscription is $7 annually.)

Successful Woman, The
Successful Woman
Box 160
Sun Prairie, Wisc. 53590
(Written by Dr. Norman Vincent Peale, costs $5 a year.)

Vocational Guidance Manuals
620 S. Fifth St.
Louisville, Ky. 40202
(This company publishes a series of manuals, each of which gives an overall view of a specific profession—what it is, the educational preparation required, has kind of work it involves, and the opportunities it offers in local, state, and federal agencies, private indushry, and self-employment. Salaries, licensing and registration, opportunities for women, advancement, and professional organizations and associations are included. You can write for a list of the occupations covered in the series.)

Woman Activist, The
Woman Activist
2310 Barbour Road
Falls Church, Va. 22043
(A monthly bulletin for $5 per year.)

Womanpower: A Monthly Report on Fair Employment Practices for Women
Betsy Hogan Associates
222 Rawson Rd.
Brookline, Mass. 02146

Women Today
Today Publications and News Service, Inc.
National Press Building
Washington, D.C. 20045
(This is a bi-weekly newsletter that costs $15 a year.)

Women's Organizations and Leaders Directory
Today Publications and News Service, Inc.
National Press Building
Washington, D.C. 20045
(This directory features about 20,000 entries for organizations, their leaders and prominent individuals active in the women's movement. It also identifies national and local groups and provides information about leading individuals in women's organizations and groups, government agencies, professional associations and disciplines, private business and industry, and specific areas of interest. It is an outstanding reference book and probably the world's most comprehensive sourcebook for locating thousands of specialized organizations and resource persons throughout the world. You'll find them all listed: traditional and radical; business and government; academic and professional associations and collectives; straight and gay; United States and foreign. Copies should be available in public libraries.)

Women's Rights Almanac
Elizabeth Cady Stanton Publishing Co.
5857 Marbury Rd.
Bethesda, Md. 20034
(Reference Guide for and About American Women. It costs $4.95.)

Women's Work
Wider Opportunities for Women, Inc.
1649 K St., NW
Washington, D.C. 20006
(Six issues per year cost $5 for individuals. Higher rates for organizations.)

Working Woman's Guide to Her Job Rights, A
Women's Bureau Leaflet 55
Government Printing Office
Washington, D.C. 20402

In addition to the foregoing the U.S. Small Business Administration and the U.S. Department of Commerce publish pamphlets that will be helpful if you're contemplating a business of your own. Some are free, others are sold for a nominal cost. Write the SBA for *Free Management Assistance Publications* and the Department of Commerce for information on its *Urban Business Profiles* at the addresses below:

U.S. Small Business Administration
1441 L St., NW
Washington, D.C. 20410

U.S. Department of Commerce
Washington, D.C. 20230

The SBA (and its branch offices throughout the country) offers free advice and guidance on a wide range of business problems and subjects. Consult your phone book for the office nearest you.

Two sources of free guidance from retired executives are:

Service Corps of Retired Executives
806 Connecticut Ave., NW
Washington, D.C. 20525

Active Corps of Executives
806 Connecticut Ave., NW
Washington, D.C. 20525

Afterthoughts

As you've seen in the foregoing chapters, go-and-do is today's way of life for women of every age. And, happily, as you've also observed—in good times and bad—there is always a job for women who know what's available and how to get started in the work that is right for them.

The first step—and always the hardest—is going through your own front door and initiating the action that makes things happen to you. As one woman said, "If you don't like where you are today, don't block your path to somewhere else tomorrow."

For you that first step can be anything from a rap group to some back-to-work courses—or maybe a session with yourself in which you plan your life and goals and mobilize your resources and times. Whatever it is, it begins with *doing* and making the women's movement the kind of personal liberation that gives you the right to choose your life-style and enlarge and broaden your world by working at the activity that's personally fulfilling to *you*. It may vary at different stages of life. But that's what liberation is!

In the years I have written of women in first or second careers, I've been asked many times to pinpoint the traits that help them get started and succeed. But because of the wide variety of traits I've noted in go-and-do women, putting them down in a composite form is far from easy. However, after a great deal of thought, I'd say today's woman who finds the right job and develops it to the fullest

——is an intelligent, giving person who relates to other people with genuine care and concern

——does what she can with what she has—in good times and in bad—instead of sitting on the sideline, thinking of all that she would do if only things were different

——belongs to the moment that she is in while committing herself to being productive (and pursuing, with her whole being, the things that interest her most)

——uses her personal freedom of choice to decide on the image *she* wants to create and the life-style *she* wants to live

——competes with herself to do her best and knows, as Eleanor Roosevelt once said, that people can't make you feel second-class unless you allow this yourself

——respects and enjoys her associations with men and knows that she is equal—but not identical

——maintains good human relations by accepting people for what they are, as she does what she can to build them up rather than pull them down

——listens to her critics as well as to her friends

——retains the quality of living that has always enriched our culture by refusing to sacrifice such values as gentleness and warmth, kindness and understanding, and generosity and love

——believes in equal rights for all as she dedicates her efforts toward making things happen vocationally and establishing and achieving job goals

——realizes she writes the story of her life in a chapter-by-chapter way—and that the portion she writes each day, in the end, depends upon her.

The time to write that story—and reach for the right work is now. So with warm good wishes and best of luck—remember, there's a right job for *you*!